RISK REVISITED

Anthropology, Culture and Society

Series Editors:
Dr Richard A. Wilson, University of Sussex
Professor Thomas Hylland Eriksen, University of Oslo

RISK
REVISITED

EDITED BY
PAT CAPLAN

Pluto Press
LONDON • STERLING, VIRGINIA

First published 2000 by Pluto Press
345 Archway Road, London N6 5AA
and 22883 Quicksilver Drive,
Sterling, VA 20166–2012, USA

British Library Cataloguing in Publication Data
A catalogue record for this book is available from
the British Library

ISBN 0 7453 1468 6 hbk

Library of Congress Cataloging in Publication Data
Risk revisited / edited by Pat Caplan.
    p. cm.—(Anthropology, culture, and society)
Includes bibliographical references and index.
ISBN 0–7453–1468–6
    1. Risk—Sociological aspects. 2. Risk perception. 3. Risk
perception—Cross-cultural studies. I. Caplan, Patricia. II. Series.

HM1101.R59 2000
302'12—dc21

                                                         99–048076

Designed and produced for Pluto Press by
Chase Production Services, Chadlington, OX7 3LN
Typeset from disk by Stanford DTP Services, Northampton
Printed in the European Union by TJ International, Padstow

CONTENTS

LIST OF FIGURES AND TABLES

FIGURES

TABLES

ACKNOWLEDGEMENTS

I am grateful to the people who gave seminars in the 'Risk Revisited' series at Goldsmiths College in the autumn of 1997, and who have provided chapters for this volume, including bearing my editing with patience. In addition, thanks are due to speakers in the series who were not able to contribute to this volume: Anthony Giddens, Scott Lash, Peter Kelly and Suzanne Hood. I also thank those who joined the project subsequently and wrote articles at relatively short notice: Alison Shaw and Simon Cohn. Those who attended the seminar series and joined in the discussion have also played an important role in the genesis of this collection. I also wish to thank Lionel Caplan for giving much encouragement and for commenting on several drafts of the introduction.

Practical help with the manuscript was provided by Imelda McGowan and Shefa Jahan, for which I am grateful.

It has been a pleasure to work with the team at Pluto, including Richard Wilson as series editor and Anne Beech as Editorial Director, and I am also grateful to their reviewer for incisive comments.

Pat Caplan
July 1999

INTRODUCTION: RISK REVISITED
Pat Caplan

At the turn of the century and the millennium, risk is a topic which is impossible to ignore. As I complete this manuscript, there are confrontations, sometimes violent, over genetically modified crops and other forms of biotechnology, and media discussions on the increasing predilections for engaging in 'risky' sports, and on the relative risks of accepting, in certain parts of the world, high levels of pollution in order to generate jobs. Risk is highly politicised, and the politicians constantly invoke science in their attempts to persuade the public that their policies are safe.

I became interested in the topic of risk while conducting research in Britain on people's eating habits in the early 1990s, a period which had seen a rash of food 'scares' around salmonella in eggs, listeria in cheese, and the dangers of 'mad cow disease'. The diversity of reactions by informants to the range of risks with which eating appeared to present them – ranging from coronary heart disease to CJD – needed complex explanations. In the autumn term 1997, I convened a seminar series entitled 'Risk Revisited' for the Department of Anthropology at Goldsmiths College, inviting the contributors to reflect particularly on how their own research relates to existing work on risk perception by anthropologists and sociologists. Most of the chapters in this book were given in early draft form at that seminar.

RISK: THE DEBATES

In this section, I consider the work of three prominent social scientists who have written extensively on risk: the anthropologist, Mary

Douglas, who first published on risk (with Aaron Wildavsky) in 1982, and two sociologists, Ulrich Beck, whose book *Risikogesellschaft* appeared in 1986, and in English in 1992, and Anthony Giddens who published *Modernity and Self-Identity* in 1991. In spite of the fact that they are writing on the same topic, there is relatively little dialogue between them. Neither the work of Beck nor Giddens was available to Douglas when writing her first two volumes on risk (1982, 1986), but she does refer to Beck's work briefly (and approvingly) in her 1992 volume. Beck and Giddens, however, only note in passing the work of Douglas, which is perhaps somewhat curious, and an issue which will be discussed below.

What all three authors have in common is their interest in modern (in its various meanings) societies, and their desire to engage in dialogue with others outside of their own discipline. All wish to see their discipline used for socially useful purposes, indeed, all three believe that their work not only asks interesting questions, but even provides some answers. While such a stance has a long tradition within sociology, it has historically been much more contested in British social anthropology, which had until recently tended to display hostility towards, even contempt for 'applied' work. Indeed, Douglas's early forays into studies of Western society and into contemporary issues of policy were regarded by the discipline as fairly heretical back in the 1960s (Fardon, 1999, p. xiv).

The view from sociology: Beck and Giddens

The sociologists who write on risk tend to be interested not only in seeking universally applicable theories, but also theories which are about the universalising tendencies of globalisation. The writings of Beck and Giddens, the two most widely quoted social theorists on risk, have much in common, although originally they appear to have worked quite independently.

Ulrich Beck's book *Risk Society* (1992 [1986]) has been enormously influential. He sees risk as having increased: '[I]n the course of the exponentially growing productive forces in the modernization process, hazards and potential threats have been unleashed to an extent previously unknown' (p. 19). He notes that risks have always been present in human history, but he argues that the nature of risk is qual–

itatively different today for several reasons. One is that modern risks are typically invisible, located in the spheres of physics and chemistry. A second is that they have their basis in industrial overproduction. For Beck, then, risk may be defined as 'a systematic way of dealing with hazards and insecurities induced and introduced by modernization itself' (1991, p. 21). The third difference between modern risks and the dangers of the past is that the former jeopardise all forms of life on earth, so that along with the growing capacity of technologies comes the incalculability of their consequences, which themselves come to be a dominant force in history and society. All of this has resulted in a new paradigm, that of *risk society*, a new stage of modernity.

Beck acknowledges that some people are more affected than others by the distribution of risks or 'bads': 'social risk positions spring up' (p. 23), which are not necessarily the same as the old divisions of class or region. For this reason, he contends, 'risk society in this sense is a world risk society' (ibid.). To some extent, risks continue to adhere to class patterns, given the correlation between extreme poverty and extreme risk; furthermore, in the new global order, some risks, such as those caused by hazardous industries, are transferred away from the developed countries to the Third World. However, although the wealthy can attempt to buy their way out of risk, such possibilities inevitably shrink with the intensification of risk position: the same air and water are consumed by everyone, or, as Beck puts it 'smog is democratic' (p. 36) and risk thus equalises. This is another of the contradictions which potentially allows for change. Thus while Beck sees risk society as a catastrophic society, he contends that this factor has political potential since 'averting and managing these can include a *reorganisation of power and authority*' (p. 4).

Beck suggests that the debates around these issues are still being conducted in terms of natural science, but this is now inappropriate. Indeed, the continuation of an uncritical acceptance of the claims of science means that, all too often, people, society and culture are ignored. However, in discussions on risk, there is no scientific monopoly, since there is rarely expert agreement either on what constitutes acceptable risk, or on how it may be managed; as a result public criticism and disquiet increase. At the same time, because of the degree of interdependence of the highly specialised agents of modernisation in business, agriculture, the law and politics, there is no single agent responsible for any risk : 'there is a general complicity, and the complicity is matched by a general lack of responsibility. Everyone is cause *and* effect' (p. 33) and so 'perpetrator and victim become identical' (p. 38).

The extent to which people are endangered by these risks is to some extent dependent upon knowledge, a knowledge which frequently the victims themselves do not have. For this reason, Beck suggests, the 'quality of life and the production of knowledge are locked together' (p. 55). But in recent years, there has been increasing interest in and awareness of the forms of knowledge necessary to challenge acceptance of hazards generated by modernisation. Knowledge of risks gains a new significance, and brings about another major change: 'whereas in class and stratification positions *being determines consciousness*, in risk positions *consciousness determines being*' (ibid.).

In short, then, Beck's argument is that environmental problems are not those of surroundings, but are *problems of people,* they are *social* problems. Furthermore, the old antithesis between nature and society no longer exists, since 'At the end of the twentieth century nature *is* society and society is also *"nature"* ' (p. 81).

In the second part of his book, Beck considers the processes of individualisation which are happening simultaneously with the growth of risk society. As a result of these, problems of the system are often transformed into apparent personal failure. But at the same time, out of these processes, new social movements are born, which are both the expressions of a search for social and personal identity and also of protest against the new forms of control being established, often in the name of risk management.

Finally, Beck looks at the idea of *reflexive modernisation* in the course of which 'socially prescribed biography is transformed into biography that is self-produced and continues to be produced' (p. 135). In reflexive modernisation, individuals are no longer willing to accept the truth claims of scientific knowledge, but subject them to criticism. In this way 'The "objects" of scientization also become *subjects* of it, in the sense that they can and must actively manipulate the heterogeneous supply of scientific interpretations' (p. 157 – all Beck quotes contain original emphasis). Here it would appear that there is some room for agency, and for the rise of a politics, both personal and public, of risk society.

Like Beck, Giddens (1991) sees the world today as having entered a new phase which he terms 'late' or 'high modernity'. Further, like Beck, he sees risk as central to this scenario: 'modernity is a risk culture' and one in which the concept of risk is 'fundamental to the way both lay actors and technical specialists organise the social world' (p. 3). Late modernity is viewed as apocalyptic, because it introduces new kinds of risks which previous generations have not had to face. Furthermore, in high modernity, distant happenings impinge on both local events as well as on what he terms the 'intimacies of the self'. In short, the world has become a single world.

Giddens, like Beck, contends that the study of risk can tell us a great deal about the core elements of modernity. Paradoxically, while on the one hand there has been a reduction in life-threatening risks for the individual, at the same time high-consequence risk resulting from globalisation has created an inherently unstable 'climate of risk': 'The risk climate of modernity is thus unsettling for everyone; no one escapes' (p. 124). For this reason, doubt has become a pervasive feature of modern critical reasoning and one which 'permeates into everyday life as well as philosophical consciousness, and forms a general existential dimension of the contemporary social world' (p. 3).

Like Beck, Giddens also sees a change in the way in which time is viewed. Instead of the past determining the present, because of the significance of risk in late modernity, the future, as envisaged in risk scenarios, determines decisions made in the present. For this reason, self-identity becomes reflexively organised and individuals are forced to negotiate their own lifestyle choices. Lifestyle implies choice within a plurality of possible options and is 'adopted' rather than 'handed down'. Such lifestyle choices raise pressing moral issues which can lead in one of two directions. Either 'Personal meaninglessness ... becomes a fundamental psychic problem in circumstances of later modernity' (p. 9) with the repression of the moral questions which day-to-day life poses, but which are denied answers, or there is a call for forms of political engagement which new social movements presage and initiate.

Giddens notes the work of Christopher Lasch, who has argued that modern society has produced a 'culture of narcissism', which Giddens relates to an apparent evaporation of history, and a loss of a sense of historical continuity:

> Global risks have become such an acknowledged aspect of modern instititutions that, on the level of day to day behaviour, no one gives much thought to how potential global disasters can be avoided. Most people shut them out of their lives and concentrate their activities on privatised 'survival strategies', blotting out the larger risk scenarios. Giving up hope that the wider social environment can be controlled, people retreat to purely personal occupations: to psychic and bodily self-improvement. (Giddens, 1991, p. 171)

So what effect does all of this have on earlier forms of social stratification? Unlike Beck, who sees them as being changed and less relevant in risk society, Giddens argues that they can now be partly defined 'in terms of differential access to forms of self-actualisation and empowerment', noting that modernity produces '*difference, exclusion and marginalisation*' (original emphasis) (p. 6). Yet in his 1999 Reith Lectures 'A Runaway World', as in a short recent article on the context of British politics in risk society, Giddens (1999) is determinedly upbeat: 'There can be no question of merely taking a negative attitude towards risk. Risk needs to be disciplined, but active risk-taking is a core element of a dynamic economic and an innovative society' (p. 29).

There are thus many commonalities between Beck and Giddens. Both see society as entering a new stage, that of 'reflexive modernisation' (Beck) or 'late modernity' (Giddens). Both view this phase as characterised by new kinds of risk. Furthermore, they see similar consequences arising from risk. First, the certainty which previously characterised modern societies, with their faith in science and scientists, has been eroded: knowledge (including the consequences of risk) is contested. Second, risk society is universal, and events and developments which are far away can have immediate effects. Third, the relationship between individual and society has shifted: the old social categories of modernity, such as class, have lost much of their salience, and individualisation has become of greater significance. Fourth, the modern concept of risk colonises the future, which thereby determines the present, whereas previously, it was the past which was seen to determine the present; such a view of time is also one which has little place for history. Finally, there remains an ongoing search for morality, which is sought either through individual effort, notably around the body with exercise and dietary regimes, and which some have termed 'narcissistic', or through social, including environmental, movements.

Both Beck and Giddens reject the blandishments of postmodernism, with its emphasis on fragmentation, arguing rather that it is not only possible to make sense of the way we live now, but also necessary to engage with new situations and to create policies which could be beneficial.

A view from anthropology: the work of Mary Douglas

Mary Douglas suggests that we do well to ask why the word 'risk' has come to its recent prominence and why the concept allows a new articulation of ideas. Her answer is as follows: 'The idea of risk could have been custom-made. Its universalizing terminology, its abstractness, its power of condensation, its scientificity, its connection with objective analysis, make it perfect' (1992, p. 15).

Douglas has written extensively on risk over a period of several years, beginning with a volume co-authored with Aaron Wildavsky in 1982, and continuing with two more sole-authored works in 1986 and 1992. She sees her work on risk as a continuation of her earlier writing on purity and pollution (1966), with its concern for understanding knowledge and cognition, and in some of her work on risk she also builds on her theories of grid and group (1970). Douglas is concerned to utilise the insights gained by anthropology in the study of small-scale societies and apply them to Western society, particularly North America; she wants to understand 'us' as well as 'them'.

Douglas and Wildavsky take as their point of departure the widespread concern about pollution in North America, the society about which they are writing:

What are Americans afraid of? Nothing much except the food they eat, the water they drink, the air they breathe, the land they live on, and the energy they use. In the amazingly short space of fifteen to twenty years, confidence about the physical world has turned to doubt. Once the source of safety, science and technology has become the source of risk. (1982, p. 10)

In *Risk and Culture*, the authors aim 'to explain us to ourselves' by posing several questions. One is why there has been a rise in alarm over risk to life at a time when health and life expectancy are better

than ever before. Another question is how people decide which risks
to take and which to ignore, since 'substantial disagreement remains
over what is risky, how risky it is, and what to do about it!' (p. 1). In
the first part of the book they consider and reject the argument that
science can give us the answers to risk and in the second part go on
to make the case for the social selection of risk. They argue that the
social sciences are themselves responsible for part of this confusion
because they have gone along with a view which treats causality in the
external 'real' world as radically distinct from the results of individual
perception: in effect, 'real' knowledge has been allocated to the
physical sciences, and illusions and mistakes to the field of psychology
and other social sciences (p. 193). They reject a psychological
approach to risk perception which is premised on some people having
personality traits which predispose them to look for risks, instead
noting that 'Between private subjective perception, and public,
physical science there lies culture, a middle area of shared beliefs and
values' (p. 194).

Douglas and Wildavsky suggest that this fear has to do both with
knowledge and with the kind of people we are. People see the weight
of risks differently, and have to prioritise between them, since plainly
no one can worry about all potential risks all the time. But in order
to rank dangers there must be some agreement on criteria, which is
why acceptability of risk is always a political issue. Since there are no
value-free processes for choosing between risky alternatives, the
search for an 'objective method' is doomed to failure and may blind
researchers, including scientists, to the value-laden assumptions they
are making. For this reason, then, 'Risk should be seen as a point
product of *knowledge* about the future and *consent* about the most
desired prospects' (original emphasis, p. 5). Furthermore, the actuarial
procedures of risk assessment will not help because *all* modes of
assessment are biased by the social assumptions they make. Yet
Douglas and Wildavsky are interested in the policy implications of
the cultural selection of dangers, denying that their argument forces
them to adopt an unscientific posture and affirming 'our capacity to
cope resiliently with risk' (p. 15).

For these authors, then, risk perception is determined both by social
organisation and by culture. They cite the example of a very different
society, that of the Lele of Zaire (where Douglas carried out fieldwork
in the 1950s), and discuss what risks people there chose to highlight,

noting that with the presence of 'all the usual devastating tropical ills', the Lele focused on being struck by lightning, barrenness and bronchitis. The authors conclude that it is 'the type of society which generates the type of accountability and focuses concern on particular dangers' (p. 7) and that this is as true of the US as it is of Zaire.

Using culture inevitably brings in morality, as Douglas had shown in her earlier work on the classification of purity and pollution (1966). Common values lead to common fears, thus the choice of risks and the choice of how to live are linked and each form of life has its own typical risk portfolio. 'Risk taking and risk aversion, shared confidence and shared fears, are part of the dialogue on how best to organize social relations' (p. 8). Culture also involves power: 'A cultural theory of risk perception would be trivial if it shirked considering the distribution of power in relation to the pattern of risks incurred by Americans' (p. 8).

Douglas and Wildavsky argue that within complex society, people who adhere to similar forms of social organisation take or avoid similar kinds of risk, and that for this reason, it is only by changing the social organisation that risk selection and perception can be altered. They identify three kinds of social organisation: market individualist, hierarchical and sectarian. They also propose that in each society there is a distinction between 'centre', which is the locus of formal power and authority, and 'border', those on the margins; each of these areas takes a different view of risk. The border sees the centre as inevitably engaged in social strategies and argues that no change ever comes from there: 'the border claims to have more credibility, itself being freer from entangling social purposes ... but it is not one whit more independent than are hierarchists and individualists' (p. 191). In other words, even those who protest are tarred with the same brush.

If, then, perceptions of right and truth around risk depend on the cultural categories created along with social relations, how can we escape charges of relativism? The authors suggest that one way forward is to describe fully the consequences of preferring one form of social organisation over others, 'to bring our moral and political judgement to bear openly on the basic assumptions' (p. 195). A second answer is to expose some inconsistencies in current thinking about risk. And a third is 'to reject the idea of knowledge as something solid and bounded and to think of it instead as the changing product of social activity' (p. 192). By thus recognising that social change is possible, it is argued that values and perceptions can change too. Indeed, 'The risk debate itself is a record of rapid cultural change' (p. 192).

Basically, then, the argument of *Risk and Culture* is that societies, and categories within societies, choose their nightmares on both social and cultural criteria, and thus their nightmares are different. The authors recognise that science does not hold the answer to such problems, since all knowledge is contested. By analysing North American society in the 1980s as an ethnographic case study, *Risk and Culture* attacks the pervasive notion that modern societies can rely on science, recognising that all forms of knowledge are socially produced. Instead, they argue for cultural analysis as a way forward, an argument which Douglas reiterated and developed in her two subsequent books on risk.

In 1985, Douglas published *Risk Acceptability According to the Social Sciences*. Her stance had shifted little from her previous work. Her questions remained the same: how autonomous is the individual? What might be meant by rational choice? How does a society meet the challenge of the provision of public goods, a topic she had already addressed with Baron Isherwood in *The World of Goods* (1978)?

Douglas sees the growing risk management industry as biased by individualism, while her own emphasis remains on the social, and especially on attitudes to blame (p. 34) and hence to morality (p. 60). For Douglas, 'Culture is the publicly shared collection of principles and values used at any one time to justify behaviour' (p. 67). It is scarcely surprising that Douglas continued to write on the topic, publishing *Risk and Blame* in 1992, since, as she notes, 'The topic of the public perception of danger had burst upon everybody's awareness ... Risk became an academic growth area, and it still is' (1992, p. 10). In asking why this is the case, Douglas suggests that not only does a culture need a common forensic vocabulary with which to hold persons accountable, but risk is also a word that admirably serves the forensic needs of the new global culture:

To be 'at risk' is equivalent to being sinned against ... America has gone farther down the path of cultural individualism, and so can make more use of the forensic potential of the idea of risk ... The neutral vocabulary of risk is all we have for making a bridge between the known facts of existence and the construction of a moral community. (1992, p. 28)

Risk and Blame is a compilation of essays published over the previous
five years, the first six of which are the subject of her further thoughts
on risk and blame. In the preface, Douglas considers the role of the
anthropologist and the anthropological project, arguing:

Typically an anthropologist tries to see individual persons in their social
environment. The anthropological project calls for a holistic view, over a
long enough stretch of generations and over a large enough number of
persons, for some pattern to appear ... in the next 20 years, the social sciences
will be looking for just such a holistic approach that they have denied
themselves by their methodological individualism. (Douglas, 1992, pp. ix–x)

Her own answer to 'methodological individualism' is what she terms
'cultural theory'. Essentially, Douglas sees the human project as one
of culture-building, which is a way of people living together in
institutions which have agreed moral standards: 'Cultural theory starts
by assuming that a culture is a system of persons holding one another
mutually accountable' (p. 31). This theme runs through all the essays
in her book:

[C]ultural theory is a way of thinking about culture that draws the social
environment systematically into the picture of individual choices. It provides
a method of analysing public debates as positions taken in a conflict between
cultures ... One of the special strengths of cultural theory is to be able to
predict what specific new perspectives appear when a social position is
changed, new foregrounds emerge and old worries are backgrounded.
(Douglas, 1992, p. xi)

For her, 'individuals transfer their decision-making to the institutions
in which they live' (p. 78) and for this reason, she argues, 'the proper
way to organise a programme of studying risk is to start with studying
institutional design' (p. 19), a topic which she had addressed earlier in
her book *How Institutions Think* (1986).

Douglas sees modern debates about risk in North America as
analogous to debates about sin or taboo held in other times and places,
since for her risk and danger are synonymous. As a result, both risk
and sin involve an exploration of blame: 'Blaming is a way of
manning the gates through which all information has to pass ... and
at the same time arming the guard' (1992, p. 19). This premise enables
her once again to draw apparently unlikely parallels between, for
example, the adversarial, litigious culture of North America, in which
for every misfortune someone is blamed or sued, and the Lele people

of Zaire, who also rarely accepted that misfortune or death were due
to natural causes.

In the course of the six chapters which make up the first part of
this book, Douglas deals with a wide variety of risk-related topics: the
politicisation of risk, the understanding of collective behaviour,
morality and its relation to politics, knowledge (including scientific
knowledge) and its ambiguity, how people make decisions, who gets
blamed for misfortune and why, social exclusion, stigma and victim-
isation, theories of probability, and how communities may be typified
(hierarchical, individualist and sectarian, in this instance). Here, as
elsewhere, Douglas' work is as much about method as it is about
theory, and 'cultural theory' is itself a method which she sees as both
objective and predictive. In Chapter Six, entitled 'The Self as Risk-
Taker: a cultural theory of contagion in relations to AIDS', Douglas
seeks to understand how different kinds of societies, and different
subgroups within a single society, will respond to the threat of AIDS,
by being either risk-averse, or risk-taking. This involves setting up a
typology of four kinds of culture, each with its theory of how
knowledge is legitimated, and with its own theory of the self. Utilising
the research carried out by Calvez on attitudes and behaviour in
relation to AIDS in Brittany, Douglas once again invokes a variant of
her grid/group model while at the same time employing an analysis
of society's use of the physical body as a social metaphor.

In short, then, Douglas is interested in difference, in explaining why
different societies, and different groups in complex societies, view risk
differently. She sees the answer to these puzzles as lying in cultural
analysis, in categorising social systems, and in terms of the knowledge
and cognition which such systems produce.

In his recent intellectual biography of Mary Douglas, Richard
Fardon (1999) suggests that *Risk and Culture* was perhaps ahead of its
time. He notes that what reviewers have welcomed in Douglas's work
on risk has been the supplying of a social dimension to debates which
had previously been dominated either by statisticians or psychologists,
and the important insight that perceptions of risk correlate with forms
of organisation and control of social groups (pp. 165–6).

None the less, Douglas's work is not without its critics. In
Kaprow's review of *Risk and Culture* in the *American Ethnologist*
(1985), she accuses Douglas and Wildavsky of reducing real risks and
dangers to metaphor: 'The authors trivialize real hazards and end up

by eliminating danger altogether' (p. 347). Further, Kaprow finds it difficult to reconcile the ubiquitousness of pollution and toxicity with Douglas and Wildavsky's confidence in the ultimate benevolence of 'the center'. Kaprow suggests that historical evidence about occupational hazard and environmental health proves rather how very opposed the interests of industry and the general public have always been.

A number of reviewers suggest that environmental concerns raised by pressure groups are more 'real' and more deserving of being taken seriously than Douglas and Wildavsky appear to suggest. Hacking, for example, in a review in the *New York Review of Books* (1982), notes somewhat acerbically that '*Risk and Culture* sometimes hovers near the anthropological fallacy of thinking that everything we perceive is a cultural artifact. Every once in a while the reader has to cry out that some pollution is real.' Beidelman too, in a review of *Risk and Blame* in the *American Anthropologist,* accuses Douglas of 'stodgy Durkheimian conservatism' (1993) for seeing the individual as entirely constrained by society, while Adams, in his book *Risk* (1995), also draws attention to her neglect of individual agency. In an article using Douglas' cultural theory to analyse his own research on pottery workers and workplace hazards, and how motorcyclists and car drivers behave on the road, Bellaby (1990) argues that grid/group analysis is a useful tool for understanding behaviour, but at the same time, it has limitations: not only does it tend to make 'static comparisons between forms' (p. 474), but it 'fails to connect perceptions with situated behaviour' (p. 476).

Douglas has been variously accused of cultural relativism and sociological reductionism. Even as sympathetic a commentator as Fardon notes that a sociological account of risk, such as that of Douglas and Wildavsky, would inevitably be caught recursively in its own arguments (1999, p. 157). He also points out that while in Douglas's work the authority of risk experts is impugned, yet the notion of 'risk' is accepted as a standard form by which to measure the apparent non-objectivity of lay perceptions. Like a number of other readers of Douglas, he takes issue with her somewhat sanguine view of 'the centre', noting that frequently sect-like organisations are close to the seat of power (the National Rifle Association, for example), and that it is not unknown for exaggerated fears to arise in the centre, as well as the border (p. 162). Furthermore, he suggests that a reduction to three types of institution (sometimes further reduced to just two, occasionally amplified to four) scarcely does justice to the complexity of American society, much less enables comparisons between societies far removed in space and time.

Fardon maintains that Douglas and Wildavsky did succeed in having their book noticed – it was very widely, even if sometimes critically reviewed, especially in America, much more so than Douglas's later books on risk. Yet curiously, neither of our two sociologists writing on risk make much reference to Douglas's work. Furthermore, few anthropologists (medical anthropologists apart, and then only to a limited and specific degree) have subsequently engaged with the topic. In current debates between academics and policy makers on risk, anthropologists are conspicuous by their absence. Even a current Economic and Social Research Council (ESRC) research programme on risk ('Risk and Human Behaviour') contains no anthropology projects. In the current rash of publications on risk aimed at the intelligent lay person, anthropologists do not appear as contributors, and are rarely quoted (for example, Franklin, 1998). Rather, the running, at least in terms of the public arena, has been made by the sociologists, notably Beck and Giddens.

THE COLLECTION

The seminar series 'Risk Revisited' began with a question about why it was that risk has become such an important discourse in the social sciences, particularly sociology, and whether the debates occurring there would look different from the point of view of social anthropology. One way of dealing with this was to consider specific ethnographic case studies in the light of the meta-theories produced by authors such as Beck and Giddens. In this book, all of the authors mix theory and ethnography, albeit to varying degrees. The ethnographic locales range from several in Britain (Caplan, Shaw, Day, Killworth and Cohn) to India (Vera-Sanso), Tanzania (Bujra), Amazonia (Nugent), and Montserrat (Skinner). Some are based on micro-level studies in specific locations (Day, Killworth, Sanso, Bujra, Skinner), while others attempt analyses of larger units (Caplan, Shaw, Cohn, Nugent).

Both Beck and Giddens contend that modern risks impact in a significant way upon personal relationships, even those which are of the greatest intimacy. Three of the nine chapters address this issue. In Chapter 1, on London prostitutes and HIV, Day compares two kinds of risk. The first is an 'old' one which sees prostitutes as a 'reservoir' of infection, thereby justifying government and other forms of control in the name of risk reduction; as a result of this, prostitutes in many countries and at many times have been punished and stigmatised. The 'new' risk comes from a discourse around HIV and AIDS, and involves epidemiology and health education, both of which prostitutes need to 'read' and negotiate. Yet prostitutes consider themselves to be professionals and are anxious to be informed about the risks to themselves and their clients; the vast majority of women in west London used condoms with their clients, and indeed, had found it easier to negotiate condom use in recent years.

At the same time, here, as elsewhere in the West, a prostitutes' rights movement has been increasingly vociferous, and its progress has been helped by the necessarily greater public openess about sexuality arising out of the AIDS pandemic; some prostitutes have even been recruited as 'safe sex' educators. Yet prostitutes have to weigh up many other risks in their lives: the risk of violence against that of HIV infection, for example. Day argues, therefore, that the analyses of Beck and Giddens omit 'the equally important sense of socially determined risks, imposed, negotiated and opposed'.

In Chapter 2, Bujra is critical of what she sees as Beck's and Giddens' universalising tendencies, and the linking of a meta-narrative of modernity with unquestioned evolutionist assumptions; she also notes that some parts of the world, such as Africa, have scarcely entered modernity, much less Giddens 'late modernity'. None the less, she does find some aspects of their work useful, particularly the extent to which a risk such as AIDS impinges upon and changes personal relations and the links made between risk and trust. She notes that Giddens' notion of trust ('a leap of faith') is similar to the way in which it is used by people in Lushoto in Tanzania. For the latter, the difficulty is that the solution promulgated by health educators – the use of condoms in sexual intercourse – actually engenders *distrust*. While condom use in commercial and non-domestic relationships is seen as acceptable by some men, its use in marital sex is considered very problematic: the partner who suggests it could either be implying that s/he had not been faithful, or that s/he suspected the other partner. Yet at the same time, men are having for the first time to question their sense of control over women, as well as their own belief in their mastery of knowledge, while some women are beginning to recognise that sexual relations will have to change if they and their children are to survive. In this way, as Beck and Giddens have pointed out, risk equalises, and hence, as Bujra contends, 'There is potential for building on this unifying effect.'

In Chapter 3, Shaw explores the increased epidemiological risks of handicap for children born of consanguineous marriages, a preferential form among British Pakistanis. Although pre-conception genetic counselling is available, as is foetal abormality screening, some women refuse both, on the grounds that each child is a gift from Allah and therefore must be received. At first sight, this appears to be a good illustration of the difference posed by Giddens between 'traditional' and 'modern' concepts of risk. Yet Shaw finds this very unsatisfactory, noting that risk perception and decision making have to be understood in their specific cultural context. For those of Pakistani cultural background, this includes the importance of *biradari* (kinship group) marriage, the significance of having children, and the principles of age and gender which govern household organisation, as well as the teachings of Islam. But it also includes the social environment in contemporary Britain.

Further, as she points out, if new information is to be effective in changing patterns of behaviour, it needs to be assimilated into lay understandings, which are, as Douglas and Wildavsky have suggested, themselves determined by social organisation and cultural values. Yet Pakistani families are not homogenous; their social circumstances are often different. Further, Islam teaches not only that a child is a gift from God, but also that suffering should be prevented and relieved; such an idea may be used as a rationale for a different set of decisions, including acceptance of some of the possibilities offered by medical science.

In India, the locale of Vera-Sanso's Chapter 4, there is a widespread perception that virtue is scarce, and that men's and women's short-term desires must be suppressed for the greater good of society. As she demonstrates, the view that women are a major threat (that is, pose a risk) to society and social order is clear from both national legislation and case law, with legislative premises deriving from the nineteenth century continuing to dominate the twentieth, and control of men being achieved through control of women. The proper place for women is thought to be in the home, but for many poor women in the kind of low-income settlements in Chennai where Vera-Sanso carried out her fieldwork, the need to earn additional income often makes living up to such norms impossible. Here, then, women have to weigh up the risks to themselves and their families of loss of reputation, which can carry severe social and even material sanctions, against the risks of not having enough money to maintain the household. Women get around this dilemma by redefining their entry into the public sphere in terms of self-sacrifice, claiming that they are acting as men do *through* the roles incumbent upon them as women and not from choice or any personal desire. Vera-Sanso, like Day and Bujra, makes it clear that the concept of risk is inextricably implicated in politics: dominant definitions of risk set moral codes which frame disciplinary regimes and these constrain action, but people also resist them.

Killworth carried out fieldwork among British troops in Northern Ireland during a period of cease-fire and, in Chapter 5, he seeks to explain why it was that infantry soldiers saw this period as being more 'risky' than other times. He uses the distinction originally made by the economist Frank Wright between risk and uncertainty – the former measurable, the latter immeasurable – to explore why the scientific calculations of risk made by the army command, based on statistical probability, were relatively unimportant to the soldiers concerned, who rather worked with uncertainties which they sought to control. For them, the only way of keeping risk low was to behave at all times as if it were high.

Killworth suggests that to the individual soldiers at the platoon level, such a notion of control was achieved by internalising dangers in two ways. The first was by explaining survival in terms of good patrolling skills: 'a soldier who was careless was thus positioned as endangering his entire unit', a view which attributed agency to soldiers' own actions. For this reason, the cease-fire, which prevented them acquiring such patrolling skills, and which was considered to be doomed to end unpredictably, was deemed more risky than business as usual. The second mode of internalisation worked by attributing to the Provisional IRA qualities similar to those of the British Army, thus rendering the risks posed by the enemy 'knowable'. At the same time, soldiers dealt with the conflict by externalising it; they never saw the British Army as a focus of explanation for the situation, or as an historical actor in the scenario, but rather viewed it as a neutral party in a conflict between sectarian enemies: 'soldiers' own narratives stressed, above all, the timeless nature of the conflict.'

A different form of agency is suggested in Skinner's account of his last days as an ethnographer on the island of Montserrat in Chapter 6. Following the anthropologist Robert Paine, Skinner argues that our modern world has not in fact been homogenised in the face of risk, and he cites Boholm's suggestion that risk is better treated as a polyseme, rather than the essentialised category of Beck and Giddens. None the less, Skinner argues that an underlying feature of all risk situations is that of management, and in this respect, risk shares with narrative the issue of control, an orderly and ordering process 'whereby the writer can take charge of self, social world and literary world by creating, destroying or amending'.

Once the volcano started erupting, Skinner found himself writing a lengthy and unsent letter to his girlfriend detailing not only events, but also his own and other people's reactions and commentaries: 'I would suggest that for me as for others, the perceived risk of the eruption, the dread that stemmed from the uncertainty of the situation, was contained by the performance of everyday activities people continued doing which constituted narrative responses.' These activities did not only include the literary, but ranged from icing wedding cakes to cleaning cars of volcanic dust. Skinner concludes that it is through such narrativity that risk can be contained.

In Chapter 7, Caplan considers responses to BSE in Britain from the early 1990s to the present. In the first part of the chapter, she discusses the symbolic meanings of beef in Britain. She then compares interviews with informants in London and Wales carried out at the beginning of this period. Here the theme of knowledge – 'knowing where it comes from' – was important in people's decision making. Where people trusted their supplier, they were more likely to continue eating beef, which partly explains why a much larger proportion of people in Wales than in London continued to do so. In the third part of the chapter she notes that, similarly, there were differences between reports in local Welsh and national newspapers, with the former adopting a very sympathetic stance to farmers, even as the national broadsheets were castigating farming for the use of modern methods which posed risks to the food chain. The fourth part examines campaigns to 'rebuild confidence' in British beef after the second BSE scare. These made use both of pre-existing symbolic notions around beef in British culture and also of the idea that trust is based on knowledge, with supermarkets seeking to guarantee consumers that their suppliers were known, inspected, and therefore trustworthy. Knowledge here includes several dimensions, including *what* and *how*, but, to be most effective (that is, to 'restore confidence'), it needs to incorporate *who* and *where*. In other words, the global risks of BSE could only effectively be countered by knowledge which is localised and dependent upon social relationships of trust.

Cohn, in Chapter 8, examines the loss of control experienced by people suffering from chronic illness. He begins by noting that since ideas about how things can happen are based on beliefs about how they happened in the past, risk perception must be examined in conjunction with theories of causation. This has long been an important theme in medical anthropology, drawing on Evans-Pritchard's idea that Western science answers 'how' but not 'why' questions. Causality has also provided an important set of debates in philosophy, with Hume arguing that the imperative to construct tangible causes is a cognitive aspect of what it is to be human, while anthropology argues that to classify is as much a moral as an intellectual process, given the cultural associations of dirt, ambiguity and taboo. Further, Cohn notes that 'The process of establishing clear causes is a way of keeping the past and the present reasonably tidy' and it is thus a way of ensuring order both cognitively and morally.

Because science is increasingly replacing mechanistic models of the body and illness by new interrelated discourses of environment, immunology and genetics, there is often growing lay frustration with scientific explanation; people experience the dissipation of cause and 'thereby the disappearance of an elementary moral resource'. The case of chronic, more than acute illness, such as diabetes, illustrates how biomedical concepts of causality are now imbued with a broader theme of uncertainty. It is thus possible that the current complexity of causal models in health discourse has severed them from lay perceptions, and consequently increased rather than reduced the impression of risk. Indeed, the belief that medical science has the answers has been significantly eroded, while many people suspect experts' and politicians' agendas: 'People are forced to ask how, if events are now presented as so complex and so potentially threatening to safety, one can do anything to prevent them.' Further, the asymmetry between the past and the future, which offered a foundation for the construction of certainty, is becoming less distinct: 'as causes are experienced as disappearing from view behind, so too the future is dissolving ahead'. Small wonder, then, that individuals feel a sense of bewilderment and also experience a loss of agency and control.

Chapter 9, while considering Amazonia, actually focuses less on local views of risk than on those taken by Western commentators, including such writers as Beck. Nugent contends that for Western commentators, Amazonia is still seen as a risk-laden natural domain, presented as a frontier almost five hundred years after its incorporation into the world system. In recent years it has acquired a 'particular iconic status' in the growth of environmental politics, its survival being seen as indispensable for the maintenance of planetary bio-diversity, sustainability and indigenous knowledge. 'Meanwhile, another Amazonia, that of complex colonial subject, has been put back on the shelf', thereby denying any explanations of a socio-historical kind. In short, Nugent contends that risk is not only an essentialising notion, but also one which is parochial and Eurocentric. He suggests that for some societies, such as Amazonia, risk has a long history, and that the risks which are highlighted by Europeans 'pale into insigificance in terms of life threat when compared to public health issues, provision of education, struggles over land, militias, corrupt politicians and other social pathologies'. Nugent concludes that risk is therefore not so much an inappropriate concept as an incomplete one.

THEMES ARISING

Tradition, modernity, late modernity and development

Most of the chapters in this book are written using the work of Beck, Giddens and Douglas, although, as we have seen, certainly not uncritically. One such critique centres around the applicability of theories developed in metropolitan societies to those lying in the South, the 'Third World', not all of which, as Bujra points out, have fully entered modernity, let alone 'late modernity'. Nugent expresses the same sentiment somewhat differently, noting that the theses of Beck and Giddens ignore uneven development, and the extent to which the development of the West has been predicated upon the underdevelopment of the rest. He argues that in Amazonia, for example, the apparent risk of the loss of rainforest with all its attendant ills, is actually the result of the impact of external systems, such as big business. Like Bujra, Nugent is critical of the unquestioning evolutionary assumptions of Beck and Giddens.

Vera-Sanso challenges Beck's contention that traditional society is a 'scarcity society', in which a preoccupation with risk similar to that in the West could not occur. Indeed, many would consider Beck's labelling of the Third World as naive, since for them, it is the West, with its endless wants, which is the epitome of scarcity society. Yet Vera-Sanso maintains that India is just as much a 'risk society' as the West, and it is thus scarcely surprising to find a highly developed environmental movement in both areas. She also notes that Beck's book *Risk Society* was published in 1986, before the reunification of Germany and the demise of the welfare state in the West, suggesting that things would look very different if the book were to be written now.

Knowledge, causality, temporality and scepticism

In considering risk, knowledge assumes great significance. Some knowledge is deemed to be irrefutable, such as the lay belief that the fundamental laws of nature should not be contravened by such acts as feeding animal remains to carnivores, what Gray (1998) has termed a form of hubris. But more often, knowledge is contested, with splits not only between scientific and lay understandings of risk, but also between scientists themselves. The faith of a previous generation in the ability of science to provide answers has turned to doubt, partly because scientists themselves are not in agreement, partly because the answers science now gives are much more complex and contingent, and partly because 'they' are always changing their mind.

In her recent book, *Naked Science* (1996), Laura Nader argues that science is never autonomous, neither is it free of culture: 'rather it is full of it' (p. xiii), and both science and culture are differentiated by gender, identity, race and class. Nader notes that 'Science is not only a means of categorizing the world, but of categorizing science itself in relation to other knowledge systems that are excluded' (p. 3). For both of these reasons, then, the politicisation of science is unavoidable. She concludes that a central issue of today is 'the primacy of a heavily dressed Science with a capital S and the consequences of its global expansion based on power rather than greater rationality' (p. 23).

Given that, as a number of chapters in this book suggest, most people are highly sceptical about what scientists and politicians tell them, they themselves have to choose what to believe, what action to take. Here they draw upon their own or others' experience: soldiers in Northern Ireland learn of the experience of comrades or relatives who served there in the past, for example. But in many of the instances detailed in this book, the risks are new, and people are uncertain of how to act. Villagers in Tanzania have only recently encountered AIDS, and the previous ways of dealing with illness are not helpful. Anthropologists' training courses do not prepare them for volcanic eruptions, only to write about whatever is happening around them, as Skinner did in seeking to cope with his own fear. None the less, in some instances, there are different, even contradictory or alternative discourses around risk, and people do have some degree of choice, points made by both Shaw and Vera-Sanso.

As Beck, Giddens and Douglas have noted, risk appears to colonise the future, since people are supposed to act in the present in terms of future risks. Day sees risk as linking the past and the future, whereas Cohn argues that, for his respondents, both past and future are dissolving. But perhaps divisions between past, present and future should not be drawn as sharply as Beck and Giddens have proposed. Douglas has argued that while risk seems to work forward, and sin and taboo work backward in explaining the causes of misfortune, matters are actually not so clear-cut, since sin can also work forward and be prophesying (1992, p. 25). Moreover, it is clear that people's scepticism about science is frequently based on their memories of the past when scientists were saying something different about the same topic.

Furthermore, neither past nor future are simple, homogenous categories: research on awareness of food risk show that perception of immediate risk (for example, of salmonella in chickens or eggs) can result in a food 'scare' and immediate change of behaviour, while information about long-term risk of, for instance, coronary heart disease occasioned by eating unhealthy food has much less effect (Davison 1989). Indeed, some longer-term risks, such as that of acquiring HIV, may be of less immediate significance than threats of violence from a partner.

Agency, control, power and resistance

Coping with or managing risk is a theme underlying many of the chapters in this book. One aspect of risk management is that, in its name, control can be asserted by governments or other bodies over populations. Thus, as Day notes, risk is 'disciplinary' in a Foucauldian sense. Further, as Gray points out, 'New Right policies rank long-term considerations of public health and the integrity of the environment a long way behind present risks to commercial profit' (1998, p. 44). Lupton too, in her article on the social and political functions of a public health discourse, points out that risk definitions may be considered hegemonic conceptual tools that can serve to maintain the power structures of society (1993, p. 431).

But the other aspect of risk management is agency. In most of the cases in this book, people display considerable resilience in coping with risk, not least in adopting an attitude of scepticism, and in reading 'against the grain'. They weigh up the risks about which they are deluged with information against other risks present in their day-to-day lives which may receive much less publicity.

A striking feature of the way in which people make decisions around risk is that they rarely do so as single individuals, even in Western society, with its apparent individualisation and plethora of 'lifestyles'. They discuss with relatives, neighbours, friends, colleagues, religious advisers, drawing upon their advice and personal experiences. In this respect, then, they appear closer to Douglas than Beck and Giddens, for the former recognises the social nature of decision making in respect of risk and danger, whereas the latter stress the trend towards individualisation in late modernity.

Here too morality enters, as Douglas has noted, since understanding risk and danger is part of a way of making sense of the world, and keeping things in their proper place. Those who are blamed for placing others at risk are thus acting in an immoral way. Just as anthropological studies of accusers and accused of witchcraft reveal a great deal about the societies in question, so too can risk be used, as Douglas suggests, 'forensically'. The work of Beck and Giddens likewise suggests that the reflexivity which is a characteristic of late modernity is a way of constructing new approaches to risk, one which takes lay critical views seriously, and allows for a science which is culturally aware. It is clear from the contributions to this book that people are dealing with new risks in new ways, while at the same time, still having to cope with many 'old' risks. Further, that looking at the risks which societies choose to highlight and how they deal with them tells us a great deal about their values, morality and politics.

THE REFLEXIVITY OF MODERNITY: ANTHROPOLOGY AND SOCIOLOGY

To what extent, then, do our authors find the work of Beck, Giddens and Douglas useful in tackling the topic of risk in their own research? While all make use of Beck's work, often to criticise it, not all refer to Douglas, and those who do so make use primarily of her important insights that risk is socially constructed and that we need to explore and understand difference; none seeks to apply her cultural theory to their own data. In retrospect, it is a pity that they were not asked why this was the case. My guess, which I hazard very tentatively, is that some would find her methods reductive and positivist, that some of her comparisons, while striking and enabling new understandings, might also be deemed on occasion inappropriate, and her positionality conservative.

Giddens has suggested that anthropology is today 'directly embroiled in the institutional reflexivity of modernity' and that for this reason 'anthropology thus becomes indistinguishable from sociology' (1994, p. 100). It should by now be clear, however, that while the respective approaches of anthropologists such as Douglas, on the one hand, and sociologists such as Beck and Giddens, on the other, have some common features, in many essentials their work is very different, both in theoretical premises and in methodology. Douglas deals in the social and cultural, she bases her theory on ethnographic examples; Beck's and Giddens' work rarely uses ethnography, and it seeks to describe universalising tendencies, including a tendency to individualisation.

There is another important difference between anthropology and sociology which, paradoxically, has been noted by a sociologist, Scott Lash, who distinguishes between the reflexivity of anthropology (citing Clifford, Rabinow, Marcus et al.), which he argues is influenced by Bourdieu's reflexive sociology, and the 'cognitive reflexivity' of Beck and Giddens, which can ultimately be traced back to Cartesianism: 'For Beck and Giddens it tends to involve the bracketing of the life-world to arrive at individualized, subject-object forms of social knowledge. For reflexive anthropology, it involves bracketing subject-object knowledge and situating knowers in their life-world' (1994 p. 156).

The form of reflexivity espoused by Lash, and indeed by many anthropologists, is hermeneutic and also communal or communitarian. It is not, perhaps, one which would be shared completely by Douglas (although she has written on a particular version of reflexivity – 1992, Chapter 14). She might well, however, share Lash's view that, while it is true that in the West there has been an increasing process of individualisation and decline of existing social structures, the latter are being replaced by other kinds of *cultural* structures, notably those deriving from the information and communication revolution and from the realm of aesthetics, which are equally susceptible to sociological (and anthropological) analysis. This seems to me to highlight not only the ongoing differences between anthropology and sociology, which are both theoretical as well as methodological, but go some way to explaining why the authors in the present volume find risk, especially as used by Beck and Giddens, a useful concept, but also one which is 'incomplete'. In the chapters here, it is argued that what is required for such completion is first of all, an ethnographic method which considers risk in particular times and places and through the voices of particular informants. Such an approach needs perforce to consider the global as well as the local, but it does not assume pre-existing dichotomies such as 'tradition' and 'modernity'. It is interested in difference, including cultural difference, and is thus relativist rather than universalist. Secondly, an analysis of risk needs to incorporate an awareness of the dimensions of power, including agency, control and resistance. Finally, such an approach sees individuals in their social

26 *Risk Revisited*

context, as embedded in networks of relationships which have an important bearing on their perceptions of risk.

BIBLIOGRAPHY

Adams, J. (1995) *Risk* (London: University College Press).
Beck, U. (1992) [1986] *Risk Society: Towards a New Modernity* (London: Sage Publications).
Beck, U. (1994) 'The Reinvention of Politics: Towards a theory of reflexive modernization' in Beck, U., Giddens, A. and Lash, S. (eds) *Reflexive Modernization: Politics, Tradition and Aesthetics in the Modern Social Order* (Cambridge: Polity Press).
Beck, U. (ed.) (1995) [1988] *Ecological Politics in an Age of Risk* (Cambridge: Polity Press).
Beck, U., Giddens, A., and Lash, S. (eds) (1994) *Reflexive Modernization: Politics, Tradition and Aesthetics in the Modern Social Order* (Cambridge: Polity Press).
Beck, U. (1998) 'Politics of Risk Society' in Franklin, J. (ed.) *The Politics of Risk Society* (Cambridge: Polity Press in association with the International Policy Research Institute) pp. 9–22.
Beidelman, T. (1993) Review of *Risk and Blame* by Douglas, *American Anthropologist*, vol. 95, no. 4, pp. 1065–6.
Bellaby, P. (1990) 'To risk or not to risk? Uses and limitations of Mary Douglas on risk-acceptability for understanding health and safety at work and road accidents', *Sociological Review*, vol. 38, pp. 465–83.
Clarke, L. (1993) 'Social organisation and risk: some current controversies', *Annual Review of Sociology*, vol. 19, pp. 375–99.
Davison, C. (1989) 'Eggs and the sceptical eater', *New Society*, 23 November 1989, pp. 45–7.
Douglas, M. and Wildavsky, A. (1982) *Risk and Culture: an Essay on the Selection of Environmental and Technological Dangers* (Berkeley: University of California Press).
Douglas, M. (1966) *Purity and Danger: an analysis of the concepts of pollution and taboo* (London: Routledge and Kegan Paul).
Douglas, M. (1970) *Natural Symbols: explorations in cosmology* (London: Barrie and Rockliff).
Douglas, M. and Isherwood, B. (1978) *The World of Goods: Towards an Anthropology of Consumption* (New York: Basic Books).

Douglas, M. (1985) *Risk Acceptability According to the Social Sciences* (New York/London: Russell Sage/Routledge).

Douglas, M. (1986) *How Institutions Think* (Syracuse, NY: Syracuse University Press) (also 1987, London and New York: Routledge).

Douglas, M. (1992) *Risk and Blame: essays in cultural theory* (London and New York: Routledge).

Durant, J. (1998) 'Once the Men in White Coats Held the Promise of a Better Future' in Franklin, J. (ed.), *The Politics of Risk Society* (Cambridge: Polity Press in association with the International Policy Research Institute) pp. 70–5.

Fardon, R. (1999) *Mary Douglas: an Intellectual Biography* (London and New York: Routledge).

Franklin, J. (ed.) (1998) *The Politics of Risk Society* (Cambridge: Polity Press in association with the International Policy Research Institute).

Giddens, A. (1991) *Modernity and Self-identity: self and society in the late modern age* (Cambridge: Polity Press).

Giddens, A. (1994) 'Living in a Post-Traditional Society' in Beck, U., Giddens, A. and Lash, S. (eds) *Reflexive Modernization: Politics and Aesthetics* (Cambridge: Polity Press).

Giddens, A. (1998) 'Risk Society: the Context of British Politics' in Franklin, J. (ed.) *The Politics of Risk Society* (Cambridge: Polity Press in association with the International Policy Research Institute) pp. 23–34.

Giddens, A. (1999) 'The 1999 Reith Lectures: no. 2. Risk' (extract published in the *Observer* 18 April 1999, p. 29).

Gray, J. (1998) 'Nature bites back' in Franklin, J. (ed.), *The Politics of Risk Society* (Cambridge: Polity Press in association with the International Policy Research Institute).

Hacking, Ian (1982) 'Why are you so scared?', *New York Review of Books*, vol XXIV, no. 14, pp. 30–32 and 41.

Kaprow, M. (1985) 'Manufacturing Danger: Fear and Pollution in Industrial Society', *American Anthropologist*, vol. 87, no. 2, pp. 342–56.

Lash, S. and Wynne, B. (1992) 'Introduction' to Beck, U., *Risk Society: towards a new modernity* (London: Sage Publications).

Lash, S., Szerszynsky, B. and Wynne, B. (eds) (1996) *Risk, Environment and Modernity: towards a new ecology* (London: Sage Publications).

Lupton, D. (1993) 'Risk as moral danger: the social and political functions of risk discourse in public health', *International Journal of Health Services*, vol. 23, no. 3, pp. 425–35.

Nader, L. (ed.) (1996) *Naked Science: Anthropological Enquiry into Boundaries, Power, and Knowledge* (London and New York: Routledge).

1 THE POLITICS OF RISK AMONG LONDON PROSTITUTES

Sophie Day

INTRODUCTION

Two views of risk currently compete for attention. The first is a 'new' kind of comparative risk: 'The centre of risk consciousness lies not in the present, but in the future. In the risk society, the past loses the power to determine the present. Its place is taken by the future, thus, something non-existent, invented, fictive as the 'cause' of current experience and action' (Beck, 1995, p. 34).[1] The second type of risk is a long-established process of government and regulation through reference to risk.

James Meikle discusses contemporary risks in the *Guardian* (7 October 1998): the balance of risks over beef on the bone, banning unpasteurised milk and eating genetically modified foodstuffs is assessed alongside risk scales featuring the relative risks for an individual of death from travel, murder, suicide and smoking and the risks for a community of measles and oral contraceptives. This list is certainly bewildering. How can an immediate illness be compared with a possible untimely cancer in the future and how can environmental damage be compared with violence? The relevant context slips away so that risk becomes the sole link between issues that are not normally compared and remain, in many respects, incomparable. A scale is achieved through the introduction of a single standardised outcome such as 'years of life lost' to a person with a normal or typical lifespan. Risk, I suggest, is thus a measure like money that enables measurement and standardisation in all spheres of life and across otherwise incomparable processes (Simmel, 1990).

29

Some believe that the uncertainties and anxieties associated with unknown and often inconceivable risks are of such significance that we should consider ourselves to live in a risk society (Beck, 1995). As traditional mainstays of family and class disappear, we are forced to live reflexively, planning and deciding between half-glimpsed and imponderable futures. In this society of free choice, individual decisions and fictive futures, risk can be used to draw connections between virtually anything at all. At the same time, these connections can become trivial, almost nonsensical, as in the comment that the former Chief Medical Officer made about BSE the week after Meikle's analysis of risk was published in the *Guardian*. Sir Kenneth Calman explained that he had not meant that there was *no* risk when he told the nation that it was safe to eat beef! (*Guardian*, 12 October 1998).

This rhetoric of unconstrained comparison allows risks to be imagined easily and to be drawn on a global scale, in an apparently objective and dispassionate way. These characteristics make the hierarchy of risks imposed through government less obvious, less unpalatable and apparently less unfair, even though they may result in dramatic inequalities. A clearly unequal distribution of risk in the here and now, shown, for example, through patterns of longevity, can be downplayed in favour of a potential chemical or other hazard that would affect us all. In some accounts, risks cease to have any reality in the world 'out there' and are *merely* perceived or constructed through various forms of discourse.

This apparently 'new' kind of risk sometimes appears to be distinct from an older form of regulation, often described in terms of the tools of government and social control, particularly through Foucault's accounts of modern discipline and confinement over the past two hundred years: 'The dialogue about risk and justice tends to be conducted in two languages: traditional English rhetoric on behalf of regulation, and mathematical language on behalf of principles of free choice ...' (Douglas, 1986, p. 3). This form of risk is closely associated with medical expertise, as discussed in detail below with reference to ideas about the medicalisation of life (Illich, 1976).

It is unclear to many of us much of the time which risk is which, new or old, and how they interconnect, if in fact they do connect at all. In this chapter, I attempt to show that both these forms of risk are relevant to London sex workers: the one about unrestrained comparison and the other about government (and opposition). I show that the varying interconnections made between these two realms define a politics that is at once relevant to individual careers and to a general rights' movement.[2]

BACKGROUND: THE PRAED STREET PROJECT

During my research with sex workers at various points during the past twelve years, I have had to deal with 'risk' as a key word in the field of infectious disease, particularly HIV, as well as prostitution. The term 'risk' becomes even more central when prostitution and disease are linked.[3] As my initial research question concerned a common assumption that prostitutes would both acquire and transmit HIV, I had to address directly the questions that others asked about risk. Were sex workers at increased risk along with their clients or children and respectable society in general? Was this risk to be attributed to their generally feckless behaviour as individuals who, by definition, behaved irrationally or to the unfair advantage exercised by clients who were easily able to assert their own preferences in commercial exchanges? Was it state interference which made it impossible to work safely or, perhaps, pre-existing cultural categories that bore no relationship to actual life chances in society but meant that prostitutes would be blamed for the ills of the world, whatever they did?

As the above comments indicate, I was unsure how to include myself within this field of enquiry. In 1986, I began a research project with female sex workers in west London, based initially in the genito-urinary medicine clinic at St Mary's Hospital. I had proposed a research project in response to early prejudices about so-called risk groups and AIDS. While gay men were ineluctably twinned with the epidemic in North America (initially known as Gay Related Immune Disorder (GRID) – see Oppenheimer, 1992), it was female (heterosexual) prostitutes who were associated with AIDS elsewhere. Early reports from East Africa suggested that over 80 per cent of prostitutes in Rwanda were infected with HIV (Van de Perre et al., 1984) while in Nairobi, tests showed an increase in the prevalence of infection among prostitutes from 4 per cent in 1981 to 61 per cent in 1985 (Piot et al., 1987).[4] These early reports encouraged calls for regulation in the UK around the mid-1980s. In my proposal, I argued that regulation was misplaced until it was clear whether London prostitutes were at risk and whether they (consequently) posed a risk to others.

I soon began to work with Helen Ward, a clinician who later trained as an epidemiologist, and together we worked on various dimensions of the business, including HIV and other sexually transmitted infection (STI) risks among women participating in the research. Our research was based on a cohort of women and the research methodology combined structured interviews and conversations, clinical and laboratory examinations, fieldwork and other observational studies of working areas and other places, such as magistrates' courts.

The methods depended partly on site. A small study with sex workers had already been conducted at St Mary's Hospital (Barton et al., 1987) and we established specific clinic sessions for these and other women in 1986, which later became known as the Praed Street Project clinic. Helen Ward provided diagnosis, treatment, vaccination, health promotion and referrals; she also acted as a 'general practitioner'. After 1988, when she began a larger epidemiological study with research staff, we were able to spend more time than previously outside the clinic. Fieldwork included informal interviews and observation but contact was rarely maintained for more than a few months with women unless they also visited the project. We established a drop-in centre that gradually came to be used regularly by some women, particularly street and flat workers. While some women never visited the clinic or only went to 'the doctor' once they knew the project well, a larger number visited the clinic exclusively. In addition, we interviewed other people involved in the sex industry, concentrating particularly on clients (Day et al., 1993).[5] My position helps to explain the difficulties I experienced in addressing the topic of risk. In brief, I seemed to align myself with a process of social control to which medical doctors have contributed so much in the delineation of an occupation, 'prostitution', and its regulation. Whilst nineteenth-century experts in the UK tended to equate prostitutes directly with disease, the health profession has drawn increasingly upon concepts of risk since the 1960s. Looking for risks through interview and examination, we in the Praed Street Project might simply reinforce the associations between sex work and disease – finding risks wherever we looked. As in other spheres of government, we might also operate with an unduly narrow notion of risk (for example, associated with purely negative outcomes) and a non-relational one (focusing largely upon individual sex workers). As 'participants in this process of government', it is thus unclear whether we are the best people to comment upon it (Overs, 1994). In what follows, risk is explored from several disciplinary perspectives (anthropological, clinical and, later, epidemiological). I hope to make explicit the role that this concentration on risk might play in an account of sex work by focusing on politics, specifically the question broached by my initial research, that of regulation, an issue raised in Parliament and the media in the mid-1980s.

I hope to build upon the benefits of these research methods as well. Two are particularly important to this chapter. First, we did not collect words alone, but also made other observations. These unique longitudinal data allowed us to correlate ideas and behaviour, facts and values, the visible and the invisible: for example, we could relate infections with the values and activities that women reported. This allowed us to avoid different forms of reductionism associated with health and social sciences respectively. We were able to avoid reducing risk to its 'real' individual and bodily manifestations, associated especially with various medical perspectives on risk. Sometimes, the epidemiological measurement of risks 'out there' in people's bodies makes people look like the agents of their own misfortunes; certainly, this could be said of the reports of STI found in prostitutes or cancers found in smokers which 'blame the victim'. Likewise, we were able to avoid the view that risk is a veritable conjuring trick through which the governed can be better watched, controlled and marshalled, an approach associated especially with various social and historical perspectives on risk. Sometimes, the sociological analyses of the risks constructed through government and discourse over the longer term make the immediate and material lives of people irrelevant and therefore 'ignore the victim'. As I show below, risks may be real or imaginary, material or discursive as far as sex workers are concerned and, indeed, one of my central conclusions concerns the effort that sex workers continually deploy to 'read statistics against the grain' and differentiate the 'true' from the 'false'.

Second, the length of follow-up and the repeated interviewing enabled us to track career and life changes and to assess the validity and reliability of our data as we came to know each other. In what follows, the data derived through this method are central to the association I draw between a personal and a broader political platform associated with rights and with risks. I conclude that the two are closely twinned in the views of London sex workers. In particular, I suggest that 'risk' becomes a marker of sex workers' attempts to recover some agency through the transformation of risk into safety, civil rights, and career developments.

GOVERNING RISK: HIV, THE PROSTITUTE AND THE STATESMAN

Risks are measured statistically in governmental, medical and other expert systems of knowledge and interventions generally follow: 'It is evident that the statistics of this class [the prostitutes], if followed and made precise according to age, family condition, and movement will be found very useful to the statesman in determining the first motives for bad morals, the lifestyle, the probability of culpability, and the organization of surveillance' (*Congrés international de statistique: programme de la sixième session*, Florence 1867, p. 93, quoted in Hacking, 1990).

Nineteenth-century statistics were applied to 'other' classes, that is, the governed, and especially to the labouring, criminal, or colonised classes. Thus, *les misérables* included brigands, beggars, vagabonds, abandoned children and prostitutes (Hacking, 1990, p. 120). As many histories of nineteenth-century England show, these people were gradually institutionalised – confined in asylums, orphanages and the like, or encouraged to adopt more respectable behaviour and confine themselves inside the house, created in the image of a bourgeois home.

Statistics such as these have been considered alongside medical and legal developments in order to show how the very categories of 'prostitute' and 'risk' can be understood as exercises in social control. The creation of the contemporary 'professional' in sex work is a product of expertise. In several countries, this history has been analysed in terms of the wide-ranging imposition of risk by government upon whole classes of people. For example, Walkowitz (1980) has produced a particularly fine analysis of the Contagious Diseases Acts in some English garrison towns during the nineteenth century. Various legal measures and particularly those related to the control of disease were crucial to the application of 'bourgeois' ideals of respectability to poor women. Such women, as Corbin (1990) indicates, were forced then to approximate either to the respectable (confined at home) or to the unrespectable (plying their trades on the streets). Through this process, respectable (apparently safe) workers and families have been created in the modern era alongside professional (and apparently unsafe) sex workers.

The Contagious Diseases Acts of the 1860s and 1870s were applied to poor women who had combined sex work with the provision of food, drink, lodgings, agricultural work and so forth. These 'public women' could be forced to undergo well-publicised medical examinations for gonorrhoea and syphilis and they could be confined if infected. Those who provided them with lodgings could also be punished (and were increasingly penalised themselves after the repeal of the Contagious Diseases Acts in the 1880s). Through these measures, working-class women were progressively separated from their communities. Walkowitz suggests that this process of displacement also put prostitutes under the control of agents and protectors such as 'pimps' (Walkowitz, 1980).[6]

Nineteenth-century reforms in the UK involved a process of discovery: what were the statistics that governed crime, disease or unrest and how then could the conditions under which those laws applied be changed?[7] Many accounts of HIV risk today dwell upon continuities in government over the past 150 years and AIDS is commonly seen to have provided a golden opportunity for the further surveillance and regulation of certain categories of people. Thus, epidemiological knowledge today follows in the same statistical traditions. What is the world like: what are the risks of HIV, the dominant routes of transmission, where and in what classes of people? How can these be changed? As Hacking indicates, the 'governing classes' change the laws that apply to the 'governed'.

All in the cause of risk reduction, women who *might* be working as prostitutes have been locked up in many countries – from Sweden to India and the United States – and confined over a period of years, just as they were in the nineteenth century under contagious disease legislation. More benign interventions have continued to insist upon the mandatory testing of sex workers (Mak, 1996), to repatriate immigrants who might be working in the industry and to deny compensation for HIV infection to the 'undeserving', whilst rewarding the 'deserving', such as haemophiliacs who have been 'innocently' affected (Buckley, 1997). It has been assumed that sex workers will be at increased risk of infection and so it is thought that their regulation will lessen the risks, as if reservoirs of infection that might harbour malaria or other dangerous pathogens were being drained (Brandt, 1985; see also the title of D'Costa et al., 1975 noted above).[8] HIV has provided an excuse to lynch and murder sex workers and to prosecute them for knowingly infecting their clients. Such risks and dangers are often compounded within a figure of an 'other' that combines prostitute, foreigner and drug user.

There is little to indicate that an apparently more liberal discourse in the UK today, where prostitutes are *at risk*, involves any less social control than its predecessors, where prostitutes posed a risk to other people through the 'cesspit', 'sewers' or 'reservoirs' of disease that they created. Indeed, these different visions of prostitution often coexist and mutually implicate each other. Yet histories of this process tend to focus on government alone, and to provide only a view from the top down. Even looking exclusively at processes of governing, it seems foolish to ignore how AIDS and HIV risks have led to appropriate and accessible service provision for sex workers and support for decriminalisation of the industry (Mak, 1996; Kempadoo and Doezema, 1998). Is this simply more government and more medicalisation?

MEDICALISATION AND RISK

The governed classes, deemed to be vulnerable (that is, at risk) and also to pose a risk to other people (that is, of risk), have often been portrayed as passive or effectively docile recipients of the governing process. For example, it has been suggested that the definition of ill health in medical as opposed to social terms leads to depoliticisation and individualisation (Zola, 1975; Freidson, 1988; Illich, 1976; see also Taussig, 1980; Scheper Highes, 1992). In a famous case study of this process of medicalisation, Taussig showed how the care of a New Yorker led to her social relationships being represented as though they were things in the patient's own body. Despite the sick person's attempts to situate her suffering in more social and structural terms, the experts won, as they do in capitalism more generally (Taussig, 1980).

Concepts of risk may produce an imaginary edifice through which medicalisation is extended as social relationships are reduced to things that cannot even be seen and which may never materialise. Although the term 'anticipatory care' was not coined by the Royal College of General Practitioners until 1981, similar concepts had long been part of medical general practice in the UK. Early diagnosis was part of a preventive outlook, which pushed the identification of illness back in time. The earliest possible intervention was justified in terms of protecting the future and therapy was merged with health education and health promotion. David Armstrong writes, 'By, as it were, intervening in the past the future could be made secure because the past and future were directly linked' (1985, p. 218). Armstrong emphasises how this view creates populations that are constantly at risk. Screening becomes more and more important to the surveillance of populations composed of pre-patients or the not-yet-ill.[9] Of course, as Armstrong and others have argued, such futures may never occur. It is this futurology that seems to explain the virtually free associations made between one topic and another in conversations on the subject of risk. Since the material world ceases to anchor such references to risk, comparison can become more and more unreserved, as in the illustrations given above.

Sex work in the HIV era seems to provide a perfect case study of medicalisation. The literature suggests that prostitutes have been further equated with disease, and thereby stigmatised and excluded (see, for example, Alexander, 1988). As noted above, the repression of sex workers has often been savage. Yet, it is hard for even the casual observer to fail to notice that a social movement for prostitutes' rights has also expanded enormously during this period. While it is possible that this process of medicalisation (involving depoliticisation and individualisation) exists independently from the active collective struggle for civil rights, I suggest below that they are linked.

In order to make this argument, it is necessary to distinguish crudely between two contrasting medical approaches to risk, which I associate with epidemiology on the one hand and public health (including health education and health promotion) on the other. Epidemiological measures of various probable outcomes provide a 'basic' science that enables the quantification of risk and these measures are commonly expressed in mathematical terms. They correspond to the earlier statistics that I discussed above with reference to the creation of the 'Western professional prostitute'. Risks for HIV infection are calculated according to various parameters including the prevalence of infection that has been measured – initially through AIDS cases and later through cases of HIV infection – alongside measures of sexual activity or the lack of a clean blood supply and so forth.

These statistics have promoted the image noted in the background section where female prostitutes in 'Africa' paralleled gay men in 'the West' by the mid-1980s as the major embodiment and source of disease. In the later 1980s, statistics were read in terms of high and low prevalence areas but, by the early 1990s, interest had shifted to trends over time as the prevalence of HIV was shown to change very rapidly indeed in parts of the world such as areas in Africa, Thailand and India. At the same time, it has become clear that HIV in sex workers reflects the local situation and not some decontextualised essence to prostitution itself. Thus, rates of HIV tend to be higher in those who have used needles or live in areas of high prevalence and lower in other groups.

Epidemiological calculations have been very important to sex workers using the Praed Street Project. As some of the examples given below show, women want to know the 'real' risks and apply a reliable set of measurements to their own lives. However, as those examples suggest, the figures were never easy to interpret. In the late 1980s, was a prostitute in Nairobi equivalent to a prostitute in London in any way at all, or more like a gay man in New York? It must always have been particularly difficult for women in the clinic to trust global and national statistics, since these purveyed such a negative image of sex work.

Another medical language, that of an applied public health, relies upon these basic statistical measures and epidemiological readings. Risks that are knowable or known can be avoided or at least minimised, since public health is concerned more with safety than with an epidemiology of risk. In our research, this language of risk reduction plays a very different role to the language of statistics. While women themselves struggled with figures on HIV risk and prevalence, not knowing which to believe nor how to dispute the statistics without extensive technological expertise, they found the language of public health at least potentially inclusive.

In brief, I argue that sex workers have used public health arguments about safety in a platform for prostitutes' rights. This can be shown by looking both at public debates and at research results from the Praed Street Project. The domain of public politics provides ample evidence of these arguments about safety while the more local ethnographic data will be used to argue for some continuity between 'personal' and 'political' attitudes to risk and/or programmes for change. Through these examples, it will be seen that medicalisation among sex workers is not all of one piece, but has both positive and negative connotations. In contrast to what might be imagined from much of the literature, medicalisation in this study did not simply lead to a willed dulling of the senses, a narrowing of vision and the constant anticipation of possible futures. Rather, as I have already implied, sex workers turned ideas about risk on their head.

COMPARISON: RISK AS A MEASURE OF ALL THINGS

I found that health status, earnings, personal relationships, bodily integrity, activities on the part of police and other state functionaries, and the use of condoms and other physical barriers during sex were all linked by reference to this term 'risk' which also related to images of danger, safety, chance, luck, discrimination, fate, and uncertainty as well as the joys of 'hustling'.[10] Sex workers engage in elaborate efforts to define and measure risks, assessments which are comparable to epidemiological constructs of probability. Jane once asked me precisely how much sperm was needed to transmit HIV and she told me this story:

There was this bloke. We used a condom and everything but I just had this feeling and I felt sperm down there. Well, my friend didn't think it was sperm, but I did. I took two E. [brand name] condoms – they're not extra good by the way, they're thin and they break but they do have spermicide. I pushed one right up and left it there. I turned the other inside out and left it in for a couple of hours. If there had been a leak, what does it mean?

Jane spoke of another episode at work when, as far as I could tell, she had oral sex with a woman who had just had sex with her boyfriend. Jane reasoned as follows: the colleague, this woman, had douched before she and Jane enacted a lesbian scene for a client; Jane said that the colleague's boyfriend had reported a negative HIV test; the woman had never had a test but she must have been negative because her boyfriend was, and they had been together some time: 'But, how possible would it be [to transmit infection through oral sex]? I don't go down that end [practice active oral sex]. I've heard [that] it [HIV] is in vaginal fluids but does it go up through the cervix or how? I had a bloody big mouth ulcer ...'

Examples are easy to find, but not always so complicated. Another woman asked, 'What is it *exactly* about AIDS in Africa and all this carry on? Is it that bad, is it high risk?' A third woman asked, 'Is it true that you have a one in two hundred chance of contracting the virus on a one-off contact?' A fourth queried the usefulness of spermicides.[11] These examples concern women who were attempting to understand epidemiological or medical constructs of HIV risk, and who were also attempting to relate these constructs to the risks they experienced in their own lives.

Such risks can be ranked in terms of their relevance. For example, a possible and distant outcome, such as an infection, might be considered less relevant than an immediate lack of money or threat of violence, and different types of work yield different risk scales (Jackson et al., 1992). Much of the sociological literature about HIV risk in prostitution deals precisely with this issue of relative risks from the perspective of sex workers themselves, who are considered to be rational actors. The social context can be summed up in the words of the women studied in West London during the 1980s, where a popular saying listed two risks: first, mugging and second, a client dying on you. These two risks are about work and I understand both to refer to the difficulties of making your money; the first adds the problem of frequently violent theft and the second adds the problem of state attention, which might involve official records, arrest, imprisonment and/or widespread publicity. In their personal lives, women also had other worries: they found it hard to move on, to set up a home, to have children and so forth (Day, 1998).

While these socially inscribed and negotiated risks are central to any description of the industry, I should also like to note the distinctive language that women used, an issue which has not been addressed in the literature. In references to risk, women made all sorts of unexpected comparisons. Jane's attempts to calculate HIV risks were elaborate, and often compared apparently dissimilar situations.

Such conversations led to talk about virtually anything at all: risk, luck, trust and protection; boyfriends and clients; health and money; law and the workplace. Sometimes, risks appeared remote as in talk of the streets among those who worked indoors but, in other conversations, it was an immediate concern. Often, a reference to risk provided a semantically empty clue to what would follow, namely, discussion of personally significant issues such as health or relationships.

It was not clear to me whether and how comparisons such as these were related to other ideas about risk, whether these addressed research into HIV or the sense that I outlined of a 'governing risk' (see above). Further examples suggest, however, that these personal and autobiographical comments were part of a collective politics.

A SOCIAL MOVEMENT

Power is not simply exercised by doctors in the manner of kings, nor accepted passively by patients in the manner of the subjects of a kingdom, as implied at times by early commentators (Foucault, 1986). Moreover, stigmatised identities are often reclaimed through a process of reverse affirmation (for example, Foucault, 1976). As noted (see note 3), the term 'whore' has been embraced in the same way as the term 'gay' by activists objecting to their marginal status. Other terms such as hustler, prostitute and sex worker have also been used explicitly in the struggle for social recognition, to assert the dignity of work, and to claim particular professional skills.

A social movement that has developed in opposition to the abolitionist view of sex work is described by several commentators (for example, Phetersen, 1989; Kempadoo and Doezema, 1998; Phetersen, 1996). Not all prostitutes are slaves; some voluntarily choose their jobs in preference to alternatives, not just through economic motivations that lead many to jobs they would rather not do, but for positive reasons such as the apparently flexible hours, good money, and freelance or self-employed status. Commonly, activists and advocates have demanded the international decriminalisation of prostitution so as to assure prostitutes of basic human rights and some control over work conditions (see, for example, the World Charter for Prostitutes' Rights in Phetersen, 1989).

The links made between disease and sex work have affected the form of this rights' movement in at least two ways. First of all, increased financial support has been particularly important to a social movement composed of local self-help groups with few funds and little organisation. Finance for international meetings and other AIDS programmes has enabled sex workers and rights' advocates to gather more easily in the 1990s and develop international dimensions to local and often Western rights' groups (see Kempadoo and Doezema, 1998 for examples). Secondly, advocates have stressed their status as professionals in safer sex. A measure of success for these campaigns can be found in relatively high-profile jobs for sex workers and activists, who have been hired in health programmes to promote risk reduction. Sex workers might demonstrate how to put a condom on a man without his knowledge or produce videos and leaflets about the erotic pleasures of non-penetrative sex. In this way, images of healthy, professional sex have become more credible outside the industry.[12]

The public success of this movement can be discerned in greater acceptance of the central arguments: prostitution is work and prostitutes are professionals in 'healthy' or 'safe' sex. Thus, Reuters reported in August 1998 that the International Labour Organisation (ILO) 'urged governments to officially recognise the booming sex industry and treat it like any other business' (Kaban, 1998). In the Netherlands, it is expected that new legislation will make (voluntary) sex work subject to local government regulations in the same way as other businesses.[13] I was struck by the similarity between ideas about HIV, risk and safety in this relatively public domain and in our own research among women who were unaware of, or uninterested in, public advocacy and activism. The similarity, I suggest, can be attributed directly to the long association between sex work, risk and disease.

INSIDE, NOT OUTSIDE THE STATE

Sex workers participating in Praed Street Project research constantly objected to stereotypes about disease, dirt, risk and commercial sex, like the activists and advocates for prostitutes' rights mentioned above. I was asking Karen about her work one day. She said that she used to come to the clinic every three months for a check-up but now she came every month. She was more comfortable with monthly check-ups, she said, and she came to find out if she had any infections. She continued:

'Cos they [the press] give prostitutes a bad name. They reckon prostitutes are the most dirtiest things on earth. I think there should be more said [in opposition to that view] because, like, it is cutting business down. That's because people think prostitutes have AIDS. Because a prostitute is in a high-risk group and I don't see why they should be such a high-risk group 'cos most of the girls look after themselves. Well, I do anyway.

In protecting herself from what is an occupational hazard, Karen found that she was also able to dispute the stereotype of 'dirty' prostitutes within the *cordon sanitaire* of a high-risk group. Karen countered the negative process of medicalisation with a positive interest in check-ups, which would both detect problems and demonstrate that she was responsible, safe and clean.[14] She had seen a programme about HIV in sub-Saharan Africa on television and she disputed the association between prostitution and disease along with the construction of a 'typical' prostitute, who travels from Africa to the UK, classical Rome or India to the contemporary world. She simply turned the stereotypes on their head. For Karen, the sex industry involved workers and it was associated with cleanliness and health, not disease.

Despite anxieties about HIV infection, research participants considered that public health platforms had enabled them to take more effective control of commercial exchanges. For example, from around 1988, two years into our research, women said that it was much easier to insist on condom use. They noted in amazement that some clients even provided, and insisted on using, their own condoms. Jacky said how good it was that the men were now frightened and explained how this had facilitated more professional, explicitly negotiated, services. Only, she added, some clients thought that gay men and drug addicts were the only people who could get AIDS, and some would not wear such a 'cheap' thing as a condom. Jacky then had to adopt her educational role (see below on images of the clinical profession among sex workers). Women talked with relief about the possibility of avoiding 'sex' (intercourse, penetrative sex) altogether. Interviewed in 1989, one woman said, nowadays, you could have less contact with clients and, in her words, 'You sit on top of them, as you're more in control.' Indeed, many explained how worries about AIDS had allowed them to demonstrate and develop their skills in sex work through a changing repertoire involving more fantasy, domination and lesbian scenes as well as different kinds of physical contact with customers which included more foreplay or masturbation and less penetration.[15]

Karen spoke of her attempts to maximise safety when she explained how clean and how safe she was, and how frequently she attended for check-ups. She had likewise raised the possibility of providing domination:

K. An' I ain't particularly into that. I suppose a lot of people are going to be asking for domination now and not actually having sex ... Safer.
S (SD). And you don't like doing that?
K. Well I need someone to teach me basically, 'cos I'm a bit frightened.
S. Is there anyone ...?
K. Don't know, ask around. Bind yourself, you know – like domination, bondage, stuff like that. I mean, you don't know what's going to happen – are they going to turn round and beat you up, or tie you up and not let you go or something? Whereas if you're with another girl, at least you hope she's going to let you go or nothing's going to happen to you.

Karen was trying to assess the risks of infection against possible violence and potential help from colleagues.

During this same period, Anna said that she was 'a little paranoid' about her work. She explained how she avoided touching clients as much as possible and asked whether a particular brand of condoms was safe. She came to the clinic once for the results of an HIV test and explained that she would want to know if she were infected, as she would stop working; she would feel a responsibility to herself rather than to other people. Anna elaborated, 'It's the press about prostitution. It makes you feel really bad.' She was referring to the conventional associations between sex work and disease. There had been a report about an infected woman working in Glasgow, and Anna felt the need to demonstrate her own contrasting sense of responsibility and, at the same time, she expressed some cynicism about these press reports, unsure whether they were true or false.

Talk of risk frequently led women to voice their opposition to this form of 'government' through the media. While Anna and Karen focused on the press, others were led directly to the conspiracy position that was so common in the later 1980s. Kate, for example, noted, 'Anyway, AIDS is probably manmade and they already know the cure.' I understood this comment to suggest that both the disease and its future cure were, in fact, part of an exercise in power and social control. This position was not held for long as Kate then went on to contrast an oppressive, technological, state medicine with nature: 'Cures for AIDS and all diseases will come from in the earth, because that's where the disease comes from. The cure is already there but we haven't found it yet.' As far as Kate was concerned in this part of the conversation, all men were to blame for her risk, 'You're at risk from everybody ... from all men. [It] comes from semen itself.'

Women also made use of more specifically clinical images of cleanliness and hygiene. One woman explained how to avoid HIV infection through a safer sex that meant 'to be clinical, particular, cautious and clean'. Another explained simply, 'you are very, very clinical' and she said that her clients had to remove the condoms themselves. Prostitutes appear to borrow further images from the clinic in this process of asserting a professional status. Just as doctors are experts who direct interactions with their 'clients', so too are prostitutes experts who scrutinise clients for dirt and infection, refuse some, make them shower, look for warts or other signs of disease. Like (other) health workers, sex workers educate as well as examine their clients. I have been told how clients were sent home shamed to their wives because they asked for sex without a condom.

This form of professionalisation also brought financial advantages. In 1987, Tracy had a client who was so frightened of AIDS that he supported her financially, and helped her to come off methadone. This man had insisted that they both have an AIDS test before she stopped working. Tracy said that there was no point in having a test as she did not share needles and had not even used needles since a hepatitis scare in her youth long before HIV had emerged, but she had a test anyway: 'it keeps them quiet.' She agreed to act as though her friend/client were her sole partner.

In all these ways, AIDS seems to have enabled sex workers to construct more forcefully a professional relationship with their clients, modelled at least in part on the relationships between doctors and patients. Some forms of risk were repudiated (particularly those posed by sex workers), while others were acknowledged and addressed (for example, those posed by clients). As I have shown, some sex workers positively medicalised themselves through attending the clinic for what were probably clinically unneccessary check-ups more frequently than they had in the past in order to counter the stereotype and some of the epidemiological data that link prostitution with disease, and to reassure themselves. Far from marginalising, individualising and depoliticising sex workers, references to risk reduction and risk avoidance have enabled sex workers to argue about their professional status and for a position inside civil society.

By and large, public health messages appeal to images of a utilitarian individual, who makes rational calculations about her behaviour. It is not necessary to review the extensive literature on health promotion[16] to note striking continuities between public health messages, public claims about sex workers' rights and the more personal arguments made by participants in the Praed Street Project. Sex workers are concerned with safety and risk reduction in the context of an overall assessment of costs and benefits at work, including the epidemiological data on risk. Whilst health beliefs and other psychological models of risk behaviour have been rightly criticised for their oddly impoverished views of human subjects, they are perfectly compatible with ideologies of (though not necessarily activities in) the market. It is because these women *work* with sex that they approximate so closely to this public health construct of an individual. Sex workers, like other people providing services for money, cost different activities explicitly and they price specified amounts of times and a range of services. They also publicise their services in advertisements and through agreed peer norms. Unlike most of the audience for health promotion, sex workers may well perceive themselves as vulnerable to infections which have serious consequences but from which there is effective protection, and they are likely to consider that the benefits of protection easily outweigh the costs, at least, when they are working (see Bloor, 1995, pp. 88–9 on health belief models).[17]

There is an elective affinity between models of working and models of health promotion. Because these women work with sex, they make good consumers of public health messages. As indicated above, public health messages about safety have enabled women using the Praed Street Project since the later 1980s to insist more successfully upon controlling their own working practices and making decisions about occupational standards of health and safety. It is relevant to note how these concerns are reflected in our statistics: only just over half the women we knew in 1986 used condoms for all vaginal sex at work; five years later the figure had risen to more than 90 per cent (Day et al., 1988; Ward and Day, 1997). Health messages delivered through the media, in the clinic and elsewhere made sense to prostitutes in at least two ways: they offered women potentially useful information on safety at work and they provided a means for arguing that this really was work, and not some form of deviant behaviour.

I have written previously of the symbolic importance associated with HIV risk reduction, for example, in the 'physical' barriers constructed by a prostitute between her inner, personal self (who might have a relationship at home) and an outer working mask interacting with clients (Day, 1990). In the present context, a more obviously political claim is equally relevant. General health education materials have been associated with images of those who avoid risk, 'responsible citizens', as opposed to those who embrace risk, the 'gambler' and, in the context of HIV, the 'promiscuous person', 'prostitute', or 'drug addict'. This implicit contrast between outside (risk taker) and inside (risk averse) is highly relevant to the politics of prostitution. The inside, often conceived as a nation or welfare state, is seen as a safe place for citizens. Prostitutes, I suggest, lay claim to this inside space when they emphasise their own professional practices.

It is not surprising that sex workers make such good consumers of civic messages relating to public health, but it is perhaps ironic that they have achieved success despite the image they appear to provide for the general population. Sex workers commonly contrast their own responsible behaviour with that of clients and/or state agents; these men and the state in general are seen to make it impossible for women to take effective charge of their own health and safety at work (see Day, 1996). Further, parallels are drawn between the public domain, where sex is work, and public health so as to argue about rights and duties among co-workers, -nationals and -citizens. Moral behaviour and civic responsibilities *should* elicit reciprocal behaviour on the part of other citizens and, in particular, the welfare state. Prostitutes, exemplary citizens in the realm of public health, deserve some recognition; by right, this exemplary exercise of duties should place sex workers inside, not outside, the polity.

A public health platform constitutes a powerful argument for inclusion and belongs both to the public movement for civil/human rights and to more personal statements about social injustice. In publications and speeches about prostitutes' rights as well as conversations in the Praed Street Project, similar themes appear: work is part of a domestic territory inside the state; prostitution concerns a public realm and not some aberrant private morality. In these different settings, public health language provides an opportunity to make a

claim to the centre, that is, to claim basic rights of the workplace and
an expanded citizenship.

In summary, I have shown that the use of a 'public health' language
is built upon and contrasts with the 'epidemiology'. In disputing their
own high-risk status, sex workers show how safe they are and
construct a domain of public health at work through which they
claim to be part of society. Talk of risk – or rather of safety and health
– involves ideas about civil/worker rights. I have argued that medicalisation in this group of women involved both negative and
positive aspects, which were associated as much with opposition as
with the business of government itself, with collective – as opposed
to individual – and, by implication, effective critiques of social
inequities. These data on sex workers in London illustrate an
awareness of social labelling, and an explicit rejection of the negative.
They illustrate a process of literally reversing the labels, substituting
safety for risk and health for disease. Women in the Praed Street
Project have thereby used a language and a history through which
they have previously been controlled to new ends.

RISK AND REFLEXIVITY

In my account of medicalisation, I have attempted to distinguish
different medical languages of risk. Epidemiological references are
read variously by sex workers. Women constructed 'real' risk
measures and objectively established statistics that were reliable and
generalisable because they could be applied from one situation to
another. As Mary Douglas has written, such talk of risk acquires the
neutrality of 'scientific discourse': 'Its universalizing terminology, its
abstractness, its power of condensation, its scientificity, its connection
with objective analysis, make it perfect' [for international debates
about justice and welfare] (Douglas, 1992, p. 15).

This sort of risk, although specialised, is similar to calculations that
sex workers make all the time (along with many other people) as they
go about a relatively dangerous job. On the whole, London sex
workers thought they made a better job of the epidemiology than the
experts because they could filter out some of the prejudices that
blinded most people to the real risks of the job. Although the idea of
a basic epidemiological science appealed to notions of objectivity and
detachment, it was by no means obvious to most sex workers whether

the figures actually reflected facts 'out there' or mere prejudice. As I have shown, women disputed conventional imagery and tended to read statistics 'against the grain' (see also Buckley, 1997). They expressed distrust and scepticism that had the effect of resisting the implication that a scientific method yields universally valid, as opposed to historically and regionally specific, generalisations. In this way, sex workers were forced to adopt a critical stance towards majority views. They necessarily became involved in reaffirming or questioning common stereotypes, including those that label prostitutes 'risk takers' with their own lives, 'at risk' of disease and other negative outcomes and 'of risk' to the rest of society. This critique intensified the way in which risk functioned as an ideological marker.

I have shown how sex workers made use of a second medical language of risk relating to public health in opposition to this kind of government. This second language was couched in terms of risk reduction or avoidance rather than risk *per se* and it involved claims to safety, professional status and full citizenship in civil society.[18]

Having looked first at activism in the public domain and then at political and personal reflections in the Praed Street Project, it can be seen that collective and individual aspects to a politics of risk are interconnected. At the local level in the Praed Street Project, the counter-claims illustrated in this chapter interweave grand politics with analyses of possible personal futures and potential change, often of career. Research suggests that effective arguments for civil rights are built precisely from individual and personal reflection. Sex workers engage in analysis, reflection and critique both in public and private in opposition to illegitimate government and social stigma. Resistance that is readily invested with collective, even non-rational dimensions by anthropologists interested in the implicit and habitual dimensions of everyday life can be seen just as easily in this Praed Street Project research in utilitarian, explicit and rational terms. These examples show that the process of individualisation so often located in medical relationships is not synonymous with depoliticisation but, on the contrary, connotes effective agency.

CONCLUSION

I have attempted to describe various, often contradictory, aspects to medical relationships, and to indicate in particular the positive, enabling, resistant strands that are so often downplayed. These multifaceted medical relationships include positive notions of the self and of political emancipation as well as passivity and political apathy, and they combine personal and public aspects to the process of social change.

References to risk differ considerably and, in this chapter, I have contrasted unfettered comparison of all sorts of issues on the one hand with the business of government on the other and, within the medical domain more narrowly, statistics with safety. Although I have focused especially on medicalisation, I have attempted to show how epidemiological assessments and statistics depend upon comparison whilst processes of government draw upon ideas about the safety of citizens within a bounded territory. Risks can be measured and ranked, compared in all sorts of ways, but it is not always clear how.

This sense of endless comparison as compared to a determinate outcome can be captured equally through more traditional references to statistics where the quantity of risk is of no interest to that individual who either lives or dies, wins the lottery or not (the risk being zero or one). I have shown that it was by no means obvious most of the time where to locate a previously unconsidered risk. Was it personal or public, part of government or opposition, about comparison or control? The constant attempt to discriminate 'real' infection risks, for example, from the (illegitimate) exercise of power promoted an attitude among London sex workers where risk became largely an ideological tool for, or marker of, reflection and explicit argument. The realms of the possible were enlarged further by an orientation towards an (imagined) future, rather than reference to the (historical) past. Risk and safety had many dimensions.

The broad comparative sweep made possible by references to risk and the indeterminacy associated with possible futures, combined with the critique of government that I have outlined, are not unique to sex work. In fact, these characteristics may help to explain the popularity of the term in other situations, remote from sex work, where risk connotes a general anxiety about what to compare and what may happen. I gave general examples from the media, opening this chapter with a citation from the *Guardian* on risk scales and a comment about risk and safety from the Chief Medical Officer. Risk provides a vehicle for linking aspects of life that are simultaneously represented as discrete, even fragmented, entities: unknowable chemical or nuclear hazards, the lack of trust in intimate relationships, ecological degradation. In contemporary accounts, it sometimes seems as though risk can be used to talk about anything at all under this rubric of uncertainty, as with the setting I have described. We live in a risk society, faced with unfamiliar hazards and unclear trajectories in life. In Beck's analysis, to return to the sociology cited at the beginning of the chapter, we have lost traditional moorings such as family and class (Beck, 1995). Now, we are forced to plan our lives reflexively as individuals, free to choose between alternatives that remain empty of content because the risks cannot be determined.

However, this 'reflexive risk' picks up only one set of referents that I have described for London sex workers and excludes another. Unrestricted comparison can accommodate a contemporary sense of rapid change drawn on a huge canvas, but it can also exclude the equally important sense of socially determined risks, imposed, negotiated and opposed. Much of what Beck describes for the middle classes in Germany today has long been standard for those without much money or control over their lives. Many, perhaps most, individuals have traditionally found it difficult to read the future, to remain in one place with their families and jobs; in brief, to determine their own lives.

While 'modern' risks of government and opposition may seem to have been supplanted by 'postmodern' risks of the life course itself, and particularly its anchorage in space and time, this ethnography from London should indicate that these different risks are inextricably linked and have long been interconnected in the lives of prostitutes. The relatively poor and disadvantaged have continually suffered excess government, leading to extreme dislocations in space and time: witness simply the mobility of sex workers from one country to another. These people have rarely exercised extensive self-determination. In an account of the politics of risk among sex workers in London, it is therefore impossible to divorce contemporary anxieties from older and more certain processes of exclusion.

Disadvantages can promote an orientation away from the unpleasant details of everyday life and towards an imagined future. Stigma, more than poverty, led many research participants to bracket off the here and now in favour of a golden future. Dramatic discontinuities between different epochs of life − future, past and present − led sex workers to imagine constantly that they might be lucky, make their money, move on and establish successful enterprises. Risk therefore involves a temporal orientation that has an affinity with other views of the world among sex workers, towards a possible future that none the less may never happen and cannot be certain.

As other classes of people come to suffer similar uncertainties today, this way of dealing with disadvantage may be construed as an advantage. Certainly, much contemporary fiction and reports in the media construct sex work as an exercise in freedom and enterprise rather than constraint (Day, 1998). Yet, in conclusion, it is worth emphasising the more material ('modern') dimensions of risk alongside these discursive ('postmodern') insecurities. At the beginning of this chapter, I wondered whether it was possible to comment on sex worker risks from the position that I occupied in a medical setting, which was associated with the inscription of risks on prostitutes' bodies, and in a research setting, which was liable to find what it looked for. I conclude that the risks of violence and disease are real enough – the quantities can be measured and compared with the risks that non-prostitutes face. In our cohort study, the risks we measured were greater for sex workers than for other women of similar ages: in the last two years of this study, four women died (Ward and Day, 1997). Two had AIDS: both were infected when they joined our study, one through injecting drug use and the other probably through sex with an infected boyfriend. The prevalence of HIV infection had remained at around one per cent throughout the research period (Day et al., 1988; Ward et al., 1993). The other two women did not have HIV; they were both murdered. Sex workers in London had good judgement about the risks that affected them; they could estimate which were likely to be serious and which might remain everyday hazards that could be accommodated within their lives. While women could not predict the future, they were able to estimate the local risks of the industry accurately, and they were attuned to the mutual constitution of these risks through the discursive and material dimensions of life.

Acknowledgements

This research was initially supported by AVERT, later by the North West Thames Regional Health Authority and currently by the

Wellcome Trust. I am grateful to those who have listened patiently to various meandering thoughts about risk over the years, including audiences at anthropological seminars in UK universities, Maria Phylactou and Jonathan Webber. I should like to thank research participants for their help as well as colleagues associated with the Praed Street Project, and particularly Helen Ward.

NOTES

1. In the seminar series leading to this book, we were asked to discuss two key contemporary figures: Ulrich Beck and Anthony Giddens (for example, Beck, 1995; Giddens, 1991). This chapter draws especially on the former.

2. A third positive language of risk is equally central to the ethnography as a whole and concerns hustling or making your money. I do not discuss this form below (but see Day, 1998 for an account of ideas about market trade or the risks of 'hustling' 'on the game').

3. I use the term 'prostitution' loosely as a synonym for the sex industry (and likewise, for prostitute and sex worker). Sex work describes what these women consider they do, a job, but some people avoid the term. Others use and identify with the terms prostitute or whore, in a process akin to the reclamation of gay and other identities. The most commonly used synonyms by women I knew in the late 1980s were business girls and working girls.

4. The earliest reports to attract widespread attention included the following from Rwanda and Kenya: Van de Perre et al. (1984); D'Costa et al. (1985); Clumeck et al. (1985); Kreiss et al. (1986); Piot et al. (1987).

5. See Ward and Day, 1997 for a brief history of the Praed Street Project. In December 1991, the District Health Authority agreed to support the drop-in and outreach project as part of HIV services, and the clinic continued to be supported in part through research grants and in part through routine clinic services. Whilst Helen Ward and myself continued to be involved both in the research and in establishing the NHS services, we did little of the day to day work. We are now embarking on a study, supported

by the Wellcome Trust, of changes in the industry, in which we shall attempt to contact the women we knew during the period 1986–91, when we collected most of the data on which this chapter is based.

6. Later legislation on an apparent white slave trade and the age of consent to sex had similar effects in disciplining poor women (Walkowitz, 1980).

7. In *The Taming of Chance*, Hacking dates this new kind of government through statistics to the 1820s (Hacking, 1990, p. 118).

8. The contemporary popularity of the trope, 'core goup,' which is thought to be disproportionately responsible for most disease transmission, can be seen in a similar light (see for example the special issue of the *Journal of Infectious Diseases*: Padman et al., 1996).

9. This applies to a wide variety of conditions. I continue to focus on HIV and other STI but see, for another example, Lock, 1998 on the 'breast cancer gene.'

10. Although I am focusing on HIV risks and on negative outcomes, it should be appreciated that some risks are evaluated in very positive terms (see note 2). Personal names are pseudonyms.

11. Spermicides are used as virucides that may destroy any virus but which may simultaneously disrupt epithelia, and increase susceptibility to infection. See debates in the literature over the use of nonoxynol-9, previously the most common virucide used against HIV infection, for example, in Stone and Hitchcock, 1994.

12. This applies to the international as well as local level; for example, in the World Health Organization as well as local projects (Mak, 1996).

13. It is unclear how to prevent processes of legalisation/normalisation/decriminalisation from making the situation still more difficult for immigrants and those involved in illegal activities (such as drug use and under age sex). Whilst there has been a general shift towards deregulation during the past twenty years, the movement for prostitutes' rights must have contributed to a mood of toleration.

14. Karen and other women also requested clinical reassurance from Helen, my colleague (and a physician). This aspect of conversations about risk is not addressed in this chapter.

15. We found substantial agreement about these changes among more than a hundred clients of female sex workers whom we interviewed from 1990–91 (Day et al., 1993).

16. Many reviews are available; see Rhodes, 1997 for one related to HIV prevention.

17. On risk in particular, Bloor notes that interview studies may emphasise unduly a 'calculative orientation to risk behaviour' (Bloor, 1995, p. 92).

18. It should be appreciated that epidemiologists and public health workers do not necessarily agree in their interpretations of risk. For example, epidemiologists rarely consider that behaviour change at the level of individuals could stop an epidemic, which has its own 'natural' curve (see, for example, Anderson and May, 1991).

REFERENCES

Alexander, P. (1988) 'Prostitutes are being scapegoated for heterosexual AIDS', in Delacoste, F. and Alexander, P.(eds) *Sex Work: Writings by Women in the Sex Industry* (London: Virago).

Anderson, R.M. and May, R. (1991) *Infectious Diseases of Humans: Dynamics and Control* (Oxford: Oxford University Press).

Armstrong, D. (1985) 'Space and Time in British General Practice', in Lock, M. and Gordon, D.R. (eds) *Biomedicine Examined* (Dordrecht: Kluwer).

Barton, S.E., Taylor-Robinson, D. and Harris, J.R.W. (1987) 'Female prostitutes and sexually transmitted diseases', *British Journal of Hospital Medicine* 1987; 38: 34–45.

Beck, U. (1995) [1992] *Risk Society: Towards a new modernity* (London: Sage).

Bloor, M. (1995) *The Sociology of HIV Transmission* (London: Sage).

Brandt, A. (1985) *No Magic Bullet: A Social History of Venereal Disease in the United States since 1880* (New York and Oxford: Oxford University Press).

Buckley, S. (1997) 'The Foreign Devil Returns: Packaging Sexual Practice and Risk in Contemporary Japan', in Manderson, L. and Jolly, M. (eds) *Sites of Desire, Economies of Pleasure: Sexualities in Asia and the Pacific* (Chicago and London: University of Chicago Press).

Clumeck, N. et al. (1985) 'Seroepidemiological studies of HTLV-III antibody prevalence among selected groups of heterosexual Africans', *Journal of the American Medical Association*, vol. 254, pp. 2599–602.

Corbin, A. (1990) *Women for Hire: Prostitution and Sexuality in France after 1850* (Boston, MA: Harvard University Press).

Day, S., Ward, H. and Harris, J.R.W. (1988) 'Prostitute women and public health', *British Medical Journal*, vol. 297, p. 1585.

Day, S. (1990) 'Prostitute women and the ideology of work in London', in Feldman, D.A. (ed.) *AIDS and Culture: the Global Pandemic* (New York: Praeger).

Day, S. (1996) 'The law and the market: rhetorics of exclusion and inclusion among London prostitutes', in Harris, O. (ed.) *Inside and Outside the Law* (London: Routledge).

Day, S. (1998), 'Hustling: Individualism among London prostitutes', in Day, S., Stewart, M. and Patapaxiarchis, A. (eds) *Lilies of the Field: marginal people who live for the moment* (Colorado: Westview Press).

Day, S., Ward, H. and Perrotta, L. (1993) 'Prostitution and risk of HIV: male partners of female prostitutes', *British Medical Journal*, vol. 307, pp. 359–61.

D'Costa, L.J., et al. (1985) 'Prostitutes are a major reservoir of sexually transmitted diseases in Nairobi, Kenya', *Sexually Transmitted Diseases*, vol. 12, no. 2, pp. 64–7.

Douglas, M. (1986) [1985] *Risk Acceptability according to the Social Sciences* (London: Routledge and Kegan Paul).

Douglas, M. (1992) *Risk and Blame: Essays in Cultural Theory* (London: Routledge).

Foucault, M. (1976) *The History of Sexuality. An introduction* (New York: Pantheon Books).

Foucault, M. (1986) *The Foucault Reader*, ed. Paul Rabinow (Harmondsworth: Penguin Books).

Freidson, E. (1988) [1970] *The Profession of Medicine* (Chicago: Chicago University Press).

Giddens, A. (1991) *Modernity and Self-identity: self and society in the late modern age* (Cambridge: Polity Press).

Hacking, I. (1990) *The Taming of Chance* (Cambridge: Cambridge University Press).

Illich I. (1976) *Limits to Medicine: Medical nemesis: the expropriation of health* (London: Boyars).

Jackson, L., Highcrest, A. and Coates, R.A. (1992) 'Varied potential risks of HIV infection among prostitutes', *Social Science & Medicine*, vol. 35, no. 3, pp. 281–6.

Kaban, E. (1988) 'U.N. body urges governments to recognise sex trade', (Geneva: Reuters) 19 August. Press release of this report at 'A plea for labor rights for prostitutes' http:///www.ilo.org/public/english/235press/pr/1998/31htm

Kempadoo, K. and Doezema, J. (eds) *Global Sex Workers: Rights, Resistance, and Redefinition* (London: Routledge).

Kreiss, J.K. et al. (1986) 'AIDS virus infection in Nairobi prostitutes', *New England Journal of Medicine*, vol. 314, no. 7, pp. 414–18.

Lock, M. (1998) 'Breast Cancer: Reading the Omens', *Anthropology Today*, vol. 14, no. 4, pp. 7–16.

Mak, R. (ed.) (1996) *EUROPAP: European Intervention Projects for AIDS Prevention among Prostitutes* (Ghent: Academia Press).

Oppenheimer, G.M. (1992) 'Causes, cases and cohorts: the role of epidemiology in the historical construction of AIDS' in Fee, E. and Fox, D. (eds) *AIDS: The Burdens of History* (Oxford: University of California Press).

Overs, C. (1994) 'Sex work, HIV and the state: an interview with Nel Druce', *Feminist Review* vol. 48, pp. 114–21.

Padman, N.S., Aral, S. and Holmes, K. (1996) 'Individual and Population Approaches to the Epidemiology and Prevention of Sexually Transmitted Diseases and Human Immunodeficiency Virus Infections', Supplement 2, *Journal of Infectious Diseases*, vol. 174.

Phetersen, G. (ed.) (1989) *A Vindication of the Rights of Whores* (Seattle, WA: The Seal Press).

Phetersen, G. (1996) *The Prostitution Prism* (Amsterdam: Amsterdam University Press).

Piot, P. et al. (1987) 'Retrospective seroepidemiology of AIDS virus infection in Nairobi populations', *Journal of Infectious Diseases* vol. 155, no. 6, pp. 1108–1112.

Rhodes T. (1997) 'Risk theory in epidemic time: Sex, drugs and the social organisation of 'risk behaviour'", *Sociology of Health & Illness*, vol. 19, pp. 208–27.

Scheper-Hughes, N. (1992) *Death Without Weeping: The Violence of Everyday Life in Brazil* (Berkeley: University of California Press).

Simmel, G. (1990, 2nd edn) *The Philosophy of Money*, ed. Frisby, D. (London: Routledge) [1900, rev. 1907].

Stone, A.B. and Hitchcock, P.J. (1994) 'Vaginal microbicides for preventing the sexual transmission of HIV', *AIDS*, vol. 8 (suppl. 1), pp. S285–93.

Taussig, M. (1980) 'Reification and the consciousness of the patient', *Social Science & Medicine*, vol. 14B, pp. 3–13.

Van de Perre, P. et al. (1984) 'Acquired immunodeficiency syndrome in Rwanda', *The Lancet*, vol. 2, (14 July) pp. 62–65.

Walkowitz, J. (1980) *Prostitution and Victorian Society: Women, class and the state* (Cambridge: Cambridge University Press).

Ward, H. and Day, S. (1997) 'Health care and regulation – new perspectives', in Scambler, G. and Scambler, A. (eds) *Rethinking Prostitution* (London: Routledge).

Ward, H. et al. (1993) 'Prostitution and risk of HIV: female prostitutes in London', *British Journal of Medicine*, vol. 307, pp. 356–8.

Zola, I.K. (1975) 'In the name of health and illness', *Social Science & Medicine*, vol. 9, pp. 83–88.

2 RISK AND TRUST: UNSAFE SEX, GENDER AND AIDS IN TANZANIA

Janet Bujra

'All right husband, you are home and let's celebrate, but use that condom! And if you haven't got one, then I'll go and sleep elsewhere! Or if you keep forgetting, then buy them for me to keep!' (A middle-aged village wife rehearsing what she will say to her husband on his return from the town: Women's workshop, Lushoto, 1996)

'Condoms on sale in village shops? No, the religious leaders would not condone that. It would lead to immorality.' (Elderly man, mosque treasurer: in group discussion, Lushoto, 1998)

Two key concepts, 'risk' and 'trust', are central to the work of Ulrich Beck (1992) and Anthony Giddens (1991, 1992) They have also figured large in analysis of the global AIDS epidemic, especially that produced by social scientists. Whilst Beck and Giddens may be cited in this work, it is other approaches to risk and trust which predominate. The reasons for this are explored through a reconsideration of the theories of Beck and Giddens in terms of their value in illuminating features of the AIDS crisis in Africa. I look in more detail at one example drawing on recent research in Tanzania.[1]

The twin concepts of 'risk' and 'trust' are also central to discourse around AIDS in Tanzania. Given the breadth of the subject, I restrict myself here to the issue of 'safer sex' in order to explore some of its contradictions. These can be summarised as follows: condoms are a device encapsulating safer sex and adopted to reduce risk – particularly in situations where there is no trust.[2] At the same time, as I show for Tanzania, condoms are themselves seen as risky and dangerous, whilst their use, rather than inducing trust in partners, actually symbolises and augments distrust.[3] The form in which trust is invested is socially constructed; the risk of AIDS disrupts the investiture and puts time-honoured social relations in question: to trust is now to court risk. If trust is as basic to human security and to 'inner authenticity' as Giddens argues (1991, p. 215), then how can people rebuild trust whilst at the same time fighting against the risk of AIDS?

BECK AND GIDDENS: RELEVANT PARADIGMS?

Although neither Beck nor Giddens has a specific concern with HIV/AIDS, there are several points where their argument appears particularly pertinent. At other points, there is a jarring difference, where the formulations seem inapplicable. Their general argument is that 'risk' is at the heart of 'late' or 'reflexive' modernity, generating a new kind of society or social condition (called 'risk society' by Beck). Giddens is more concerned with how the individual relates to this new order.

Let me begin by summarising the arguments presented by Beck and/or Giddens which have some purchase on the AIDS issue. First, there is the claim that in risk society there are distinctive 'diseases of modernity' (or as Beck puts it, 'diseases of civilisation', 1992, p. 27), though it is also argued that in such societies the technological capacity for diagnosis has outstripped the ability to deliver cures (Beck, p. 204). Indeed science and its claims to truth are at issue in risk society.

More generally it is asserted that modern risk is 'universal'. First, risks are no respecters of existing social or economic divisions: 'risks display an equalising effect' (Beck, p. 36). Second, risks are globalised in such a way that no disengagement is possible (Giddens, 1991, pp. 22, 30). In the spreading of risk, 'perpetrator and victim soon become identical' (Beck, p. 38). In order to survive or to make a livelihood, risks are confronted and indeed multiplied (Beck, p. 43). The risks themselves are often defined in relation to invisible threats whose presence may require confirmation through 'scientific' procedures (Beck, p. 27). There is a tendency for the risk society to generate authoritarianism (Beck, p. 79).

Giddens adds that the universalisation of risk impacts most forcefully on relations of intimacy and trust (Giddens, 1991, p. 19). In late modern society, with sexual intimacy no longer tied to reproduction or concealed in the realm of the private, the 'negotiation' of sexuality is increasingly subject to social pressure (Giddens, 1992, p. 96).

We may rephrase these points in terms of AIDS in Africa. A disease which is transmitted predominantly through heterosexual intercourse, AIDS at first afflicts those who are 'on the move': its incidence is highest in areas of urban in-migration, the 'service stations' of international highways, the battlegrounds of armies and camp-followers, and the sites of economic development. It is thus a disease associated with 'modern life'. Later the disease is taken home to wives, husbands and sexual partners in more homogeneous and settled areas where economic development is limited. People are first infected through seeking or carrying out activities on which their livelihoods come to depend (the labour migration of men and women, the commercialisation of sex); the disease is then spread, not only through sexual desire, but in a natural bid to reproduce.

If the risk of AIDS does not discriminate between men and women, neither does it recognise material distinction. The rich may be endangered through their capacity to purchase sex with many partners (though these are usually rich *men*, rather than women, and the partners generally of a lower socio-economic status); the poor are at risk because they must earn a livelihood and once infected have few resources to keep themselves healthy. Those who carry the virus usually do so unknowingly at first. They become perpetrators in passing it on, but then succumb to its ravages. The position of medical experts is enhanced by their role in testing and treating opportunistic infections, but at the same time their inability to offer a cure undermines their authority as well as trust in science and in 'Western expertise'.

In Africa, as elsewhere, AIDS has opened up the whole area of sexuality to public scrutiny whilst exhortations to practise safer sex have raised the issue of how this might be negotiated in private relationships. Governments are also under pressure to act, but their responses have sometimes been authoritarian: testing procedures (more or less compulsory for many pregnant women), plans to punish 'perpetrators' (presently under debate in Zimbabwe), the outlawing of homosexual relations or the rounding-up of 'vagrants' (especially women working as prostitutes) and so on.[4]

AN INAPPROPRIATE FRAMEWORK?

If, for Beck and Giddens, 'risk society'/'risk culture' is defined as entailing distinctively new kinds of risks encoded in the transformations characterising modernity or industrial society, risks which severely try and often fracture established relations of trust, then this conceptualisation seems initially very relevant to the AIDS crisis. However, there are points at which the argument seems inappropriate to the case of AIDS, or at least of AIDS in Africa.

Whilst the patterns of transmission and spread of AIDS in Africa may be linked to the changes wrought by capitalist penetration, the disease itself is not a product of 'science', that is, equivalent to pollution, toxicity, the nuclear threat or genetic engineering.[5] In Africa, more than in the developed countries, transmission may be effected in under-resourced medical settings via inoculations or blood transfusions, but most often the 'responsible parties', as Beck puts it (p. 55), are ordinary unsuspecting members of the public. This does not prevent people apportioning blame, but it does distance the problem from that being explored by Beck and Giddens (and perhaps makes it harder to address).

'Globalisation' is also at issue here. It is true that AIDS is spread along the paths that draw the world closer together and homogenise its patterns of organisation: through investment, trade, tourism, political involvement, aid and so on. However, the globalisation argument is often over-stated, downplaying the way in which contexts can transform globalising tendencies (at least for a time), as blue changes into green when it is washed over yellow.[6] The case of AIDS is instructive here with different patterns of transmission in Africa and North America. When news of the epidemic first hit East Africa, people thought of it as a 'white homosexual disease' (Kaleeba, 1991, p. 4).[7] When it began to spread in Africa, however, it was predominantly through heterosexual relations, thus putting *all the adult sexually-active population* potentially at risk. It may well be that in North America, the infection was at first largely contained within the gay community precisely in consequence of the liberatory social movement which allowed male homosexuals to come out and to contract gay relationships openly.[8] Even if AIDS had first taken hold in Africa amongst homosexuals, the moral climate there was very different. Hostility towards gays is generally virulent, with homosexual relations often hidden and disguised through outwardly heterosexual activities (see Phillips, 1994 on Zimbabwe; Porter, 1995 on Kenya).[9]

Given gender inequality and physiological vulnerability, women are at greater risk of contracting HIV in Africa than men, whether through coercive sex or inability to negotiate safer sex. Given that women are married or seduced at a younger age than men, they are also infected earlier. Sero-positive women tend to be weakened by pregnancy and to die faster. Both these patterns are evident in statistics (see for example NACP, 1997).[10] If the incidence of AIDS is different in Africa from patterns in Europe/North America, the way governments, communities, families and individuals perceive it is also distinctive. Just because AIDS is a global phenomenon, with infection knowing no national boundaries, strategies of containment which have worked in one place may not work everywhere in the same way.

The final and obvious point about applying Beck's or Giddens' theories to this situation is that nowhere in Africa could we legitimately speak of conditions of 'late modernity' (Giddens' term). Even 'modernity' cannot be said to be securely established (in their definition: Giddens, 1991, pp. 15–16), with industrial development limited and halting in many areas, the penetration of capitalism incomplete, the nation state built on insecure foundations and 'the regularised control of social relations across ... time-space distances' (p. 16) extremely shaky. Responses to the AIDS crisis reflect this backwardness, with African governments unable to support the medical expenditure to treat or test all those infected, and, given the lack of a developed pharmaceutical industry, very much at the mercy of multinational drug companies profiting out of tragedy.

These features appear to set Africa outside of the theoretical frame within which Beck and Giddens operate. That this resurrects a barely disguised meta-narrative of 'modernisation', with its evolutionist assumptions and its unquestioning presumption that the 'West' will show the Rest the way, is notable in this work of Beck and Giddens – though it is a darkly-hued version of modernity and late modernity which is purveyed here.

RISK AND TRUST IN THE AIDS LITERATURE

The concept of risk has been much worked over in the literature on AIDS. Although reference may be made to Beck and/or Giddens in this context, it is often by way of paying lip service to the idea that risk symbolises the contemporary social condition rather than exploring its validity for AIDS research (see, for example, Bloor, 1995, p. 84). Foucault makes more of a splash in the AIDS literature. The key debate in terms of AIDS risk analysis is not with Beck and Giddens, but between epidemiological accounts and those written from a more sociological perspective.[11] Amongst those who view AIDS in its social aspect, epidemiological approaches, based on large-scale surveys and testing regimes, are suspect, as the predominant sociological mode of AIDS research is largely based on interactionist perspectives. Epidemiology's narrowly quantitative methods, framed in positivist assumptions, are rejected, and it decries the consequent treatment of the data as an aggregation of individual cases. Epidemiological analysis is said to lend itself to medical models of disease and a reliance on technical fixes; epidemiology is also seen as potentially an arm of the authoritarian state bent on surveillance and control through screening and testing. By delineating social categories where prevalence is high, it contributes to their stigmatisation as 'high-risk groups'. It sets up 'risk management' as the goal.

The rejection of epidemiological approaches generally extends to their sociological analogue, KAPB studies (that is, large-scale surveys which presume that there is an unproblematic link between knowledge/attitudes/beliefs and practice).[12] Much preventive work has been based on the outcomes of such work which Friedman dismisses as 'individualist approaches that treat infection risk and transmission risk as due to individual pathology or cognitive failure' (1998, p. 138).

By contrast, sociological accounts have generally sought out qualitative data and adopted a relativistic stance. The focus here is not on individuals *per se*, but on their *relationships* and on the *social contexts* in which risk behaviour might occur. The aim is to uncover the diversity and to explore the meaning of risk behaviour to participants, investigating *how* they manage risk. Consequently the notion of 'high-risk groups' is rejected and a more nuanced picture of risk *behaviour* in social settings is offered. The concept of trust, absent from epi-demiological accounts, is a significant one here. Stigma is seen as a consequence of labelling processes. Technical fixes (condoms, for example) are derided in favour of investigation into how they are perceived and employed in practice. The proponents of these views are more likely to argue for community-level or sub-cultural responses rather than looking to the state. Overall, these approaches have been anti-authoritarian, and range from the liberal to the subversively libertarian.

The work of Beck and Giddens finds little echo within sociological accounts of AIDS, for it proposes Grand Theory rather than micro-analysis. In its meta-narrative of late modernity, it is universalistic rather than relativistic, whilst its subject is Society in a specific historical epoch rather than everyday social interaction. Rather than endorsing the technicist theme of risk management or exploring the micropolitics of managing risk, Beck and Giddens are asserting that risk is precisely *not* managed in late-modern society. In points of detail there may be overlap in these perspectives and occasional strong convergence, as for example when Beck notes the dangers of medical autonomy from processes of social consent, or when he writes: 'Surreptitiously the mastery of nature [by science] becomes technical control of the subject' (1992, p. 207). But for the most part, these are divergent conceptions of the world.

DEFINING RISK AND TRUST IN THE TANZANIAN CONTEXT

Although my own approach was anthropological, there are many points of parallel between my data on Tanzania and that in other diverse settings, emphasising the way that AIDS exposes both the human condition (modern, pre-modern or postmodern) as well as more localised responses.

The concept of 'trust' is central to the way people in Tanzania talk about AIDS. Giddens defines the term as 'the vesting of confidence in persons or abstract systems, made on the basis of a "leap of faith" which brackets ignorance or lack of information' (1991, p. 244). I queried this definition at first, seeing in the term a set of *anticipations based on experience*[13] rather than faith, though on further thought I conceded that the more intimate and personal the relationships the more often one operated in terms of 'hope' or 'aspiration' rather than predictability! The Swahili term for 'trust' (*uaminifu*) underlines the same assumption, as it derives from the word for belief or *faith*.

The concept of risk is defined by Beck in an exclusive way that equates it with modernity: it is 'a systematic way of dealing with hazards and insecurities induced and introduced by modernisation itself' (p. 21), as opposed to 'older dangers', or what Giddens refers to as 'inclement nature' (1991, p. 19). It embodies reflexivity and doubt. It also implies calculation.[14] The term most often used in Swahili – *hatari* – is more straightforwardly applied to a known or certain outcome. People try, with homespun metaphors, to render the threat of AIDS predictable: 'If there is a lion in the forest you don't go in'; 'If you see a rotten tree you don't wait underneath until it falls' and so on. But most people recognise that AIDS is a danger and a risk of a very uncertain kind. People acknowledge this by using the word 'fear' or 'anxiety' more often than danger. The 'fear' is of a faceless enemy or enemies: 'You can't know them'; 'We are not sure who they are'; 'You can't tell who has it, so you might make friends with someone, unknowing'.[15] This invisible danger, this terrifying unknowingness, this threat which undercuts the possibility of rational action, actually throws people back onto faith or trust – even as this in itself compounds the risk.

AIDS IN LUSHOTO

The research which I am discussing here was carried out in Lushoto in northeastern Tanzania as part of a larger comparative project on gender relations and AIDS in Tanzania and Zambia. The people in this poor and mountainous area are Sambaa by culture and pre-dominantly Muslim by religion. They are largely peasant/subsistence farmers who, due to soil erosion and land pressure, have migrated out from the area for at least the last three generations. Initially, it was men who migrated to work in tea estates or sisal plantations; others became dockworkers, labourers, factory workers or domestic servants in newly industrialising towns like Tanga, Dar es Salaam or Mombasa. Wives were left at home to cultivate, though husbands returned regularly; young men went home to marry. By the 1990s, male migration more commonly takes the form of trading rather than wage-work, and women are now also migrating independently, especially young women. They may go simply to 'visit', but they often seek work or find themselves in prostitution or bar work (Bujra, 2000).

Despite a long history of migration, this is not an area with a very high HIV prevalence in Tanzanian terms.[16] The reasons for this are unclear, although it is evident that AIDS is now making inroads into the local population and is perceived to be a threat by local people. It is clear that people's perceptions do not simply reflect the recorded statistics; their sense of danger may magnify its real extent. Our own surveys in the capital, in Mbeya and in Lushoto show that the level of *perceived* local impact (63 per cent) is as high in Lushoto as in higher-prevalence Dar es Salaam; though Mbeya records a realistically greater awareness (with 92 per cent seeing it as a local problem). Asking about people's personal sense of risk, however, discloses a ranking which better reflects reality, with only half of respondents in Lushoto feeling themselves to be personally at risk (compared to a realistically higher proportion in Mbeya and Dar es Salaam).

Within these percentages, there were contrasts between men and women, particularly in Lushoto, on which I now focus. In Lushoto, women were approximately half as likely to feel themselves in personal danger as men (33 per cent compared to 59 per cent) – or at least to concede that they felt so. Women in rural Lushoto are constrained by a culture of shame in relation to sexual matters: before AIDS, sex was unmentionable in public and any display of knowledge was regarded as morally reprehensible. Young women in particular were expected to feign ignorance. The onset of the AIDS epidemic has dramatically challenged these norms of modest female behaviour, and forced people in general to be more open, name the unnameable, speak the unspeakable. But we still found young women who denied any knowledge of AIDS or its modes of transmission. Women in general claimed less knowledge than men. This is not ignorance (there were often inconsistencies in the responses which betrayed more knowledge than was at first claimed!): it is more a bid to be acknowledged as morally upright.

EXPLAINING AIDS IN LUSHOTO

In Lushoto, several competing and socially defined explanations are given for the catastrophic onset of the AIDS crisis. Whereas most people can explain in 'scientific'/rational terms how the disease is transmitted and indeed how it can be avoided, the explanation for why it strikes some rather than others is formulated on different grounds.

One argument, much favoured by young men, puts AIDS outside of any rational explanation but locates it in a thrusting conception of masculinity. AIDS is likened to *'ajali kazini'*: accidents at work. The 'work' (sex) is that of men; the accidents cannot be predicted and occur randomly. We might say, 'that's life'; except that it really means, 'that's death' – unanticipated and beyond human control.

More commonly, however, people subscribe to a view of the world in which events are the outcome of willed action. If some succumb whilst others do not, then this may be because of the malevolence of people who practise witchcraft – people who must be identified and exposed. The problem of AIDS is here narrowed down to one amongst many forms of misfortune that evil people may wish upon others. The grudges which sustain it may have nothing to do with sex or its moral charge.

Most often, however, people in rural Lushoto subscribe to a moral diagnosis of AIDS. Those who succumb are not simply people who have sex with the infected, they are 'adulterers', 'immoral people', 'those who love money', 'fornicators', etc. AIDS may then be understood as divine intervention, with the more religious (and especially elderly men) seeing AIDS as 'God's Big Stick' – punishment for those who break his commands, and especially the adulterers and fornicators whose behaviour has become outrageous. Here it is the immoral behaviour which is seen as threatening rather than the outcome, which is regarded as deserved, the wages of sin.

Whilst there is no single explanation of HIV infection, respondents most often pose the issue in moral terms. The point they wish to make is that they themselves are respectable and decent – the problem is with others. The formulation is often in terms of 'trust': 'I trust myself' they will say, but, 'You can't trust [husbands/wives/ strangers/people who come back from town/hospitals etc].' These formulations should dictate certain kinds of action, but what people say, and what they actually do is not always the same thing, especially where the required actions demand the rupture of time-honoured social arrangements. In Tanzania, the question of protection has often been posed in individualistic terms: people may 'choose' abstinence, fidelity – or condoms. In practice, people – and especially women – may find that the choices are made for them by others, or by the circumstances in which they live. Safer sex becomes a matter of hope/aspiration, that is, trust, rather than a goal consciously planned and achieved through negotiation between equals.

In rural Lushoto, women are not in a strong negotiating position for a variety of reasons. Given a rule of patrilocal marriage residence, women leave the familiarity and support of their natal homes on marriage to reside with strangers. Married women are expected to provide sustenance for their families through cultivating their husbands' land. Husbands expect to be in control of their wives and to determine their movements, their access to resources, their sexuality and reproductive capacity. Women are virtually unrepresented in the political and religious hierarchy of the village. Men leave as migrants and may enter into liaisons unchecked, whilst women should stay behind faithfully and support the family. Young unmarried women are in a particularly dependent position and may find themselves subject to violent seduction. It is anticipated that widows will be inherited by a male relative of their dead husband.

These women are not entirely helpless victims. There are associations, especially of older women, which allow for some mutual support (Bujra and Baylies, 1999). Younger women may leave for towns to escape parental domination or following divorce or widowhood. One or two women have gained minor positions of local political leadership.

Gendered inequality presents a different face when AIDS enters the picture. Men's labour migration as well as their inheritance of widows are suddenly rendered dangerous. Women care for the sick and dying but then find themselves uninheritable and unsupported (one such case occurred whilst I was doing fieldwork). Men insist on sex and may do so coercively, despite wives' or girlfriends' justifiable suspicions that they could be infected. Young women (and young men) run off to towns and may come back infected. Young women, however, because their behaviour is seen as particularly transgressive, are often blamed for bringing AIDS to the area.

But perhaps most dramatically, men suddenly begin to see women as dangerous – their 'trust' in wives (and daughters) and other partners is put in question. Whereas women have always had a healthy distrust of men and find in this new situation simply an augmentation of long-held doubt, for men this is something new, a situation in which they can no longer take their own power and capacity to control women for granted. What AIDS has done here, in Beck's formulation, is to equalise risk, and consequently to bring gender relations into question.[17]

Whilst both men and women regretted the way that AIDS had transformed trust into doubt, especially in the most intimate relations, it was men who spoke of it more. Although men will say dogmatically that 'a wife trusts her husband' (and they may add 'and he trusts his wife'), and they are generally confident that they can trust themselves and are therefore safe, doubts soon crowd in: 'I trust myself. But the one I live with – what of her?', 'You are worried that your wife might have it, that she might not be faithful to you ...', 'A wife can infect her husband!' And tellingly, 'Adultery holds more danger now than it used to, so there is more anxiety and lack of trust.' And in consequence, these days, 'People are not trusting each other.' Inconsistently perhaps they also put their faith in trust: 'If there is trust between you, then it's safe.'

VARIETY OF MALE RESPONSES

Some men claim that in response to AIDS they now discuss sexual relations with their wives or partners, trying to make a compact between them for fidelity (a very novel notion here – both infidelity and discussion of sex between partners were previously male prerogatives and not usually negotiable). Some claim to *be* more faithful, and some wives express pride in their husbands: 'I know my husband doesn't run after other women', 'He doesn't stray.' Most are sceptical: 'My husband goes out and you don't know where he is or what he is doing.' Some men simply watch their backs, warily sizing up opportunities for sex in terms of whether the person is 'trustworthy' or not.

This calculation is often expressed through the language of 'inside' and 'outside', a conceptualisation which women also voice. The simple verb 'to go out' stands for many activities which have now become risky: to go away to urban areas to work or trade, or to commit adultery. Men typically 'go out' or have this right, which now puts them in danger. Some are beginning to rethink, and talk of 'staying at home' as a prophylactic, meaning not committing adultery and thinking twice about going to town: 'When I go to Dar es Salaam [the capital] these days I don't do anything and I come home quickly.' The mixed metaphor of sex and travel is potent in these comments. Women, by contrast, have always stayed at home, paradoxically giving them a false sense of security. Thus many women protested that they would be safe because 'I have never been anywhere', 'If I stay here I should be all right.'

There is a clear hierarchy of risk in many people's minds with those deemed 'inside' (at home, not moving) to be safe, whereas those 'outside' represent a series of levels of danger. As one man put it: 'There is sex here at home, that is good. There is sex there outside and that is dangerous.' But within the local area, a known sexual partner, even if not the spouse, may be trusted, whilst someone who is unknown cannot be trusted. It is best to avoid those 'who have been away'. 'Strangers' who pass through are even more dangerous and sex in distant parts is the most dangerous of all, as people there are untrammelled by moral imperatives as well as being unknown – there is 'mixing' of people from different areas with different customs and 'too much sex' and too much drinking.

An example of this reasoning was presented to me on a recent visit. 'Fortunately', I was told, 'of those people who stayed in the area and did not go away, no one has died recently of AIDS.' Three AIDS deaths had occurred, however: one a young woman whose death was easily explained: 'She worked in a bar in [Lushoto] town.' The other two were a local man and his wife who returned sick from Dar es Salaam. A male relative of the husband explained: 'After his wife died he told us that he too was dying of AIDS. But it was not his fault. Whilst they were in Dar es Salaam he and his wife had quarrelled and she found another *bwana* [literally boss, but here it means sexual partner]. Then later they were reconciled, but it was too late.' The couple died 'within forty days of each other'.

The 'stranger/outsider' metaphor is employed in explanatory mode in both these cases, with towns both near and far a source of danger. The metaphor is overlaid with a gendered moral significance, for it is women who go to work in bars and wives who may be blamed as untrustworthy, as well as 'not one of us'. The problem with this imagery – which also plays its part in calculations about the use of condoms – is that the home is actually the most dangerous place of all, since the assumption of trust leads people to suspend judgement about potential risks.

There are some men who respond to the breakdown of trust (which is rather for them a breakdown in control over women) by aiming to assert a 'renewed patriarchy'. As one man put it: 'I drove away one of my wives because she was behaving badly and I feared the outcome.' And another assured us that: 'If the government in your house is bad then you will get [AIDS] – you need to rule your wives so that they don't go straying.'

WOMEN'S RESPONSES

Certainly men expected to hold undisputed authority within the home and women acknowledged this: 'Men just go out, but we must beg permission', 'He has become like your parent', 'You are under his foot, under his rule', 'He has married a woman to stay at home and serve him.' They concede that husbands have the right to beat wives if they misbehave, even though most do not. And in the context of AIDS they feel powerless against 'husbands who go away and come back with the disease'. Can they refuse sex? As one of the male respondents put it: 'It's the man who refuses' – in other words, only he has this right and privilege. And hence women say: 'You can't do anything.' Or as one put it: 'There is no protection for wives. Can you stop a man from taking what he wants outside?' And another: 'Men are never satisfied – they're like chickens' (who scratch outside and are promiscuous in their sexuality).

But the AIDS epidemic has led even women to take unprecedented steps. One case, reported by several people, was of a woman whose husband came home from town, infected as she believed. She did refuse sex and left him: 'And she is still alive.' This potent example had led other women to imagine such possibilities, of running away, of demanding divorce, refusing sex, or even: 'I sometimes think that it is better to live alone.'

In the workshops we held in connection with this project, women sometimes spontaneously rehearsed how they might be more assertive with men. In one meeting, a middle-aged woman called Farida[18] expounded on how women might become infected:

Let's say, my husband is in Dar es Salaam or Tanga – he is away and he comes home – that's how you get it! After four years he's been away, and then you hear a knock on the door: 'Mama open up!' You welcome him. He has brought many presents – because all this time he has been away he sent nothing. And he makes out he 'loves you so much!' [spoken derisively]. He used to be fat, and now look at him – he has lost weight. My man has got so thin! Well, what do you do?

The room was now in uproar, some telling her to be ashamed for speaking so, and others concurring excitedly at this blunt statement of their common dilemma. An elderly woman behind Farida said vehemently: 'You can't do anything – he is your husband and if you refuse he will be angry ...'. The debate continued:

Farida: Well, we have heard there *is* a way – there is this thing called condom! [There was excited embarrassment and shock from the other women.] All right husband, you are home and let's celebrate, but use that condom! And if you haven't got one, then I'll go and sleep elsewhere! Or if you keep forgetting, then buy them for me to keep!

The other women were bowled over by this frankness and were now howling with laughter and shame, covering their faces with their wrappers. The elderly woman intervened: 'Some men get drunk and they refuse to use these things and they can beat you!' Farida, engaging with this, responded: 'Yes! It's true. He will beat you, but at least you have told him plainly! Better to be beaten than to die!'

CONDOMS AND SAFER/UNSAFE SEX

Let me end by elaborating on the perception of the condom as the ultimate in safer sex. On the whole, people in rural Lushoto do not use condoms, though most people know about them. Despite the AIDS epidemic, condoms are not freely available except in guesthouses in the nearby town or at family planning clinics.

Condoms may be purchased in the same town, but rural shops did not stock them. And the price, whilst relatively low (Sh20: approximately 2p sterling) is more than most people could afford on a regular basis. But the real barriers to the use of condoms are of a different order. There are three constraints – one is lack of knowledge in how to use condoms, the second is their association with shame, and paradoxically the third is tied up with the issue of trust.

Whereas nearly all men appeared to be knowledgeable,[19] in practice they were not. For example, the mistaken idea that condoms would be more effective if two were used together was occasionally voiced. Claims to knowledge vied with shame at disclosure. Like women, men displayed embarrassment and shock even at the naming of this item. At one of the men's workshops, the AIDS Coordinating Officer from the town demonstrated how to put one on, using a penis mould. This generated considerable hysteria amongst those present, revealed in my notes, along with evidence of men's assertions of knowledge. In the following dialogue, the facilitator is a middle-aged woman from Dar es Salaam whilst the AIDS Coordinating Officer is male and referred to as 'doctor' – though in fact he was not qualified as such; Jamal and Paul are men in their thirties, seen locally as 'young men' (*vijana*), whilst Mzee Martin is an elderly man who is the hamlet chairman.

When asked for suggestions about protection from AIDS, Jamal burst out: 'We can help ourselves by using condoms! But those things – sometimes when you use them they split! When I used them myself – it tore. They say they help, they protect you, so I bought them – I don't know if they had expired, but they were useless!' Other men are embarrassed by his frankness, but the facilitator confirms Jamal's statement:

'Yes, we can use condoms, but it's true, sometimes they split. Do you all know them?'
Paul: 'Not everyone knows about them.'
Facilitator: 'You don't know?'
Paul: 'Of course I know.'
Facilitator: 'Let the doctor show you how to use it so that it doesn't split.'
Doctor [taking out several packets]: 'One thing is, that if you leave them in your back pocket for a week or more the rubber can perish with your body heat. Also when you use them you need to pinch this bit at the end –'

Jamal: 'But listen! I bought mine just there at the bus stand – I went and I used it straight away! After the job, I found it was split!' [Men are hooting with laughter.]

Doctor: 'You need to look at the expiry date – approximately five years after the manufacturing date. Like this one – it was manufactured in [he shows where it is written] – January 1995, so it will expire in around 1999. Let me show you – they are sold in sets – open the packet carefully so that you don't tear the condom. There is this little teat at the end. Pinch it, and when your male thing is ready–' [He gets out the penis mould.]

Jamal: 'So that's how it's done! Aiya!' [He laughs uncontrollably in shocked embarrassment, hiding his face in his hands. The other men are embarrassed both by the mould and by Jamal!]

Doctor: 'Look, this is how we put it on – '

Jamal: 'Eh! Mzee Martin – ! [He is ashamed to have the respect which younger people generally adopt with elders so publicly and rudely interrupted, but he is also excited and giggling.]

Mzee Martin [reasserting the authority of an elder]: 'You need to know this.'

Younger men felt that the respect they owed to older men was transgressed by the demonstration and did not know where to put themselves. The male need to assert knowledge is also powerfully expressed here. It is also notable that a 'young man' felt no inhibition in referring publicly to a casual sexual encounter. No woman, young or old, would have dared to do so.

When men were asked individually if they would ever use a condom, only 56 per cent of them agreed. Many were suspicious of the whole idea. Their faith in Western medicine had been undermined by its failure to come up with a cure for AIDS, and condoms were regarded as a foreign imposition, politically suspect if not indeed an element in a genocidal conspiracy: 'They are an alien thing for Africans', 'They are infected with HIV', 'They are made elsewhere and you don't know those who made them – they could be defective' (the implication again is that unknown persons cannot be trusted). Amongst those who said they might use them, the circumstances were telling. As one man said: 'Outside you use, inside you don't use them.' Again, 'outside' has a double meaning. It means when men are away from home, for example, 'In Dar es Salaam, you don't know them and they have no shame, you could be in danger.' But it also means outside marriage, with partners whom you don't trust: 'Each one has doubts.' But even here there is calculation: 'If I know and trust them, then I don't use condoms', said one man. Another said he wouldn't use them with 'those who haven't been anywhere'.

The last place men would use condoms would be at home. Not only is this the place where they expect to trust, they are also conscious of the deductions that would be made by their wives if they did so. First of all, she would assume that he suspected her of infidelity: 'A woman can't agree to using condoms – she will say: "Don't you trust me?"' Second, she would immediately suspect him of having affairs or of being infected, leading to accusations of trust betrayed. So despite the fact that his wife is more important to him than extra-marital partners (her illness or death would undermine his capacity to survive and to parent his children), he is unable openly to protect her. This is the domestic politics of risk from the perspective of men.

The situation for women is different. Some women may be ignorant about condoms, but many more deny the knowledge: 42 per cent claimed never to have heard of them. When we asked if they would consider using them (or rather having them used), only 12.5 per cent said that they would. Even where they would feel safer if they were protected by men's use of condoms, they are dependent on men's goodwill to effect this. As the AIDS Coordinating Officer said in one of our women's seminars: 'The problem with the male condom is that he has to agree to wear it. You can't force him!' To demand the use of condoms would be to court another risk – of being beaten or driven away. As one man said: 'The one who asks for a condom is not a wife but a prostitute.' Women fear to ask in case they are thought to be infected or immoral themselves: 'He will ask, where have you been?!' A wife might ask when she knows or suspects that the husband is infected. But in raising the issue, she undermines further the trust between them. And so, although few women genuinely trust their husbands, the *appearance* of trust must be there.

Elaborate games are played out in the conjugal bed with each partner pretending to trust the other, because the consequences of not doing so will in themselves induce mistrust. Women persuade themselves that marriage will protect them from AIDS whilst also noting that the unmarried do not even pretend to trust: 'You don't hear of prostitutes dying – they use their wits. And condoms.'

There are echoes here of insights drawn from quite different settings in which AIDS has taken hold. Bloor comments on the way in which commercial sex allows for a negotiating moment when the price is determined and on which can be grafted an insistence on the use of condoms.[20] Non-commercial sex, by contrast, is often the 'culmination of a mutely enacted series of events where ambiguity [is] both pervasive and functional' (Bloor, 1995, p. 82). Ambiguity limits the capacity of either partner to negotiate for safer sex. As Green puts it in another context: 'unsafe sex implies closeness, trust, honesty and commitment and leaves rosy facades and dreams of monogamy and security intact' (1995, pp. 145–6). From the point of view of rural people in Lushoto, the safest sex would be 'immoral sex'; proper conjugal relations require sex which, in an era of AIDS, is unsafe sex.

CONCLUSION

AIDS is a global phenomenon but as a disease of modernity it is spreading to areas of a very different character from those on which Beck and Giddens focus. Despite this, their work opens up significant and stimulating vistas of enquiry about cultures in which new forms of risk are becoming embedded. Its relevance lies not so much in the model of risk society itself, but in hypotheses about what globalising risk does to social relations. Giddens' exploration of 'transformations of intimacy' discloses a new world in which sexuality is no longer hidden in the private domain but opened up to public negotiation and discussion.[21] He traces this development most powerfully to the combined impact of modern forms of contraception and feminism, but we can see that in Africa similar effects have flowed from a more sombre cause. AIDS has drawn sex and sexuality into the realm of public discourse in Africa.

If sexuality is on the public agenda in Africa, is it also more negotiable? Or to put this in a different way, can gender inequity offer fertile ground for negotiation? We have seen that women may rehearse scenarios of 'negotiation'; in practice they are more likely to be silent or to be beaten for questioning men's prerogatives. Holland et al. argue that Giddens overstates the case for sexual transformation in late-modern society, pointing to the enduring power of 'masculine hegemony' (1998, pp. 193–4). It is worth pondering the implications of quite another scenario in the African context. In Lushoto these days, if a woman returns from the ante-natal clinic with free condoms and advice to 'rest after her pregnancy', then husbands generally accept this advice. Here 'trust' is invested in medical 'experts' whose advice has a halo of scientific credibility. Use of the condom does not imply any moral judgements, or lead to poisonous and corrosive doubt within the conjugal relationship. To seek better health for oneself and one's family is seen as commendable and normal. That the condoms are free also eases the process, avoiding potential embarrassment in their purchase. Even Muslim religious leaders now accept 'spacing of births' as a legitimate and proper reason for using condoms. This scenario leaves masculine hegemony intact. In the short run, it also protects wives from unsafe sex. What it does not offer is an opening for negotiating gender inequity.

Trust and risk counterpoint each other in the setting of rural Lushoto. Trust enhances the dangers of infection; but risk also equalises, putting both men and women into a situation where the Other could kill. I have shown that trust is gendered unequally, for men linked indissolubly to control of women and to the display of knowledge, for women more of a hope or aspiration. AIDS (amongst other factors) is challenging men's sense of control over women as well as their mastery of knowledge. Men's trust has therefore received a considerable jolt. Women's dependence in the old order renders them extremely vulnerable in the new context of risk, their sense of trust more fragile, but its performance more critical. Trust is in question all round; risk equalises. There is the potential for building on this unifying effect, but that is another story.

NOTES

1. Research was carried out in 1995–97 as part of a wider project funded by the ESRC ('Gender relations as a key aspect of the fight against HIV/AIDS in Tanzania and Zambia'). Directed by the author and Carolyn Baylies of the University of Leeds, it involved a team of African social scientists and AIDS activists carrying out field research in three sites in each country. Lushoto in Tanzania is the site reported on here. A base line survey complemented close observation and participatory action research (see Bujra and Baylies, 1999).

2. Note the fortuitous but compellingly appropriate metaphor used by Giddens when he writes of a 'cocoon of trust' allaying the existential anxiety of late modernity (1991, p. 126).

3. This may be universal (see Holland et al., 1991) – though compare the alternative scenario described in the Conclusion of this chapter. Certainly in Africa it is not restricted to Tanzania. Amofah writes of Ghana: 'Condom use has the connotation of infidelity in many of our cultures' (1992, p. 5).

4. References to human rights and their violation in this field, especially by autocratic states, are cited in the *Newsletter* of the African Network on Ethics, Law and HIV (1996). See also Seidel, 1993, on Africa in general; Phillips, 1994 on Zimbabwe; and reports in many issues of *AIDS Analysis Africa* (e.g., vol. 2, no. 4, 1992; vol. 3, no. 2, 1993; vol.7, no. 2, 1997). Conversely African governments struggle to contain the epidemic and treat those affected on diminishing budgets. None is as authoritarian as Cuba – though the measures implemented there have indeed stemmed the spread of AIDS (Scheper-Hughes, 1994). Many Tanzanians support harsh measures (Lwihula et al., 1993 report that people in Kagera – where prevalence rates are very high – commend the 'isolation of patients on fortified islands in Lake Victoria or giving them lethal injections': 1993, p. 354). Cleland and Ferry's survey revealed that many older people in Africa respond to AIDS by demanding the repression of young people (1995, p. 218).

5. That AIDS in Africa might be a product of Western science is discussed by (amongst others) Chirimuuta and Chirimuuta (1987, pp. 7–8). The claim is that the HIV virus was formulated in a US laboratory and then exported to Zaire where the CIA had a base in the 1970s. See also Lwihula et al., 1993, p. 351.

6. Giddens recognises the problem as one of the dialectical relationship between the global and the local: 'events at one end of a distanciated relation often produce divergent or even contrary occurrences at another' (1991, p. 22).

7. A similar account from West Africa is in Amofah (1992, p. 5).

8. On the American gay epidemic see Altman (1994). On the role of restricted sexual networking in the social containment of risk, see Friedman et al. (1998, pp. 148–9).

9. This is not true everywhere in Africa. Male and female homo-
    sexuality is situationally/subculturally tolerated in the East
    African coastal region, as I know through research and residence
    in the area (see also Shepherd, 1987; Porter, 1995), whilst South
    Africa has a long-established though mostly white homosexual
    community. Male homosexuals are beginning to 'come out' in
    other places too – particularly those where the state is most
    oppressive, like Zimbabwe.

10. The Tanzanian statistics confirm a general pattern. The highest
    rates of HIV infection and AIDS cases amongst women begin in
    the 20–24-year-old category, whilst amongst men, infection is
    pronounced from the later age of 25–29. Moreover, the
    prevalence of HIV infection is now higher in women than in
    men (NACP, 1997, pp. 14, 20). AIDS statistics must be treated
    with considerable caution. In Tanzania, 103,185 reported AIDS
    cases are contrasted with a more realistic *estimate* of 520,000 cases
    (NACP, 1997, p. 6). Tanzania is one of the worst affected
    countries in Africa.

11. The characterisation of these opposing positions is taken from a
    range of writers on the social aspects of AIDS: see for example
    Frankenberg, 1993; Bloor, 1995; Hart and Boulton, 1995;
    Rhodes, 1995; Friedman et al., 1998. Within the sociological
    camp, differences of approach and emphasis in regard to risk are
    explored particularly by Bloor, but see also contrasts between
    Douglas, 1992 (who devises an almost Durkheimian
    explanation); Seidel, 1993 (drawing on discourse analysis); Schiltz
    and Adam, 1995 (combining survey analysis with phenomeno-
    logical reflection); McFadden, 1992 and Holland et al., 1998
    (informed by feminism), etc.

12. In Tanzania the most extensive use of KAPB studies has been in
    school surveys (for example, Ndeki et al., 1994). A fairly reflexive
    and critical account is offered by the authors of one of the most
    wide-ranging surveys of this kind, investigating sexual behaviour
    and AIDS in developing countries (Cleland and Ferry, 1995).

13. Giddens' conception is not altogether consistent: he also defined
    trust as 'accountability and openness' rather than blind faith
    (1992, p. 187).

14. The degree of calculation involved in AIDS risk behaviour is
    contested. Where sociologists reject 'rational choice' theories of

action, they may associate calculation with this. Moreover they may argue that, 'risk related action is often a product of socialised habituation rather than calculation' (Rhodes, 1995, p. 129; Bloor, 1995). Conversely they may see risk behaviour as calculatedly rational where choices are being made *between risks*: between courting infection or repelling affection, for example (see Rhodes, 1995; Schiltz and Adam, 1995).

15. Most of the comments cited hereafter derive from the 1996 baseline survey in the rural hinterland of Lushoto town. A structured sample of 100 was sought, reflecting gender, age, and socio-economic position. Half of those interviewed were women. The interviews were in Swahili and allowed for discursive elaboration and discussion. My two local assistants (one male, one female) followed a standard mode of questioning; I recorded answers, inflections, body language, etc., and probed further where this promised to be productive. Other quotations are culled from my field notes based on extensive participant observation in the area.

16. Much higher rates are found in the capital and other urban areas, in Kagera near the Uganda border, or areas straddling international highways to the south or north (like Mbeya, our third site). Between 1991–97, cumulative AIDS cases showed Tanga Region (of which Lushoto is one district) ranking twelfth. It ranked ninth in terms of the prevalence of HIV infection, with sero-positivity levels of 8 per cent found amongst blood donors (NACP, 1997, pp. 11, 19). Lushoto had a comparable rate of only 5.6 per cent (data culled from documentation at Lushoto District Hospital).

17. Giddens (1992) argues that (in the Western world) effective means of contraception had already severed the relationship between sex and reproduction, and thereby between sex and fear (of pregnancy or of death in childbirth). He describes this as 'a phenomenon with truly radical implications', equalising relations between the sexes and underpinning the impact of the feminist movement. Only later does AIDS reintroduce the 'connection of sexuality to death' – but with the sting for men that, 'AIDS does not distinguish between the sexes' (1992, p. 27). In Lushoto, few women practice contraception (especially modern forms such as the pill), except for those who do this in a limited way to space births. The possibility of using 'the pill' to deceive (especially

absent) husbands is, however, not beyond women's imagination (Bujra, 2000). Men's control over their wives' sexuality is still largely intact here – it is AIDS which is putting this in question, not feminism.

18. All names are pseudonyms.
19. In our other two research sites (in Dar es Salaam and Mbeya), no respondent denied knowledge of condoms.
20. This does not always follow. In Africa, the clients of prostitutes are generally able to insist on having sex without the use of condoms and will pay more for this.
21. The most potent example to date is the Clinton–Lewinsky saga.

REFERENCES

African Network on Ethics, Law and HIV (1996) *Newsletter*, no. 1.
AIDS Analysis Africa, various issues.
Aggleton, P., Davies, P. and Hart, G. (eds) (1991) *AIDS: Responses, Interventions and Care* (London: Taylor and Francis).
Aggleton, P., Davies, P. and Hart, G. (eds) (1995) *AIDS: Safety, Sexuality and Risk* (London: Taylor and Francis).
Aggleton, P., Davies, P. and Hart, G. (eds) (1997) *AIDS Activism and Alliances* (London: Taylor and Francis).
Altman, D. (1994) *Power and Community: Organisational and Cultural Responses to AIDS* (London: Taylor and Francis).
Amofah, G.A. (1992) 'AIDS in Ghana: profile, strategies and challenges', *AIDS Analysis Africa*, vol.2, no. 5, p. 5.
Beck, U. (1992) *Risk Society: Towards a new Modernity* (London: Sage Publications).
Bloor, M. (1995) *The Sociology of HIV Transmission* (London: Sage).
Bujra, J. and Baylies, C. (1999) 'Solidarity and Stress: gender and local mobilisation in AIDS work in Tanzania and Zambia', in Aggleton, P., Davies, P. and Hart, G. (eds) *AIDS: Family, Culture and Community* (London: UCL Press) pp. 35–52.
Bujra, J. (2000) *Serving Class: Masculinity and the Feminisation of Domestic Service in Tanzania* (Edinburgh: International African Institute).
Chirimuuta, R.C. and Chirimuuta R.J. (1987) *Aids, Africa and Racism* (Derbyshire: Richard Chirimuuta).

Cleland, J. and Ferry, B. (1995) *Sexual Behaviour and AIDS in the Developing World* (London: Taylor and Francis).

Douglas, M. (1992) *Risk and Blame* (London: Routledge).

Frankenberg, R. (1993) 'Anthropological and epidemiological narratives of prevention', in Lindenbaum, S. and Lock, M. (eds), *Knowledge, Power and Practice: The Anthropology of Medicine and Everyday Life* (Berkeley: University of California Press) pp. 219–42.

Friedman, S., Neaigus, A. and Jose, B. (1998) 'AIDS Research and Social Theory', *Research in Social Policy*, vol. 6, pp. 137–58.

Giddens, A. (1991) *Modernity and Self-Identity: Self and Society in the Late Modern Age* (Cambridge: Polity Press).

Giddens, A. (1992) *The Transformation of Intimacy* (Cambridge: Polity Press).

Green G. (1995) 'Sex, love and sero-positivity: balancing the risks', in Aggleton, P., Davies, P. and Hart, G. (eds) *AIDS: Safety, Sexuality and Risk* (London: Taylor and Francis) pp. 144–58.

Hart, G. and Boulton, M. (1995) 'Sexual behaviour and gay men: towards a sociology of risk', in Aggleton, P., Davies, P. and Hart, G. (eds) *AIDS: Safety, Sexuality and Risk* (London: Taylor and Francis) pp. 55–67.

Holland, J., Ramazanoglu, C., Scott, S., Sharpe, S. and Thomson, R. (1991) 'Between embarrassment and trust: young women and diversity of condom use', in Aggleton, P., Davies, P. and Hart, G. (eds) *AIDS: Responses, Interventions and Care* (London: Taylor and Francis).

Holland, J. et al. (1998) *The Male in the Head: Young People, Heterosexuality and Power* (London: Tufnell Press).

Kaleeba, N. (1991) *We Miss You All: AIDS in the Family* (Zimbabwe: Women and AIDS Support Network).

Lwihula, G. et al. (1993) 'AIDS epidemic in Kagera region, Tanzania – the experiences of local people', *AIDS Care*, vol. 5, no. 3, pp. 347–57.

McFadden, P. (1992) 'Sex, Sexuality and the Problem of AIDS in Africa', in Meena, R. (ed.) *Gender in Southern Africa: Conceptual and Theoretical Issues* (Harare: Sapes Books) pp. 157–95.

NACP (National AIDS Control Programme, Tanzanian Government) (1997) *HIV/AIDS/STD Surveillance*, Report No. 10 (Tanzanian Ministry of Health, June 1966).

Ndeki, S.S. et al. (1994) 'Exposure to HIV/AIDS information, AIDS knowledge, perceived risk and attitudes toward people with AIDS among primary school-children in Northern Tanzania', *AIDS Care*, vol. 6, no. 2, pp. 183–91.

Phillips, O. (1994) 'Censuring sexuality and gender in Zimbabwe: a look at some moral panics', (unpub. paper delivered to British Sociological Association's Annual conference, Preston) pp. 133–53.

Porter, M. (1995) 'Talking at the margins: Kenyan discourse on homosexuality', in Leap, W. (ed.) *Beyond the Lavender Lexicon: Authenticity, Imagination and Appropriation in Lesbian and Gay Languages* (Amsterdam: Gordon and Breach).

Rhodes, T. (1995) 'Theorising and researching 'risk': notes on the social relations of risk in heroin users' lifestyles', in Aggleton, P., Davies, P. and Hart, G. (eds) *AIDS: Safety, Sexuality and Risk* (London: Taylor and Francis) pp. 125–43.

Scheper-Hughes, N. (1994) 'An essay: AIDS and the social body', *Social Science and Medicine*, vol. 39, no. 7, pp. 993–1003.

Schiltz, A. and Adam, P. (1995) 'Reputedly effective risk reduction strategies and gay men', in Aggleton, P., Davies, P. and Hart, G. (eds) *AIDS: Safety, Sexuality and Risk* (London: Taylor and Francis).

Seidel, G. (1993) 'The competing discourses of HIV/AIDS in sub-Saharan Africa: discourses of rights and empowerment vs discourses of control and exclusion', *Social Science and Medicine*, vol. 36, no. 3, pp. 175–94.

Shepherd, G. (1987) 'Rank, gender and homosexuality: Mombasa as a key to understanding sexual options', in Caplan, P. (ed.) *The Cultural Construction of Sexuality* (London: Tavistock) pp. 240–50.

3 'CONFLICTING MODELS OF RISK': CLINICAL GENETICS AND BRITISH PAKISTANIS

Alison Shaw

INTRODUCTION

This chapter suggests a framework for exploring the range of attitudes towards genetic risk that may be found in modern Britain, with particular reference to British Pakistanis. It considers some general aspects of current 'scientific' concepts of genetic risk, and then discusses those genetic risks that have been shown to confront British Pakistanis in particular. With reference to detailed case material, the chapter then explores the social and cultural factors that influence Pakistani perceptions of genetic risk in the context of genetic counselling. It suggests that we need to move beyond typological classification of risk perception – as, for example, 'traditional' or 'modern' – in order to understand the social and cultural variation that may exist and the processes through which risk perceptions change.[1]

'THIS IS MY QISMAT (FATE)'

Shamim is thirty-six and came to Britain from a village in northwest Panjab, Pakistan, when she was eighteen, to marry a cousin. She has had six children. Her eldest child, a daughter, is now seventeen. Her second child was a boy whose birth brought great joy to the household. Shamim's husband hired a Rolls Royce to bring his wife home from hospital, and, more in accordance with tradition, distributed *laddu*s (South Asian sweets) to his family's Pakistani friends and neighbours. Their joy was short-lived, however, for the boy was rushed back into hospital and into intensive care within a few days of his birth. Over the next five years, he required 24 hour nursing care. He hardly grew, his limbs remained thin and rigid, he suffered from seizures, he was incontinent and could not feed himself. He was frequently admitted to hospital for intensive care because he was prone to infections and during his sixth year he failed to recover from a bacterial infection and died in hospital. Shamim was devastated at his death, inconsolable for weeks.

During the investigations into the possible causes of their son's handicap, Shamim and her husband were advised that the condition was probably a consequence of parental consanguinity, and that there was a one in four risk that they would have a similarly affected child again. Yet when she was next pregnant, Shamim and her husband turned down foetal anomaly screening, on the grounds that it was against their religion. 'There is no purpose in having the test', Shamim considered, 'For one thing, the test might harm the baby. The second thing is that even if the baby is sick, it is against my religion to abort it. Abortion is sin. It is the murder of unborn children.' She continued: 'God gave me my son as a test of my faith. It was my duty to look after him as well as I could. Of course, I would like all my children to be strong and healthy, and I pray to God that my next child will be healthy. But if God wants to test my faith again, then I must accept it.'

She proceeded to have a healthy baby, another daughter. When Shamim became pregnant for the fourth time, she and her husband again received genetic counselling and again turned down the offer of foetal anomaly screening. Their fourth child, another daughter, was born with handicaps very similar to those of her brother who had died.

The birth of this second handicapped child put a huge strain on Shamim's household, because of the round-the-clock nursing care involved. Shamim's household was already under pressure: Shamim's father-in-law was an invalid and Shamim's husband was the only wage earner, working long anti-social hours at a local factory, while her brother-in-law and one unmarried sister-in-law studied. Shamim's mother-in-law suffered from depression and her other unmarried sister-in-law had been diagnosed as schizophrenic. Before her second child was born, Shamim had sometimes attended English classes, leaving her baby daughter with her mother-in-law. However, alongside the birth and subsequent death of her handicapped grandson, Shamim's mother-in-law's physical and mental health had deteriorated considerably. The burden of the domestic responsibilities, of cooking, cleaning and washing clothes for seven adults, in a small terraced house, as well as caring for two lively young daughters and a severely handicapped child, now fell on Shamim's shoulders.

However, this time, Shamim was more willing to share the burden of caring for this second handicapped child with the local health and social services. The child would be collected by mini-bus and taken to a local day-care centre three or four times a week. She also received regular health checks at home, including physiotherapy, during which the therapists would show Shamim how to exercise her daughter's limbs to prevent the disabilities worsening. Even so, Shamim was constantly afraid that her daughter's health would deteriorate and that she would succumb to an infection and have to be rushed to hospital. Like her brother, this child eventually failed to recover from a bacterial infection and died at five years of age.

With the next pregnancy, when Shamim and her husband again received genetic counselling, they once again turned down the offer of foetal anomaly screening. This fifth pregnancy brought them a much desired, healthy son. When she was pregnant for the sixth time, Shamim again declined antenatal screening, and her sixth child, a girl, was born with severe handicaps very like those of her affected brother and sister and died six years later.

Shamim herself recognises that in her village in Pakistan each of her affected babies would probably have died at birth or soon after, for the medical facilities which enabled her handicapped children to live as long as they did are absent. Since caring for each child has placed a considerable burden on both this household and on the local social services, it is something of a mystery to those who have been professionally involved in the care of these children that, with each pregnancy, knowing from experience what would be involved in the care of another severely handicapped child, Shamim has consistently turned down the offer of foetal anomaly screening and selective abortion.

The justification Shamim herself gives is that foetal anomaly screening, together with the option to abort an affected foetus, is against her religion. 'Each child is a gift from Allah' she says, 'Whether the child is a boy or a girl, clever or stupid, strong or weak, Allah decides.' She considered it her duty to God to look after each child as best she could: 'This is my *qismat* (fate); this is Allah's decision, and if Allah decides to make my child healthy, he will. It is up to him.' Shamim, like many other Mirpuri and Panjabi Pakistani Muslims, considers that human intervention in this process is an attempt to defy the will of God, to thwart fate. As such, it is a sin indeed, one for which the sinner will pay at the final judgement. 'You will burn in hell for ever', Shamim says, 'and hell is seventy times hotter than a gas fire turned up to maximum.' What is at issue, at least on the face of it, is not the genetic risk in this life but the certainty of divine punishment in the next.

This appears to be a good illustration of a 'traditional' as opposed to a 'modern' conception of risk within the framework of Giddens' analysis of the relationship between self-identity and modernity in industrial society (1991). According to Giddens, beliefs in an all-powerful God or in a destiny ultimately external to individual control, which also carry powerful moral values, characterise the 'pre-modern' outlook on risk. By contrast, in the modern era, 'sureties of tradition and habit' are replaced by diverse claims to knowledge which are by their nature provisional, because they are constantly revised by experts, and which require the individual self-consciously to weigh up and choose between various possible risk scenarios (Giddens, 1991, p. 2). For example, if I decide against a particular course of action such as foetal anomaly screening because it is wrong, a sin in the eyes of God, then this is a 'traditional' response in relation to external moral constraints. By contrast, if I decide either for or against it, not on moral grounds, but as a result of balancing the advantages against the disadvantages of producing a handicapped child for the quality of my own life and of those close to me, then this is a singularly modern risk calculation. It is what Giddens would call 'reflexive life planning', involving 'consideration of risks ... filtered through contact with expert knowledge' (1991, p. 5). It is this approach to risk as an inevitable concomitant of modernity that enables Beck, in an earlier argument (1992, 1986) which parallels Giddens' analysis, to describe 'post-industrial' society as a 'risk society'. His terminology is not meant to suggest that life is more risky than it used to be, for in most respects it is far less so; the point is that in modern society we think about risk 'reflexively' (Giddens, 1991, p. 28; Beck, 1992).

In the terms of these arguments about risk and modernity, Shamim's attitude to genetic risk could therefore be described as 'traditional' or 'pre-modern'. This description may indeed be broadly accurate in some if not many cases, and not only among British Pakistanis or other 'ethnic minorities'. A significant minority of 'white' British women refuses pre-natal testing, and this may well be for complex 'pre-modern' reasons, only some of which involve religious motivations. It follows then that Giddens' theoretical typology would need considerable revision in relation to local empirical studies within so-called 'modern' industrial society, where people may in fact be portrayed as operating with a range of 'traditional or 'pre-modern' as well as 'modern' (or even 'postmodern') attitudes. A further problem with such typologies is that they may have little explanatory power when we begin to explore the processes involved in the range of possible responses by Pakistani or any other group of women to a proposal of foetal anomaly screening and to information conveyed through counselling about genetic risk.

CLINICAL VIEWS OF GENETIC RISK

From the viewpoint of modern molecular genetics, we are all in some respect genetically 'flawed' in that we all carry mutations, which are variant forms of genes, or genes copied with 'errors'. Mostly these 'defects' are masked, because, with the exception of the genes on the sex chromosomes, we inherit two copies of each gene and if one of them is faulty, the other one usually compensates. The unaffected owner is then a 'carrier' of the disease gene.

However, inheriting two copies of the same genetic mutation, or else inheriting a mutation with a 'dominant' effect may sometimes cause disease or death. The risk of inheriting a genetic disorder varies considerably between populations. For example, thalassaemia and sickle-cell disease, both recessively inherited blood disorders, are relatively common in the Mediterranean and in Africa respectively, because inheriting one copy of the mutation for these diseases confers resistance against malaria. Today, carrier testing and prenatal screening is available for those identified as 'at risk' of these diseases. New 'risks' constantly come to light as research in molecular genetics advances. One recent discovery shows Caucasians to be at particularly high risk of inheriting haemochromotosis, a disease of excessive iron accumulation in the body; one in ten Caucasians are carriers. Since treatment is simple, it is likely that widespread population screening will become routine for whites in Europe and the US (Feder et al., 1996).

Small, relatively immobile, populations or those with high rates of endogamy have very different spectrums of congenital disease (Flint et al., 1993). For instance, European Finns have a unique set of genetic disease, while Ashkenazi Jews are at significantly higher than usual risk of inheriting Tay-Sachs disease, for which, following the discovery of the gene, carrier-testing is now available (Jones, 1997, pp. 64–5, 67, 75–7). World-wide, about one-fifth of all births occur within populations in which consanguineous marriage is common (Bittles, 1990). In parts of the Middle East, North Africa, the Indian subcontinent and Japan, 20–50 per cent of marriages are consanguineous (Bittles et al., 1991). Epidemiological evidence from these populations shows consistently that parental consanguinity is associated with an increased risk of recessively inherited disorders and with higher rates of infant mortality and morbidity (Bittles et al., 1991; Jaber et al., 1998).

GENETIC RISK AND BRITISH PAKISTANIS

In Britain, several studies have shown that Pakistanis have higher rates of infant mortality and more birth defects than any other group (Young and Clarke, 1987; Chitty and Winter, 1989; Bundey et al., 1990). One five-year prospective study of 5,000 babies born in Birmingham concluded that, although constituting only one-fifth of the population studied, Pakistanis produce far more genetic disease than the other ethnic groups and contribute 40 per cent of the total disability (Bundey and Alam, 1993). Extrapolations from this study for the whole of the UK suggest that Pakistanis, who represent less than 1 per cent of Britain's population, generate 2 per cent of all births and produce 5 per cent of the congenital abnormalities and handicapping diseases.

The reasons for this high morbidity and infant mortality are complex and have been hotly debated. They include low socio-economic status, poor nutrition, a high proportion of older mothers, lack of immunity to infections like rubella in mothers born in Pakistan, restricted access to medical services and the increased risk of genetic disease in the children of consanguineous parents (Proctor and Smith, 1997). Of these factors, consanguinity has received particular attention. If a child's biological father is not a biological relative of the mother, the probability that the child will have no genetic disease is 95 per cent, whereas if the child's father is the mother's first cousin, this probability drops to 90 per cent. The probability of producing a 'normal' child also decreases further if the father is a first cousin related in more than one way, as is the case with many British Pakistani marriages, which take place preferentially within the *biradari* (extended kinship group). More than half of the Pakistani children in the Birmingham study were of consanguineous parents. Bundey and Alam (1993) found a three-fold increase in adverse birth outcome among the children of consanguineous parents and estimated that consanguinity accounts for 60 per cent of infant mortality and severe morbidity. The most obvious implication is that if Pakistanis were to stop marrying their cousins, the rate of congenital abnormalities in this population would be reduced by 60 per cent.

THE CLINICAL VIEW IN SOCIAL AND CULTURAL CONTEXT

This conclusion has fuelled concerns with the adverse genetic consequences of consanguineous marriage and, by implication, with the disproportionate use of health service resources that may result, because the financial costs of long-term care for children and adults with congenital disorders and with learning difficulties are very high (Young and Clarke, 1987). Yet there are immense dangers in singling out and stigmatising Pakistanis by placing undue emphasis on the practice of consanguineous marriage, a practice which is customary in many societies, including parts of the Middle East and North Africa, where it can bring considerable socio-economic advantages (Modell, 1991). One critic suggests that the preoccupation with 'consanguinity and related demons' distracts attention from more pressing issues such as racial exclusion, and is itself an expression of racial prejudice (Ahmad, 1996). The question is indeed politically sensitive:

community education programmes designed to reduce the rate of consanguinity because of the association with increased infant mortality and morbidity could be interpreted as a 'eugenicist' policy singling out a disadvantaged ethnic minority (if eugenics refers to a policy aimed at altering in some way the reproductive patterns of a particular group). It is important, therefore, to be aware of the extent to which racial prejudice or political pressure may influence the clinical or 'scientific' formulation of any proposed solution of this 'problem'. It is also the case that for many English people the idea of marrying a cousin touches very deep prejudice – although cousin marriage was quite common among Victorians.[2] Pakistani families may thus bear the brunt of racial prejudice in the particular context of reproduction. Pakistani parents struggling to care for a handicapped child have sometimes been told, 'What do you expect if you marry your cousin?' and at other times been accused of deliberately burdening the UK health services with handicapped children.

However, in relation to these fears of either invoking or being accused of racism, I would make two points concerning the 'reality' of the clinical 'problem'. First, the extent to which consanguinity, as opposed to other factors, contributes to adverse birth outcome in this particular population can be measured mathematically in relation to particular observed incidence rates; it is a question which geneticists or epidemiologists rather than social scientists or political activists are best trained to try to answer. This is not to say that epidemiologists or geneticists necessarily have a monopoly over 'truth' – prior cultural assumptions may, of course, affect which variables are selected for analysis and different mathematical procedures may produce different patterns of results – but that establishing the genetic contribution to a particular epidemiological profile is a statistical question. To date, no equivalent epidemiological research has effectively challenged the Birmingham study.[3]

Second, genetic disorders are 'real' in that they are directly observable, and it is also a biological reality that cousin marriage increases slightly the risk of having a congenitally affected child; the difference is that this 'reality' is one we observe as a mathematical risk calculation. Such risks are not 'absolutes' – they may be recalculated, as the technical process of estimating them is refined – but the risk remains nevertheless. We are therefore faced not only with ideological positions on this issue, but also with a 'real' practical problem which may cause a great deal of suffering and distress to the families of affected children. Furthermore, from a political standpoint, British Pakistanis have as much right as any other group to avail themselves of the genetics and pre-natal services. And in this process, their attitudes to congenital handicap, genetic risk and the possibilities offered by preconception counselling, genetic family studies, pre-natal diagnosis and foetal anomaly screening cannot be assumed but need to be established empirically. This point is important both scientifically and clinically, and returns me to my main argument.

CLINICAL SOLUTIONS

The problem that faces clinicians is how to reduce infant mortality and handicap within consanguineous populations world-wide in a culturally sensitive way. Recognising that the practice of consanguineous marriage may be fundamental to the social structure of many communities, clinicians consider that the solution to this problem lies in community education and in pre-natal genetic counselling (Jaber et al., 1988, p. 16). In Britain, there are now some trained South Asian workers employed within Regional Genetics Centres who interpret in clinics and distribute audio-cassettes, leaflets and posters giving information about the genetic risks of parental consanguinity and about how families may obtain further advice should they want it. In one Centre, a local *imam* (Muslim priest) has worked with clinicians in the making of a video-cassette tape.

There is, however, considerable potential conflict even at the most pragmatic level between a clinician's probabilistic model of the genetic risks of parental consanguinity and a client's understandings of inheritance and handicap, even without the potential complications of 'ethnic' or 'cultural' difference between clinician and client. For example, where both parents are carriers, the risk of having a child with a recessively inherited disorder is one in four. Yet clients quite often understand this risk to mean that if they have had one affected child, the next three will be unaffected – not that the same risk applies at each pregnancy. (Geneticists sometimes explain recessive inheritance with the rather culturally inappropriate image of tossing coins: which are 'tossed' simultaneously with each conception.)

Furthermore, although the information about genetic risk conveyed by a genetic counsellor is given to enable 'clients' to make their own decisions regarding pre-natal screening and abortion, there is inevitably an implicit cultural value attached to the information given and it is often difficult for any pregnant woman – regardless of 'ethnic' or 'cultural' background – to refuse the tests now routinely offered (Marteau et al., 1992; Clarke, 1991). Yet, as Shamim's case suggests, Pakistani clients may bring distinctive perceptions of risk and handicap to the counselling situation.

As Martin Richards (1996) has shown, information about genetic risk, if it is to be effective in changing patterns of behaviour, needs to be assimilated into 'lay' understandings of inheritance and risk. Even where the client is of the same 'ethnic' or cultural background as a clinician, and even when the clinician is also a client, lay models of risk and lay understandings of inheritance may have far more power than information acquired within a clinical consultation (Richards, 1997). For example, Davison's work (1997) in south Wales shows that the results of genetic tests may be given more (or less) meaning than clinicians intend, when interpreted within the framework of lay perceptions of the process of inheritance and conceptions of kinship.

It does not necessarily follow, then, that community education programmes and genetic counselling will alter Pakistani patterns of genetic risk-taking: they may do for some; for others they will not. Nor will it necessarily be sufficient to enlist the support of religious authorities in attempts to define the Islamic position on pre-natal screening and termination of pregnancy. This is not, of course, to suggest that these measures should not be taken, but my point here is that information about risk will be received and interpreted within a pre-existing framework of social organization and cultural values.

PAKISTANI ATTITUDES TO RISK IN SOCIAL AND CULTURAL CONTEXT

In a collaborative theoretical essay on risk, which preceded the work of Beck (1992) [1986] and Giddens (1991), Douglas, a social anthropologist and Wildavsky, a political scientist, (1982), proposed a social and cultural theory of risk. They argue that the perception of risk is a social process in which some risks are highlighted and others suppressed, and that how people choose which risks to take and which to avoid is a reflection of social organisation. Since 'people select their awareness of certain dangers to conform with a specific way of life, it follows that people who adhere to different forms of social organization are disposed to take (and avoid) different kinds of risk. To alter risk selection and risk perception, then, would depend on changing the social organization' (Douglas and Wildavsky, 1982, p. 9).

Understanding Pakistani perceptions of risk, in this formulation, therefore requires first of all understanding the social organisation within which perceptions of risk are embedded. What, then, are the main features of the social organisation of British Pakistanis? Comprising, according to the 1991 Census, the third largest British 'ethnic minority' after Indians and Afro-Caribbeans (Ballard, 1996, p. 16) British Pakistanis are themselves a heterogeneous population, sharing certain features of religion and heritage in some contexts but divided according to region of origin, rural or urban background, caste, socio-economic class and religious allegiance in others. However, the majority (perhaps 95 per cent) of those who came to Britain from the late 1950s onwards are of rural origin (Dahya, 1972–73; Shaw 1988, pp. 16–17). The following account outlines the main features of the socio-economic background of this category of migrants.

The 'pioneer' migrants of the 1950s and 1960s were single or bachelor-status men from small-scale landowning families in particular parts of rural Pakistan: mainly Jhelum and surrounding districts in northern Panjab, Mirpur district in Azad Kashmir and from districts such as Faisalabad in the south. Neither simply 'pushed' by socio-economic conditions at 'home' nor 'pulled' by the temptation of financial rewards in Britain, these families made an initial investment in sending abroad a man whose remittances to the village would be used to improve landholdings, build a better house, start a business or provide a dowry. A 'pioneer' migrant might subsequently sponsor the migration of a relative; in this way, a pattern of 'chain migration' developed in response to local work opportunities. From the early 1970s, the wives and children of the 'pioneers' began to settle in Britain and this in effect consolidated the kin- and village-based structure of most British Pakistani settlements.

Kinship is the predominant principle of social organisation at village level in rural Pakistan. Local kinship networks link households within particular villages and households in other villages in the area. These kinship networks, called *biradari*s, bear the names traditionally associated with castes or sub-castes in the Indian subcontinent. Indeed, in some areas, they are referred to by the term *zat*, which denotes caste among Hindus in India. Whether Pakistani Muslim *biradari*s or *zat*s should be regarded as castes has been much debated (Shaw, forthcoming). It is worth noting here that Pakistani *biradari*s are ranked in that families of *ashraf* (noble) status such as Sayyed or Sheikh consider themselves superior to *zamindar* (landowning) families such as Gujar and Arain, while these in turn rank themselves above the artisan groups such as Kumhar (potter) and Nai (barber). In a given local context, especially one of migration, the details of this ranking may be challenged and contested.

Marriage within the *biradari* is the principle mechanism for maintaining *biradari* structure, and thus, in effect, the hierarchy of castes. Pakistanis say, 'We prefer to marry relatives,' or, 'We like to marry within the family', although, as Hastings Donnan has argued (1985), the fact that a majority of marriages are in practice with first cousins is not a question of 'blindly' following a cultural rule, but the result of pragmatic deliberations which very often coincide with this cultural preference. Actual rates of cousin marriage may vary considerably: the practice may occasionally be a strategy for upward mobility, but it may also be characteristic of socio-economic insecurity. There is no evidence that rates of close-kin marriage among British Pakistanis are declining; in fact, and possibly uniquely among consanguineous populations world-wide, the opposite seems to be the case. Of course, there are immense problems with documenting and comparing rates of cousin marriage; these notwith-standing, current rates among British Pakistanis have been estimated at 50–60 per cent, with the majority of marriages involving a bride or groom from Pakistan marrying a cousin raised in Britain (Darr and Modell, 1988; Shaw, forthcoming).

A hierarchy by gender and age also governs relationships within households. Men have formal authority over women and older relatives have authority over younger kin. Deference and respect should characterise the relationship between a woman and a man, or a younger and an older relative. A new bride, such as one who has recently arrived from Pakistan to marry a cousin in Britain, often has the lowest status in a household: she must defer to her husband, her mother-in-law and to any older sisters-in-law; it may only be with her husband's younger brother or sisters that she has a more free and easy relationship. When she begins to have children, however, especially sons, her influence and authority within the household increases.

This idealised portrayal of the structure of domestic power relations has of course been altered in various ways by migration, in Pakistan as well as in Britain. The wives of pioneer migrants in Britain often had a degree of autonomy they would have lacked in their mother-in-law's household; likewise, girls raised in Britain may bring to marriage expectations of domestic authority rather different from those of their husbands from Pakistan (Shaw, 1997). Yet traditional ideals or expectations often remain important, even where they are contested. In the context of the domestic power structure and women's careers within it, it would be difficult to exaggerate the importance to women, perhaps especially to a new bride from Pakistan, of producing children. Moreover, in rural Pakistan, infant mortality is high, and children, sons especially, are seen as an investment for the future, although too many daughters are viewed as an economic burden. In Britain, even where a mother-in-law does not restrict access to birth control, it is very often unlikely that a woman will consider limiting the size of her family until she has had several children.

ISLAM, FATALISM AND THE ROLE OF SAINTS

Attitudes to issues such as birth control and to health and illness more generally are also shaped by the ideas of Unani medicine, also known as Unani-Tibb, a system long associated with Muslims in the Indian subcontinent. The Unani system has ancient origins in the Greek medicine of classical Europe, in contrast to Ayurvedic medicine which has long been associated with Hindus in the Indian subcontinent, but mutual influences and borrowings go back to ancient and medieval times (Basham, 1976). The Unani system is based on the humoral theory that all matter is formed from fire, air, earth and water, and that each element has hot, cold, wet and dry properties. Each individual has a natural humoral balance; illness follows when this balance is upset. Unani practitioners, called *hakims*, prescribe herbal or mineral remedies or offer dietary advice to restore this balance. These ideas are also incorporated into *desi ylaj* (home remedies) for a variety of ailments such as stomach cramps, headaches, menstrual pains and childbirth and are usually effected by adjusting the diet. Humoral principles may also be important in shaping understandings of fertility and conception.

In the context of genetic risk, however, ideas about the correct balance of physical elements in the body and in the diet are not as important as Islamic beliefs and practices which emphasise the role of prayer, faith and religious ritual. As already indicated, religious ideas about the causality and management of illness may influence 'risk-taking' behaviour in important ways. Such ideas are also themselves situated within and in part constituted by social organisation, for Islamic beliefs and practices are not uniform or uncontested.

Pakistani Muslims often portray their religion as a set of shared beliefs and practices, such as the confession of faith and the notion of the 'five pillars' of Islam, and these shared elements do indeed characterise Islam wherever it is found. Despite this, there is considerable heterogeneity in Islamic ideals and practices, and much dispute about what counts as 'orthodox' or 'genuine' Islam. These divergences are perhaps most marked in the context of health and illness. For Muslims, health, illness and misfortune are ultimately the consequence of Allah's will, a belief which lends itself to a fatalism which may itself be a source of comfort in cases of terminal or incurable illness. Yet it is also a religious duty to do what is within one's power to alleviate suffering. It is in this regard that disputes arise.

In many parts of rural Panjab and within many Pakistani settlements in Britain, what can be done to influence Allah's will extends beyond prayer and faith to ideas about the transformative and miraculous power of *pirs*. Within South Asian Sufism, *pirs* are saints regarded by their followers (*murid*) as spiritual intermediaries between humans and God. A *pir*'s power arises from his being a spiritual and a genealogical descendant of the Prophet or the Prophet's tribe. 'True' *pirs* are Sayyed or Sheikh, though a close follower can himself become a *pir* without having a 'sacred' genealogy, and becoming a *pir* may effect a claim to *ashraf* status. Moreover, the tombs of deceased *pirs* are popular places of pilgrimage, for a *pir*'s spiritual power extends beyond the grave. In Pakistan, popular shrines include that of Data Ganj Baksh, in Lahore, and that of Baba Farid, near Pakpattan. The famous deceased *pir*s are all men, as far as I know, though I have on two occasions been told of living female *pir*s.

Many stories reveal a *pir*'s ability to transform nature: a *pir*'s supernatural power (*baraka*) can bring speech, hearing and fertility and may even transform the sex of a child. A *pir* may also use his spiritual power to exorcise the malicious spirits (*jinn*s) which may cause psychiatric disorder. These beliefs are contested as unIslamic by some more middle-class or educated Pakistanis, although there is in fact no necessary or straightforward correspondence between socio-economic class and the belief in *pir*s; educated Pakistanis of urban backgrounds are also sometimes the devout followers of a particular *pir*. Among British Pakistanis, the ritual healing power of *pir*s continues to be a central component of health beliefs and practices, to the extent that, as I have suggested elsewhere, local challenges to these beliefs may be viewed as tantamount to an onslaught on Islam itself (Shaw, 1988).

FAMILY HISTORIES AND HOUSEHOLD DYNAMICS

It is against the background of the belief in *pir*s, the hierarchy of *biradari*s and the principles of age and gender which govern household organisation, that the attitudes to handicap and congenital disorder of women like Shamim are best understood. As I have said, the justification Shamim herself gives is religious: foetal anomaly screening, together with the option to abort an affected foetus, is against her religion. Yet to rest the case with religion would obscure more than it would explain, for it would be to ignore other aspects of social organisation which shape risk perception. Many Pakistani Muslims oppose abortion on religious grounds, but there are occasionally circumstances in which even the most fervent critics may have recourse to abortion, either themselves or in order to end an unmarried daughter's pregnancy. What I am suggesting here is that religion is but one of a number of interrelated factors involved in shaping risk perception, one to which Pakistani Muslims may sometimes appeal in order to preclude, for all sorts of other reasons, any further discussion of the issue. An attitude to religion such as Shamim's, while perfectly sincere, is thus also a reflection of other aspects of her social and domestic situation.

Shamim's family is of *ashraf* status, of Sheikh origin. 'My family is the family of the Prophet Muhammad', said Shamim. Moreover, they are the descendants of a *pir* eight generations back whose shrine in Shamim's ancestral village in north-west Panjab is to this day a place of pilgrimage. Marriages have taken place within Shamim's *biradari* for generations; marriage outside the *biradari* would be virtually unthinkable. Those of her *biradari* who have moved to the cities or who work abroad, in Britain and in the Middle East, maintain close links with relatives in their ancestral village, primarily through close-kin marriage. The fact that they are the descendants of a *pir* remains important to Shamim's family's status and religious identity in relation to fellow Pakistanis in Britain, perhaps especially since they have not prospered in comparison with some of their Pakistani neighbours.

In Shamim's family background, attitudes towards women's activities and demeanour are more restrictive than is the case within some other *biradari*s. Female behaviour, generally, is a symbol of family *izzat* (pride, respect) and governed by the ideas of *purdah*, a morally sanctioned system of gender differentiation that in practice varies considerably. For example, Shamim had considered taking up paid work outside the home when her youngest child started school, since for some of her friends part-time work provided a useful supplement to their husbands' earnings. Shamim's husband, however, considered the prospect to be totally out of the question and forbade it. Likewise, Shamim has had fewer opportunities than some of her friends to learn English or to develop a degree of autonomy outside the home. It is not very surprising, then, that her views on foetal anomaly screening and abortion are 'traditional'.

This is not to say, however, that the experience of having handicapped children, or the process of genetic counselling and screening has had no impact on Shamim's outlook. Knowledge of the genetic risks of consanguinity has not changed Shamim's plans that her daughters will marry relatives. However, she has decided that the knowledge revealed through carrier testing – that her son, like herself, is a carrier of beta thalassaemia – will be incorporated into the negotiations for his marriage. Her son is only eleven years old, but like many other Pakistani mothers, Shamim is already thinking about his marriage. 'He will still marry a relative, but we would turn down the offer of a girl who is also a carrier', she says.[4]

Shamim herself is aware that other Pakistani Muslim women might consider foetal anomaly screening and even abortion if they have a high risk of producing a handicapped child, even though for her this would be unacceptable. She also recognises that her own attitudes are related to the circumstances of her own background; for other women, these circumstances might be different. Consider, for example, Riffat, who is thirty-six, like Shamim, and comes from a middle-ranking *zamindar* family, also from north-west Panjab. Unlike Shamim, Riffat came to Britain when she was seven and attended school until she was eighteen, when she was married to a cousin who came to Britain from Pakistan after the marriage. At first, the couple lived next door to Riffat's parents. Riffat, who speaks English fluently, worked in the family shop for a few years after her marriage while her mother helped with child care. Riffat's marriage, however, had been unstable from the beginning, and Riffat pinned her hopes of repairing it upon the birth of a son, her fourth child. However, this baby was diagnosed at six weeks as having Down's syndrome. The diagnosis plunged Riffat into a depression for the next 18 months which was exacerbated by continuing marital difficulties and the fact that her husband was frequently absent from home for months at a time. Six years later, however, she is not only reconciled to the fact that her son has Down's syndrome, but regards him as a blessing from God.

The reasons for her change of heart are in large part to do with aspects of her cultural background that she has only come to appreciate since her son's birth. She discovered that not all Pakistanis view children like her son with shame. While there is no concept of Down's syndrome within the culture of her parents, Pakistani and Indian Panjabi visitors to Riffat's home sometimes call her son *saya,* a term which literally means 'shadow' or 'shade', and also sometimes means 'spirit'; in this context, it refers to someone's spiritual qualities, even supernatural powers. Sometimes Panjabi neighbours come to Riffat's house specifically to see her son; they touch or feel him or borrow an item of his clothing and they may give Riffat money and gifts. Sometimes they ask to borrow her son for the afternoon, because they believe that he will bring them good fortune. 'I used to find the money and gifts embarrassing', Riffat said, 'but I accept them more easily now.'

Being *saya (saya hona)* may also mean that the usual rules regarding purity and pollution in the context of religious ritual may be overturned. Prior to doing *namaz* (prayers), Muslims must have performed ritual ablutions (*vuzu*) to ensure that they are ritually pure (*pak*) before uttering the holy words of the Qur'an. Bodily functions such as defecation, urination, menstruation and sexual intercourse involve the escape of bodily substances which are all seen as 'matter out of place' (Douglas, 1966). Faeces, urine, blood and semen make a person *napak* (impure) and require ritual control; the ritual ablutions before prayer thus re-establish purity. Riffat's son does not speak very clearly, but nevertheless knows sections of the Qur'an very well indeed. In fact, as his mother explained:

He is so fond of reciting his prayers, especially the *qalma* [Islamic confession of faith] that he says it sometimes while he is sitting on the toilet. You know how bad that is, for our people. It made me really worried, I felt really sick. So I asked our *imam* who said to me, 'Do not worry. Your son is *saya*; he has a special relationship with Allah.'

Through an appreciation of aspects of her own cultural background, Riffat now not only views her son as a special blessing from God, but her greatest fear is that she will lose him. She sleeps in his bedroom, listening to his breathing, afraid that he may succumb to infection and die young, despite clinical reassurances that nowadays people with Down's syndrome have an average life expectancy.

Down's syndrome, although a congenital disorder, is not usually clinically linked with parental consanguinity and is not typical of the congenital disorders associated with British Pakistanis. In Riffat's case, having a Down's syndrome son has not been linked clinically to the fact that she is married to a cousin. While she was pregnant with her son, Riffat was too young to be considered sufficiently at risk to have been offered routine foetal anomaly screening. When, however, she became pregnant again, she was told that having already had a Down's syndrome child gave her a significantly higher than average risk of having another, and she was offered amniocentesis. Unlike Shamim, Riffat agreed to the test, aware that if it were positive, she would be considering a termination. When I asked her why she had agreed, she told me she had consulted a woman *pir* about having amniocentesis. She had explained her family situation, that her husband was often absent, that she had been depressed, and that she did not think she would cope with another affected child. She was told that Allah would not punish her if she went ahead with the test, because she had a duty to care for her existing children.

CONCLUSION

Information about genetic risk, itself shaped by scientific discourse, is neither given nor received in a social or cultural vacuum. As Douglas and Wildavsky (1982) have argued, the perception of risk is a social and cultural process, and changes in risk behaviour will be intimately related to changes in aspects of social organisation and culture. Pakistani families in Britain, in comparison with some other South Asian groups, are on the whole notable for their marked resistance to 'assimilation', however this term may be defined (Ballard, 1990). The key to this resistance lies in the close-knit structure of Pakistani *biradari*s, in migrants' continuing socio-economic links with kin in Pakistan and in the continuing importance of close-kin marriage. Increasingly, too, a commitment to Muslim identity provides a justi-fication for the maintenance of this social organisation (Shaw, 1994).

Within the terminology of Giddens' and Beck's arguments about modernity, rural-origin Pakistani Muslims, such as Shamim, might therefore be regarded as 'traditional' or 'pre-modern' in their attitude to genetic risk; one could add that this is to a large extent a reflection of social organisation. Refusing foetal anomaly screening or amnio-centesis on the grounds that it is not acceptable on religious grounds is, in this view, a 'pre-modern' approach to risk which invokes external moral constraints. However, this description of either a 'traditional' or indeed a 'modern' approach fails to consider the social and cultural variation that may exist within either category or the mechanisms of change. In the case of British Pakistanis, knowledge of the social background provides some general guidelines, but gives no necessary clue as to how any particular Pakistani Muslim family or individual will respond to information about genetic risk or how these perceptions may change over time. Individual socio-economic circumstance, education, religious allegiance, length of stay in Britain and the structure of authority within a household, none of which is 'fixed', all affect risk perception; religious convictions are but one factor among those which influence risk-taking behaviour. Moreover, living in Britain brings new challenges and experiences, especially to those raised and schooled in Britain, and so we cannot assume that the same expectations will apply across generations or even within one household. A person may perceive the 'same' genetic risk differently in these different social circumstances. As among non-Pakistanis or 'white' British generally, individuals will take advantage of those aspects of the service which can be accommodated within their current social circumstances and understanding of the world.

NOTES

1. This chapter presents the background and some of the framework for the research which I am currently undertaking at the Centre for the Study of Health, Sickness and Disablement (CSHSD), Brunel University, Uxbridge, Middlesex. I am grateful to two women whose names I have changed for the case material discussed here. I am also grateful to Pat Caplan and to Ian Robinson for comments on an earlier draft of this chapter.
2. Charles Darwin, for one, married his cousin Emma Wedgwood and had eight children, only later becoming worried about their 'genetic weakness' (Desmond and Moore, 1991, pp. 446–7; 629, 657).
3. Proctor and Smith (1997) present the most recent challenge, but would have to subject their findings to multivariate analysis to contest statistically the conclusions of the Birmingham study (Bundey, 1993).
4. This approach, incorporating knowledge of risk within a particular structure of marriage preferences and avoiding the issue of abortion, has been taken in order to reduce the incidence of Tay-Sachs disease in some Jewish communities in the US (Jones, 1997, p. 77; Richards, 1996; Mertz, 1987).

REFERENCES

Ahmad, W. (1996) 'Consanguinity and related demons: science and racism in the debate on consanguinity and birth outcome', in Samson, C. and South, N. (eds) *The Social Construction of Social*

Policy: methodologies, racism, citizenship and the environment (London: Macmillan).

Ballard, R. (1996) 'Negotiating Race and Ethnicity: Exploring the Implications of the 1991 Census', *Patterns of Prejudice*, vol. 30, no. 3 (London: Sage Publications).

Ballard, R. (1990) 'Migration and Kinship', in Clarke, C. G., Peach, C. and Vertovec, S. (eds) *South Asians Overseas: Migration and Ethnicity* (Cambridge: Cambridge University Press).

Basham, A. L. (1976) 'The Practice of Medicine in Ancient and Medieval India', in Leslie, C. (ed.) *Asian Medical Systems: A Comparative Study* (Berkeley: University of California Press).

Beck, U. (1992) *Risk Society: Towards a New Modernity* (London: Sage Publications), originally published as Beck, U. (1986) *Risikogesellschaft: Auf dem Weg in eine andere Moderne* (Frankfurt: Suhrkamp).

Bittles, A. H. (1990) 'Consanguineous marriage: current global incidence and its relevance to demographic research', Research report no. 90–186 (University of Michigan: Population Studies Center).

Bittles, A. H. et al. (1991) 'Reproductive Behavior and Health in consanguineous Marriages', *Science*, vol. 252, pp. 789–94.

Bundey, S. et al. (1990) 'Race, consanguinity and social features in Birmingham babies: a basis for prospective study', *Journal of Epidemiology and Community Health*, vol. 44, pp. 130–35.

Bundey, S. and Alam, H. (1993) 'A Five Year Prospective Study of the Health of Children in Different Ethnic Groups, with Particular Reference to the Effect of Inbreeding', *European Journal of Human Genetics*, vol. 1, pp. 206–19.

Chitty, L. S. and Winter, R. M. (1989) 'Perinatal mortality in different ethnic groups', *Archives of Disease in Childhood*, vol. 64, pp. 1036–1041.

Clarke, A. (1991) 'Is non-directive genetic counselling possible?' *Lancet*, vol. 338, pp. 998–1001.

Dahya, B. (1972–3) 'Pakistanis in England', *New Community*, vol. 2, no. 1, Winter, pp. 25–33.

Darr, A. and Modell, B. (1988) 'The frequency of consanguineous marriage among British Pakistanis', *Journal of Medical Genetics*, vol. 25, pp. 186–90.

Davison, C. (1997) 'Everyday ideas of inheritance and health in Britain: implications for predictive genetic testing', in Clarke, A.

and Parsons, E. (eds) *Culture, Kinship and Genes: towards cross-cultural genetics* (London: Macmillan).

Desmond, A. and Moore, J. (1991) *Darwin* (London: Penguin Books).

Donnan, H. (1985) 'The rules and rhetoric of marriage negotiations among the Dhund Abbasi of Northeast Pakistan', *Ethnology*, vol. 24, pp. 183–96.

Douglas, M. (1966) *Purity and Danger: An Analysis of the Concepts of Pollution and Taboo* (London: Routledge).

Douglas, M. and Wildavsky, A. (1982) *Risk and Culture: an essay on the selection of technical and environmental dangers* (Berkeley and Los Angeles: University of California Press).

Feder, J. N. et. al. (1996) 'A Novel MCH class 1-like gene is mutated in patients with hereditary haemochromatosis', *Nature Genetics*, vol. 13, no. 4, pp. 399–408.

Flint, J. et al. (1993) 'Why are some genetic diseases common?: distinguishing selection from other processes by molecular analysis of globin gene variants', *Human Genetics*, vol. 91, pp. 91–117.

Giddens, A. (1991) *Modernity and Self-Identity: Self and Society in the Late Modern Age* (Cambridge: Polity Press).

Jones, S. (1997) *In the Blood: God, genes and destiny* (London: Flamingo).

Jaber, L., Halpern, G. J. and Shohat, M. (1998) 'The Impact of Consanguinity Worldwide', *Community Genetics*, vol. 1, pp. 12–17.

Marteau, T. M. et al. (1992) 'Presenting a routine screening test in antenatal care: practice observed', *Public Health*, vol. 106, pp. 131–41.

Mertz, J. (1987) 'Matchmaking schemes solve Tay-Sachs problems', *Journal of the American Medical Association*, vol. 258, no. 3, pp. 2636–9.

Modell, B. (1991) 'Social and genetic implications of customary consanguineous marriage among British Pakistanis', *Journal of Medical Genetics*, vol. 28, pp. 720–3.

Proctor, S. R. and Smith, I. J. (1997) 'Factors associated with birth outcome in Bradford Pakistanis', in Clarke, A. and Parsons, E. (eds) *Culture, Kinship and genes: towards cross-cultural genetics* (London: Macmillan).

Richards, M. (1996) 'Families, kinship and genetics', in Marteau, T. and Richards, M. (eds) *The Troubled Helix: social and psychological implications of the new human genetics* (Cambridge: Cambridge University Press).

Richards, M. (1997) 'It runs in the family: lay knowledge about inheritance', in Clarke, A. and Parsons, E. (eds) *Culture, Kinship and Genes: towards cross-cultural genetics* (London: Macmillan).

Shaw, A. (1988) A *Pakistani Community in Britain* (Oxford: Basil Blackwell).

Shaw, A. (1994) 'The Pakistani Community in Oxford', in Ballard, R. (ed.) *Desh Pardesh: The South Asian Presence in Britain* (London: Hurst and Co.).

Shaw, A. (1997) 'Women, the household and family ties: Pakistani migrants in Britain', in Donnan, H. and Selier, F. (eds) *Family and Gender in Pakistan: Domestic Organization in a Muslim Society* (New Delhi: Hindustan Publishing Corporation).

Shaw, A. (forthcoming) *Kinship and Continuity: Pakistani families in Britain* (London: Harwood Academic).

Young, I. D. and Clarke, M. (1987) 'Lethal malformations and peri-natal mortality: A 10 year review with comparison of ethnic differences' *British Medical Journal*, vol. 295, pp. 89–91.

4 RISK-TALK: THE POLITICS OF RISK AND ITS REPRESENTATION

Penny Vera-Sanso

THE POLITICS OF RISK REPRESENTATION

In *Risk Society*, Ulrich Beck (1992) draws an alarming picture of the world: a world of new and intense risk arising from technological developments. He describes these dangers as global threats to life which none can escape and which, unless changes are made, will become increasingly hazardous in the future. The changes required are greater reflexivity and effective public participation in what Beck calls 'the auxiliary and alternative governments of techno-economic sub-politics – science and research' (Beck, 1992, p. 229). He argues for a politics based on reflexive accommodation between two opposing forms of knowledge, those of laboratory-based science and experienced lay persons, in order to recognise and address dangers.

In the context of these global technical risks, Beck predicts the rise of what he calls 'risk society' in which the key political issue is not the distribution of wealth but of risk. He argues that 'risk society' will be the inevitable outcome of the contradictions inherent in modernity due to technological developments, the meeting of basic material needs, ideologies of equality and individualism and the loss of faith in science. For Beck, the contemporary concern with environmental and health risks amongst some sectors of the population in Europe and the United States is a new phenomenon which will become generalised throughout society. Indeed, Beck's work itself is an attempt to generalise this preoccupation, for the language he selects is alarmist, referring to 'irreversible harm' (ibid., p. 23), 'apocalyptic catastrophes' (p. 60) and a future scenario in which society becomes habituated to birth defects (p. 83).

For Beck, this preoccupation with environmental and health risks could not be expected to occur in what he calls 'scarcity society' because 'the distribution of socially produced wealth and related conflicts occupy the foreground so long as obvious material need, the "dictatorship of scarcity", rules the thought and action of the people (as today in large parts of the so-called Third World)' (ibid., p. 20). Beck states 'On the international scale it is emphatically true that material misery and *blindness* to hazards coincide' (p. 41, emphasis added). He resurrects the stereotype that 'for these people ... chemical factories with their imposing pipes and tanks are symbols of success' and the death threat that they contain 'remains largely invisible' (p. 42).

However, it is evident that Third World peoples are not uniformly 'blind' to environmental and health hazards. Beck quotes a report in *Der Spiegel* on a steel and chemical town in Brazil where in the *favelas* corrugated roofs must be replaced each year because of acid rain, where locals call the rashes residents develop 'alligator skin' and where gas masks are sold in supermarkets. *Der Spiegel* indicates that the Brazilian military government (which invited polluting industries into Brazil) and the industries themselves justify policy and practice in terms of local poverty. Yet Beck makes nothing of either the clear differentials of interest and power within Third World countries which this example suggests nor of the obvious awareness of health hazards any population buying gas masks in supermarkets would have. Explanations couched in terms of 'blindness to hazards' and industrial buildings being seen as 'imposing symbols of success' are not just inadequate but an offensive misrepresentation of Third World people of exactly the kind (and for the same purposes) of which Said (1978) and many others have complained.

For Beck, then, the significant difference between the West and the Rest is the distribution of resources; having met its own material needs and found an acceptable level of distribution, Western societies are in a position to focus on the environmental and health risks created by technology. Here we can see that the scale of Beck's work is too grand and his statements too sweeping; he generalises from his knowledge of Germany since the 1970s, is unreflexive about his own views of the West and the Third World and is inevitably caught out by history. *Risk Society*, for example, was first published in 1986 before the unification of Germany and the subsequent conflicts over resources and before the 'welfare experiment' was declared unsustainable in the West. Contrary to Beck, the salience of class position and conflicts over access to resources are not declining; rather the situation is becoming more polarised as debates on exclusion and the development of gated communities testify.

Illich (1971), Sahlins (1972) and others would consider Beck's view that there is an obvious relationship between material goods and the perception of scarcity or poverty naïve. For them the West is the epitome of 'scarcity society', since capitalist society is founded on the ethos that one's needs are infinite and never satisfied. With such an ethos, the West will never be free of wants, will never overcome conflicts over the distribution of wealth and, if the meeting of material needs is the criterion for a focus on global hazards, will not be the prime candidate for safeguarding the global environment (as the United States stance at the 1997 Kyoto Climate Summit testifies).[1]

NUCLEAR RISK – A DISCUSSION

Despite his passing acknowledgement that the rise of risk society is essentially a rise in the perception of technological risk, Beck does not maintain a distinction between risks as hazards and the perception of risk. The epitome of modern technological risk, for Beck, is the nuclear threat; here the level of risk is incalculable, impossible to make compensationable, no one can be held individually responsible and those at risk include people not yet conceived. Even if we agree that nuclear technology poses a new hazard to the planet of the order Beck suggests, in the West its perception as such is recent and cannot be explained in terms of rising wealth or declining economic inequalities.

A quick rummage in my own past as a lay historian of the nuclear threat produces a different picture. In the mid–1960s, the first task of each day in my American fundamentalist Christian primary school was to memorise three verses of the New Testament so that when (not if) 'the Russians' (read Communists) invaded and burnt all the Bibles we, the pupils of Los Angeles' Golden West School, could reconstruct an underground Bible. During this period, sirens would sound across the city at which the class would 'duck and cover', as required by the US's policy of national readiness for Russian nuclear bombs. In our case we would duck under the desks, hands protecting our necks against falling glass, and await the nuclear bombs.

A decade later I was in England on a college trip being shown around Brighton police station. We were shown a bunker equipped with radio equipment, a few months' food and water stores and a shooting range. We heard of the arrangements for police personnel who had volunteered to leave their families for the bunker should Britain be attacked by Russian nuclear bombs. When leaving, gun mountings on the station's roof were pointed out to us. The guns were to hold back crowds clamouring to enter the bunker once nuclear war was declared. The police (and state?) were confident that after a few months it would be safe to resurface.

A decade further on and I took a break from fieldwork in 1989 in a rundown South Indian beach resort, only to marvel at history's prank that, in the space of a few years, one-time arch-enemies, in this case the passengers of two cruise ships, one Russian, one American, could be found together on the dance floor of a leading non-aligned country. By this time, the nuclear threat was perceived as an environmental risk which for some none would survive but for others would be more in the order of John Wyndham's post-Apocalyptic vision depicted in *The Chrysalids*. A 1987 survey of public attitudes in Britain reflects these shifts in attitude to nuclear weapons. It found that 82 per cent of people thought they would not survive a nuclear war between the superpowers (Jones and Rees, 1990, p. 58).

What I am arguing is that Beck is missing the point; even the perception of the most modern and devastating of technological hazards is, as Monica Hunter-Wilson (1951) said about the content of witchcraft beliefs in relation to small-scale societies, the expression of society's nightmare. From the 1950s to the mid-1980s, the communist threat was the West's central nightmare. Nuclear weapons, which for much of the time were not popularly thought of as qualitatively different from conventional bombs, were a vital deterrent. While nuclear weapons are now recognised as qualitatively different, it is instructive to note that opposition to nuclear stockpiles dissipated once communist regimes collapsed in the USSR and eastern Europe, despite the continuing development, upgrading and deployment of nuclear arms.[2]

Clearly, then, the West cannot be described as having an 'objective' view of environmental hazards. Instead, at the end of the century, the

West is undergoing millennial *angst*: uncertain about social and economic relations nationally and internationally as power becomes less localised, technological risk becomes the stand-in for distant, unaccountable, often unidentifiable, shifting 'centres' of power. In this context Dolly the cloned sheep, Chernobyl, Creutzfeld Jakob's Disease and Thalidomide are metaphors for society's nightmare. It is not the West's comparative wealth that underlies the contemporary concern with technological risk amongst certain sectors of the population, rather it is its impotence. Having failed to realise the most recent incarnation of the 'white man's burden' – global development – and unsure of their own social and economic future, certain sections of the West's population now aspire to save the world from man-made risk.

RISK AND BLAME

Following Mary Douglas (1992), I am arguing that risk-talk itself is political; it attributes blame by asserting moral positions and legitimates formal and informal disciplinary regimes. Thus risk-talk is best viewed as pointing to the fears and ethos of society as well as the distribution and sources of power within society. Risk-talk needs to be contextualised and studied in fine detail; since, however, Beck drew a distinction between the West and Third World countries I will briefly compare Britain and India before turning to a consideration of the risk-talk prevalent in India and the low-income settlements of Chennai, formerly called Madras.

A comparison of Britain and India at the end of the twentieth century does not reveal clear-cut economic and technological differences since India is highly industrialised, poses a threat to Britain's service sector, has nuclear power stations and nuclear arms, and, unlike Britain, has an independent capability to build and launch satellites. Awareness of and protest against environmental and health hazards are equally sectoral, sporadic and inconsistent in Britain and India. Greenham Common is matched by opposition to the Narmada Dams Project in taking on hugely powerful forces. The long-standing Chipko Movement's embracing of trees takes on, by similar methods, national and business interests as does the much younger anti-roads campaign in Britain. Similarly, workers' opposition to risk reductions that threaten their livelihoods is common to both countries.

The more obvious difference between the two countries is the way social risks, that is, risks to one's social status, are increasingly reduced in Britain, providing more opportunity for individual choice and self-determination. Stigmas which attached to illegitimacy, divorce, co-habitation, unwed or lone mothers and sex-outside-marriage at the beginning of the twentieth century have by the end of the century reduced to such an extent that these statuses and activities are increasingly positive choices rather than the imposition of others or of circumstance. Part of this shift is related to welfare provision and better employment opportunities for women. Part is due to the shift in popular discourse from that of inherited personalities, which reflect on other family members, to personalities moulded by individual experience. Although periodically lone mothers and broken families are singled out for blame by government this frequently backfires; it is refugees and migrants who are more commonly cited as the major source of social and economic ills.

For the majority of the population in India, on the other hand, divorce, desertion, co-habitation, unwed or lone mothers and sex-outside-marriage are rarely positive choices and illegitimacy is strongly stigmatised. The inadequacy of welfare provision and of female wages makes female-headed households an undesirable option. Additionally, socially unsanctioned behaviour implicates the whole family, on the basis of ideas about common substance (Inden and Nicholas, 1977; Daniel, 1987), poor training or the condoning of a selfish disregard for social values. Although recently, the most highly charged risk-talk attributes risk and blame to communal and caste divisions, the everyday risk on which contemporary Indian society is predicated is the threat posed by women to the social order. Like the West's predilection towards affirming itself through stereotypes of other nations, India frequently resorts to the spectre of Western liberalism which it blames for increases in illegitimacy, broken families, destitute women and the abandonment of the elderly in the West. Thus what constitutes risk and the attribution of blame is a social and political phenomenon which cannot be read apart from economic development.

To support my argument that in contemporary India women are presented as the chief risk to the social order, I first briefly examine discourses on female sexuality and gender relations as revealed in the framing and interpreting of national legislation and in Tamil ethnic politics. Despite the view that women are a major risk to society, in practice the meaning and implications of the concepts of risk and the associated notions of danger, courage and boldness are context-dependent and contested. This is illustrated by a discussion of the strategies that women employ in Chennai's low-income settlements to evade these discourses without appearing to contravene them.

GENDER AND RISK IN INDIA

In the popular Indian imagination, women are characterised both negatively and positively. These characterisations inform legal and political discourse, media representations, popular theatre and ritual as well as everyday interaction. Positive images stress motherhood, purity, chastity, modesty, forbearance, obedience and *shakti* (a power common to gods and women). The 'good woman' is hard-working, thrifty and restrained; she subordinates her needs to those of her family. Negative images present women as gullible, immodest, promiscuous, cunning, undisciplined, lazy, spendthrift and disloyal. Such women are portrayed as a danger to their husbands, their families and society for they drain the family's resources, spoil reputations and set individuals and families against each other. It is acknowledged that conforming to social roles requires the suppression of individual short-term desires for the longer term, more satisfying goals rooted in family welfare. This suppression is considered difficult and, left to their own devices, men, women and children will readily 'take the wrong path'. As Daniel puts it, '[E]vil and decadence are taken to be the normal and the expected, whereas goodness and virtue call for great effort to create and sustain' (1987, p. 203).

The main mechanism for suppressing men's short-term desires is their concern for their own as well as their family's reputation. A key measure of masculinity is a man's efficacy in providing for and controlling his wife and children, that is 'keeping them on the right path'. However, it is not enough that a man fulfils his responsibilities; for his self-esteem and reputation he must be seen to fulfil them. It is thought that if men's efforts at family maintenance and their sense of responsibility and masculinity are undermined they will have no incentive to conform to social values. Thus social order is at risk when men do not adequately maintain the family and its boundaries. Yet their ability to do such is considered easily weakened by women who are in a position to dissipate family resources, fail to care for or instruct children, have extra-marital relations and disclose family secrets. Therefore, women (and children) must be controlled by husbands and fathers with the aid of society and the state. The maintenance of social order requires that women submit to their roles as dependent, chaste, discreet wives, instructive mothers and reliable stewards in their husband's homes. Women's submission to these roles is required not just to control women but to control men. Indeed, men and women strategically utilise these discourses to control each other and, in the case of women, to expand their own sphere of action.

While the risks and control of female sexuality have a long history in India, there has been considerable variation in what is deemed to be unacceptable. This began to change in the nineteenth century when missionaries, colonial administrators and European travel writers denigrated what they saw as the degraded status of Hindu women, the incorporation of lust within marriage through polygamy and multiple unions and the barbaric practices of child marriage, female infanticide, widow immolation and temple dancers (whom they saw as prostitutes), as well as what they considered obscene entertainments enjoyed throughout the social hierarchy (Nair, 1996; Banerjee, 1989). The emerging Indian intelligentsia's response was largely to admit the colonial critique of contemporaneous practices while denying they represented authentic ancient Hindu culture. Following European Orientalist scholars, the intelligentsia examined ancient Sanskrit texts to uncover India's glorious past, pointing to the education of women and female chastity in the Vedic period (Chakravarti, 1989).

Confrontation over defining and evaluating Hindu culture sharpened with the colonial assessment that barbaric practices made India unfit for self-government (Chakravarti, 1989). Nationalists, who became increasingly involved in local and national government, moved to eradicate those practices considered inconsistent with a civilised society. They did this by undermining their material basis, by defining them as obscene and, frequently, their practitioners as prostitutes (Nair, 1996; Banerjee, 1989). In the process of regulating gender relations and introducing a prudish social attitude, prominent nationalists, who were overwhelmingly men, attempted to define women as naturally chaste and men as naturally promiscuous (Nair, 1996). This definition was challenged by female nationalists who argued that chastity was a national trait to which men must also conform (ibid.).[3]

Recourse to ancient texts in order to fight contemporaneous political struggles is not confined to the colonial encounter. It is also common to the politics of the south Indian state of Tamil Nadu of which Chennai is the capital. The Tamil ethnic movement, known as the Dravidian movement, claimed to have a superior and more ancient language and culture than that of the Aryan-Brahminic culture of north India (Dirks, 1996). It promoted an ethnic identity which rejected Brahminic claims to cultural and ritual supremacy and opposed the dominance of north Indians and Hindi in colonial and post-colonial India. Once again morality, particularly the sexuality of women, became the yardstick by which one people, in this case the Tamils, claimed superiority over another culture, that of the Aryan-Brahminic culture of north India.

Tamil identity is founded on concepts and metaphors of female chastity (*karpu*) and motherhood (Lakshmi, 1990; Ramaswamy, 1992). It emphasises the centrality of motherhood and purity for women and the role of men as heroic protectors of both their mothers and all that is termed 'mother' – mother Tamil, mother country, mother community (*tai kulam*). Female purity and chastity is seen as having a spiritual power that demands justice and ensures victory and therefore is the object of veneration. Chaste mothers who are themselves descended from chaste mothers produce valorous men. Their wombs are described as the lairs of tigers and this imagery of the courageous Tamil son can be seen in classical Sangam poetry (100 BC–AD 250) (Hart III, 1973, p. 240), twentieth-century politics and the widely popular Tamil film industry (Lakshmi, 1995). A mother who is humiliated, insulted or violated sends her sons to do battle on her behalf (Lakshmi, 1990). Unchaste mothers, on the other hand, do not produce valorous sons nor can they lend the spiritual power of their chastity to ensure the success of their sons' efforts: unchaste women are traitors to the culture and unrealised persons while the man who does not protect the mother and all that is termed mother is emasculated (ibid.).

Thus Tamil ethnic discourse evaluates women in terms of their purity and chastity and locates them in a domestic, reproductive role, whereas a man's role is a public one which requires the overcoming of outside forces to protect and avenge the mother. The discourse does not provide men with an independent source of valour and success but predicates it on their mothers' purity and, by extension, the purity of all Tamil womanhood (the *tai kulam*).

In India, discourses on female sexuality have been a critical tool for shaping, justifying and contesting social hierarchies since at least the nineteenth century. In post-colonial India, it is one of the main (and public) means by which those of a higher caste and class justify their position in the social order. It is also central to the contestation of the social order by those lower down the hierarchy. While the politicisation of the sexual abuse of poor and low-caste women by police, employers, landlords and others constitutes a challenge to their claim to moral superiority,[4] cynicism towards claims of moral superiority by higher-class and caste women is widespread. Similarly, while women agree that external controls are necessary to ensure women's conformity to their social roles, they deny that men alone have a sense of responsibility for the family or concern for the family's reputation. They claim these dispositions are more frequently the preserve of women for not only do they not indulge in the resource-dissipating and reputation-endangering practices to which men are prone (alcohol consumption, extra-marital relations and bigamy) but, unlike men, their resolve to forego short-term individual desires does not break when their spouses fail to conform to social norms.

The view that women are a major threat to a peaceful and ordered society is clear from an analysis of national legislation and case law. The ghoul stalking this body of discourse is the sexually autonomous woman. Despite rhetoric to the contrary, legislators have stepped back from supporting women's economic rights in order to inhibit female sexual autonomy. Instead, legislation frames women as properly located in the domestic sphere and dependent on men. Hence, the Minimum Wages Act (1948) ensured that women receive only two-thirds of what men receive for the same work. The much-vaunted Hindu Succession Act (1956) did little for women's right to inheritance or control of what they inherit (Agarwal, 1998). It was feared that should women have equal rights to inheritance they would refuse to marry. The Code of Criminal Procedure specifically predicates women's and girls' right to maintenance on their not taking control of their sexuality. Under the Code, a woman's claim to her natal or marital family's resources only holds while she surrenders control of her sexuality to her father or husband. A woman has a right to maintenance even after divorce provided she has not refused to live with her husband without 'sufficient' cause (which does not include adultery), has not agreed to a separation, is not leading an 'immoral life' and has not remarried. Legally, maintenance for Muslim women should come from their natal families. The reason for stipulating who is responsible for maintaining women is the fear that a woman without economic support will resort to prostitution which itself is considered a risk to the family and, hence, the social order.

In addition to inhibiting women's sexual autonomy through economic means, the legal system defines women as the sexual property of men. The Law of Torts provides for the wrongs considered deserving of compensation by the judiciary. It allows for a father to sue the person who seduces his daughter and for a husband to sue the person who deprives him of his wife's affection and society. Similarly, the Indian Penal Code punishes a man who has sexual relations with a woman without her husband's consent and provides for the husband to register an official complaint against his adulterous wife. The Penal Code, however, expressly precludes a woman from registering an official complaint against her adulterous husband. The legal system is, as the Supreme Court held in relation to Section 498 of the Indian Penal Code, 'intended to protect the rights of the husband and not those of the wife' (quoted in Swaminathan, 1989, p. 134).

Consequently, Swaminathan has argued that '… rape, kidnapping and seduction have been made offences not to protect the person of the woman but to protect the rights of a man against violation by another man' (Swaminathan, 1989, p. 134).

What we see here is that discourses on female sexuality and gender relations which took hold in the nineteenth century have continued to dominate legislation in the twentieth century. Not only does legal discourse depict women and girls as the property of men and as properly dependent on them but legislation specifically hinders women's economic independence. In basing women's claims to their family's economic resources in the transfer of their sexuality to men, it defines the sexually autonomous woman as losing her rights and status — as having cut herself off from the family.

Thus legal discourse and the discourses utilised by those engaged in culturally-framed politics define the proper ordering of social relations between men and women and the ordering of society itself as rooted in female chastity, achievable only through men's control of women. After nearly two centuries, it is commonplace to regard unfettered female sexuality as productive of the kind of society of which nightmares are made.

It would be a mistake to understand this simply in terms of patriarchal hegemony for two reasons. First, by putting men in charge of women, society (quite consciously) attempts to control men.[5] Second, as Raheja and Gold (1994) argue, it is important to recognise that this discourse is not the only discourse on female sexuality and gender relations. Rather it is the most powerful discourse underlying generalised conceptions of women and social relations and, therefore, one to which women must be seen to conform. While this discourse is difficult to contest when applied to the generality, women can and frequently do contest it when specifically applied to themselves (as will be seen below). Nor should it be understood that subscribing to the dominant discourse prevents women from having a more positive view of female sexuality and a more playful attitude to sex expressed through song (ibid.), or from engaging in flirtations (Osella and Osella, 1998) or sexual joking between women of equal status.

WOMEN AND RISK IN THE LOW-INCOME SETTLEMENTS OF CHENNAI

Discourses at both a national and regional level position women and their sexuality as the major risk to society as well as their family's social standing. They present women as properly confined to the dependent, private, reproductive sphere while the independent, public, productive sphere is reserved for men. The residents of the two low-income settlements I studied in Chennai between 1990 and 1992 subscribed to these discourses. The normal role for women is *vitle*, literally 'in the house', but is also used for 'in the family'. Women are presented and present themselves as naturally afraid, shy and ashamed to enter the public sphere: afraid to go out of the house, out of the family. Some describe themselves as ignorant, as not aware of what happens outside the home, as not knowing how to go about things or how to speak to people. Women are described as easily deceived: fooled by soft words, easily persuaded to give or loan money, easily overcharged. However, in response to family need, men and women say that the latter are forced to overcome their inhibitions and inadequacies: for the sake of their families they must enter the public sphere as men do, with the courage (*thaiyaram*) to face the inevitable risks (*tunivu*) and difficulties (*kastham*). This is the discourse that enables women to move outside their accepted sphere of activity without posing a risk to their reputations; it allows them to expand their sphere of action by defining it as self-sacrifice. There is also a negative discourse: women who unnecessarily enter the labour market are selfishly bold/brazen (they have *timir*), for in flouting social mores, they risk their family's social standing merely to fulfil individual desires (*aasai*), frequently assumed to be sexual desires.

Examining the key Tamil words used to refer to risk and risk-taking, we find, as in English, both a positive and negative view. *Tunivu*, in a positive sense, means not only the courage and confidence to take risks but that this risk-taking is based on sound knowledge. In practice, *thaiyaram*, meaning courage and confidence, and *tunivu* are used interchangeably to convey this positive view of risk. *Tunivu* can also refer to risk-taking rooted in foolish stubbornness, temerity, audacity and, when used in relation to women, in insolence, immodesty and lack of sexual reticence. *Mosham* also carries the meaning of risk, but here the risk is one of treachery and deceit, of being exposed to danger, of taking the immoral path in life. *Abayam* refers to unforeseen danger or evil, accidents and deceptions. *Tuni*, the root common to the word for risk and the verbs to sunder, cut and sever or to be sundered, cut and severed, points exactly to the consequences of not conforming to dominant values – the risk of being repudiated by family, friends, neighbours and caste.

If we look at the way these meanings are attributed to the sexes we find that women are seen as more of a risk to themselves, their family, caste and society than are men (see Table 4.1).

We can see from Table 4.1 that women outside the family are also considered a source of risk for they may lead men to neglect their responsibilities to their families, if not to desertion. Older women or women who have had previous sexual partners are not considered sexually attractive so their ability to draw men is attributed to the use

Table 4.1 Attribution of risk and blame and its consequences

Risk-taking based on	Men	Women	
Courage: (*tunivu, taiyaram*)	Expected	Depends on context	Positive value
An unforeseen danger: a danger (*abayam*)	Less vulnerable (witchcraft)	More vulnerable (to the supernatural cheats)	Neutral value
Temerity: audacity (*tunivu*)	Less frequent (by women, male friends)	More frequent (acting beyond one's gender, not submitting to authority)	Negative value
Exposing oneself to deceit (*mosham*)	Less frequent (by women, male friends)	More frequent (due to gullibility)	Negative value
Consequences of risk-taking			
To be cut, severed: (*tunika*)	Less frequent (often temporary)	More frequent (usually permanent)	
To cut, sever: (*tunikka*)	Stance taken by domestic authority towards women and junior men	Less frequent (only able to do so in concert with their families)	

of witchcraft. Girls and young women are considered easily misled by men's soft words. They are also particularly susceptible to supernatural forces which will lead them to reject their prescribed social roles by refusing to get married or to have sexual relations with their husbands (Nabokov, 1997), both of which pose risks to the future well-being of the women concerned and to their family's reputation. To maintain their social standing, families are expected to distance themselves from those who flout social values. In practice, women are more likely to be cut off than men and this is more likely to be a permanent break than it is for men. The economic and social constraints under which women live make it less feasible for women to dissociate themselves from those of whom they disapprove unless they do it in concert with the rest of the family.

Thus the discourse on women and risk, as well as the attribution of blame, prevalent in Chennai's low-income settlements is contradictory. The dominant theme is in keeping with the representation of female sexuality in legal and ethnic discourse as the major risk to society. The contingent theme based on necessity, reluctance and self-sacrifice potentially provides women with the means to escape their *vitle* condition without endangering their family's reputation.

NEGOTIATING RISK

While all Indian women must negotiate their way round dominant discourses on the risks of female sexuality and unconventional gender relations, the economic constraints under which poor women live inevitably drive them into direct confrontation with these discourses at some point in their lives. The women in the squatter settlement and municipal tenements studied were usually forced into working because their husbands' incomes were insufficient or too irregular to meet household needs. This insufficiency and irregularity might be due to ill-health or old age but for many it was due to men's high levels of alcohol consumption. In other instances, women worked because they were deserted or widowed or because their husbands could not afford to maintain the women and children of more than one union. Some women worked, not because their family was short of money but because their husbands refused to provide enough for the household budget. In these circumstances, women must negotiate the values and categories on which the discourses discussed above are based; they must find some means of appearing to conform to dominant discourses while not doing so.

Before getting to this stage, women try to goad their husbands into fulfilling their role as provider and protector. Threatening to take up work is one means. Another rather risky strategy is for a wife to claim to her husband that his reputation as a drunkard is encouraging even his own relatives to proposition her. The efficacy of these strategies tends to be short-lived but they do reveal that women utilise dominant discourses to make men live up to their prescribed gender role – to take responsibility for the family.

At a later stage in the career of a drunkard, dominant social values and gender stereotypes are turned against a woman.[6] Finding they can secure neither work nor loans, men with serious drink problems force their wives to hand over money for alcohol. A man can do this in two ways: first, by saying that he is in too much pain to eat and if he was sick wouldn't she give him money for medicine and the second is by shouting abuse at her from the street or complaining about her to neighbouring families. Thus, in addition to playing on a wife's fear for her husband's health, men exploit women's concern for their family's social reputation (*maanam*).

We can see here that while the dominant discourse ascribes the sense of family responsibility to men rather than to women, a number of men are not only willing to pursue individual desires at the family's expense but recognise and exploit women's sense of responsibility for the family.

The decision to take up work is not lightly entered into even by women running households on very tight budgets. The main reason for their reluctance is that working poses a risk to women's reputation for chastity. In addition, they feel ill-prepared and powerless in their encounters with strangers. Initially, the change of status from *vitle* woman to working woman feels humiliating and women are unsure of how they will be treated by strangers as well as how to respond to them. However, there is no lasting humiliation as long as women can convince others of the validity of their objectives. The necessity of convincing others that a woman only works to provide for her family, that she does it with great reluctance, is essential to protecting her reputation as a chaste woman. If, at any point in her working life, she fails to convince others they will interpret her actions as located solely in her desire for a '*jolly*' time.[7] This marks her as sexually unrestrained, brazen (having *timir*) and on the way to infidelity, if not already unfaithful.

Such a reputation not only shames the whole family, leaving them exposed to harassment and disrespect, but can have significant material consequences. Most commonly it decreases the likelihood of finding suitable spouses for sons and daughters. Being asked to leave private rented accommodation and having her business boycotted (unless she is a money lender on whom others depend) are not uncommon. Similar consequences affect the families of men with serious alcohol problems, but because such families are widespread the consequences are less severe. It does mean, however, that families containing serious drinkers get trapped in a drinking network for, as one woman put it to me, 'Who but a drunkard would rent to another drunkard?' and only the families of drinkers will knowingly marry into a similar family.

The reluctance with which women enter the labour force can be seen from Shantamma's account. Shantamma is a 38-year-old woman of the Vanniar caste. As her own account of being forced to confront dominant discourses graphically sets out the dilemmas, experiences and strategies of most of the women in the settlements studied, I will recount it in full. I asked Shantamma why she started working:

Shantamma: Seventeen years ago my husband worked in a private company but lost his job when he got asthma. He didn't work for over two years. During this time my in-laws didn't respect me. I could see it from the way they looked at me and spoke to me. They thought I only visited them for money and they wouldn't speak to my children. I didn't work at this time because I was worried what people would say. I was worried they wouldn't accept me. For two years I worried but I thought I wouldn't do a cheap job but do an *idly* business [making steamed rice cakes] at home. But even this felt very demeaning. I told myself 'At least it's not stealing.' My husband told me not to do the *idly* business. He said I knew nothing about it so I shouldn't do it. I persuaded him that it is the same as cooking for the family and that I could make a profit from it. As it didn't cost much to start the business he let me do it.

Penny Vera-Sanso: How long have you been selling idlies?

S: For fifteen years now. I've redeemed some of my pawned jewels, put my children through school and am paying off a loan for my daughter's marriage. I can pay for anything the family needs through the *idly* business although I'm not making as much profit as I was before because the prices [for raw materials] have gone up.

P V-S: So it's made quite a difference for you?

S: Yes. Earning money has given me a lot of confidence too. When I was married I never went out of the house for the first five or six years until my husband's elder brother's wife started taking me out. Even fifteen years ago I only went out to buy food locally. I didn't have the courage to go beyond the local area and I wouldn't speak to anybody who came to the house if my husband wasn't at home. I told them to come back later. Now I have the courage to cross town to go to the *sangham* [a women's organisation lending money to the poor] to get my loan and if people come to the house I have the courage to ask them who they are and what they want.

P V-S: Are things different at home? Do you take more decisions, for instance?

S: No, it's just the same. I don't do anything against his wishes. I have to get his agreement.

P V-S: How does your family feel about you working?

S: After coming up in life and educating my children, my brothers respected me because they didn't educate their children and I managed it even though my husband was often out of work. Actually they showed me respect throughout. Even so I didn't go much to see them because people don't respect those who have no money. They didn't feel bad because I was working. They supported me. They said 'You are only working at home and trying to improve your family.'

Although not explicitly referring to dominant discourses on the risks of female sexuality and unconventional gender relations, Shantamma's account is framed against the expectation that everyone subscribes to them. Embedded in her account lie many of the strategies women use to appear to conform to the spirit of these dominant discourses while not entirely adhering to them in practice. Shantamma takes great pains to ensure I can have no doubt that she was forced into work for the sake of her family, that it does not reflect her own desires and that she has no underlying sexual agenda. The key points are that she wrestled with her dilemma for a long time and that she had a real need to work as they had sold or pawned their assets and were not being adequately helped by others (in this case her husband's family). In addition, their *maanam* was going because their need for assistance made them unwelcome guests and their poverty was effectively cutting them off from their relatives.

Furthermore, Shantamma stresses the propriety of her work by emphasising that it is undertaken at home, that she has her husband's consent and her brothers' approval, and that she continues to submit to her husband's wishes. The latter reflects one of the key objections to women working, that if women earn independent incomes they will become arrogant and disobey their husbands. Should a woman be defined as such, her husband's reputation for having the upper hand in the family (on which his masculinity is based) and her reputation for submitting to the control of her sexuality are at risk. This is also why Shantamma emphasises the necessity for her continuing to work by stressing the commonly accepted goals of educating children, securing good marriages and redeeming family assets. It would be unacceptable to suggest her objective is to enrich the family because such entrepreneurial activity is only legitimate in men.

JUGGLING RISKS

In confronting dominant discourses on the risks of female sexuality and unconventional gender relations, women living on low incomes strive to dissociate themselves from negative traits often attributed to men and considered yet more immoral in women. They do so to avoid definitions of themselves and their motivations which risk their exposure to the material sanctions and loss of *maanam* discussed above. In doing so, women are playing off one risk against another.

While I have emphasised the risks women face in relation to their reputations outside the family, the same concern for *maanam* poses risks to women and men which can create conflict within the family. Working women pose a risk to men's reputation as providers, as husbands who are not cuckolded and hence to their self-esteem. In this context men have several options: first, to shape definitions of themselves and their relationship by defining their wife's economic contribution as unremarkable and by setting constraints on her behaviour and activities; second, by refusing to permit their wife to work and, should she not submit to this, by reducing or withdrawing financial support to the family or by taking the final option of rejecting her altogether. Thus, in relation to the extra-household sphere, women play off the material and social risks of poverty against the material and social risks of working, while in the domestic sphere, the primary risk with which they juggle is the potential loss or reduction of their husband's contribution to the household budget.

This risk is exacerbated where a woman has herself chosen her husband or partner rather than submitting to a marriage arranged by her family. Such a woman is considered to have succumbed to lust and put the welfare of her family, including her siblings' and (future) children's marriage prospects at risk. As lust is considered to be short-lived, men engaged in such relationships feel more insecure about their wife working than do men in arranged marriages, for she has already proven herself to be disloyal and sexually motivated. Consequently, they are far more likely to employ stratagems such as turning to drink, chasing other women, denying paternity of their children (thereby denying responsibility for their financial support), or threatening to leave in order to force their wives not to work or only to work with them. Thus men in love marriages are also playing off risks: in this case the risks to their *maanam* of having their reputedly sexually uncontrolled wife working as against the loss of *maanam* their own stratagems may engender.

All women driven initially by the need to raise family incomes but whose overall goal is family welfare risk not only the reduction of their husband's contribution to the household budget but also lowered social status (which itself can have economic implications) and, in more extreme cases, homelessness and the sexual harassment to which lone women are subjected. Women without the cooperation of their husbands, fathers, brothers or, in the case of widowed or deserted women, adult sons are more likely to find these risks realised than do those with their support.

Underlying the risks women balance, then, is the dominance of discourses which posit female sexuality as a major risk to family and society. In this context, women attempt to redefine their transgression of conventional gender roles by arguing that though they may be acting and interacting in ways similar to men they do so *through* the roles incumbent on them as women. That is, they are claiming the positive traits attributed to men of courage, confidence, ability and a sense of family responsibility. As Shantamma shows us, this is a source of great pride for women for they have gone beyond the timidity stereotypically attributed to them and faced the world with courage, confidence and ability. Whether we should see this as a real change brought about by working or merely a good front for assertiveness (though not for what is deemed disrespectful or arrogant) is not clear. Shantamma's story is typical of the experiences and strategies of women in the two low-income settlements studied in Chennai. Although by no means all women work from home, all female workers select and justify the job they do, the number of hours they put in and its location (all of which heavily determine income levels) as appropriate to a balance between their age and family's need (Vera-Sanso, 1995). At the time Shantamma started working, she was only 23 and working from home was the appropriate setting; working in the street (with the associated risk of sexual encounters) would not have been.

Although dominant discourses on 'proper' gender relations and the risks of female sexuality form the subtext of Shantamma's representations of herself and her motivations, this does not mean that she or the other women living on low incomes accept these ideas any more than do women elsewhere in India. Shantamma does not think of herself as a risk to her family or society but this is the discursive context in which she must operate, a context which has real material effects.

Thus risk-talk is political and has been used to constrain women's economic and social position in India since the nineteenth century. Equally it has been used by Indian women for individual and larger political objectives although it rarely works as effectively for them as it does against them. This is because the economic, jural and discursive empowering of men in order to control women frequently enables the former to side-step women's strategies. This empowering, which is intended to control men by giving them responsibility for and power over women and children, in practice enables men to flout social norms more openly than can women.

CONCLUSION

My main contention is that Beck does not question why some things or people become defined as risks and others not. Yet this is precisely our task. Beck is mistaken in attributing the West's (shifting) response to modern technological hazards to the overcoming of material needs. It is not technology itself which people worry about, but how society is organised, what its impacts are on the individual, where power lies and how it is managed, as well as the impact of individuals on society. Hence the emphasis on communism rather than nuclear weapons and the dissipation of nuclear protest once communist regimes collapsed.

Amongst Indians, the central risk perceived as such is not a consequence of the 'dictatorship of scarcity', as Beck rather glibly suggests, but a concern for social status and maintaining social order. The latter is thought best achieved by establishing stable families in which men have the main resources, rights and responsibilities, which must be protected from women except in circumstances that better serve the goal of maintaining stable families. And, indeed, engaging in discourses which argue in terms of maintaining social order is more likely to secure legal or policy changes that benefit women than arguing in terms of women's rights.

What we need to be examining is the way the concept of risk is implicated in politics; the way dominant definitions of risk set moral codes which frame disciplinary regimes, constrain action and set the terms of debate in which people engage both to enforce and resist the impact of such definitions. Such an approach prevents us from assuming, rather than investigating, the impact of poverty on risk perception. It reveals that even for those living on very low incomes the primary concern may be risks to social status and to the security ordered social relations seem to offer. In Chennai's low-income settlements, it is precisely through this lens that economic need is refracted.

Dominant perceptions of risk are collective nightmares. On the one hand, they are rooted in a failure of the imagination, a failure to envisage alternatives. On the other, they are rooted in an over-stimulated imagination which can see no boundaries to change. In both they reflect, and sometimes illuminate, the sources and centres of power and powerlessness.

ACKNOWLEDGEMENTS

I am grateful to Pat Caplan and the anthropology departments of Goldsmiths College and the University of Kent for their helpful comments on earlier drafts of this paper.

NOTES

1. At Kyoto, the United States refused to commit to stabilisation of domestic gas emissions and rejected a strong compliance regime for emission targets. Instead, it demanded unlimited emissions trading, backdating of emissions quotas and no joint buyer/seller liability for fraudulent trading. These demands would allow the US to buy other countries' emission quotas, as well as the estimated emissions Russia did not produce over the last decade (due to economic crisis) and would encourage fraudulent trading. If met, the US's demands would raise global emissions as well as increase its own emissions (Climate Action Network, 1997).
2. In the opinion of Britain's Campaign for Nuclear Disarmament (CND), the declared nuclear powers have no intention of banning nuclear weapons despite their rhetoric to the contrary. The Nuclear Non-Proliferation Treaty, which only required the

declared nuclear powers to start talking (within a period of twenty years) about the possibility of a global ban on nuclear weapons, was extended indefinitely in 1995 at their insistence. While obsolete weapons have been destroyed to much fanfare, the nuclear powers are updating their nuclear arms as well as developing and building new ones such as the 'bunker-busting bombs' designed to combat the kind of strategies Saddam Hussein employs. CND considers that the dissipation of popular opposition to the stockpiling of nuclear arms and the fragmentation of active resistance is directly connected to the fall of communism (personal communication, 1998).

3. For more detailed accounts of regional and class-based variations in how women were re-imagined during the colonial period, see Sangari and Vaid (1989).

4. For a discussion of custodial rape cases, see Nair (1996).

5. An explicit expression of this is the belief that marriage is the best means of steering a wayward son back onto the 'right path'.

6. The term 'drunkard' is the one women use to describe husbands who drink heavily ('a full time drunkard'). It reflects the way the urban poor consume alcohol, solely to get drunk. No enjoyment is expected of the flavour: alcohol is downed in one go, with eyes screwed up as though submitting to foul-tasting medicine.

7. In Chennai, English words are borrowed although the meaning may be altered. A *jolly* time or having one's *jollies* refers to the selfish pursuit of individual pleasure.

REFERENCES

Agarwal, B. (1998) 'Widows versus Daughters or Widows as Daughters? Property, Land and Economic Security in Rural India', *Modern Asian Studies*, vol. 32, no. 1.

Banerjee, S. (1989) 'Marginalization of Women's Popular Culture in Nineteenth Century Bengal', in Sangari, K. and Vaid, S. (eds) *Recasting Women: Essays in Colonial History* (qv) (New Brunswick, NJ: Rutgers University Press), pp. 127–79.

Beck, U. (1992), [1986] *Risk Society: Towards a New Modernity* (London: Sage).

Chakravarti, U. (1989) 'Whatever Happened to the Vedic Dasi? Orientalism, Nationalism and Script for the Past', in Sangari, K. and Vaid, S. (eds) *Recasting Women: Essays in Colonial History* (New Brunswick, NJ: Rutgers University Press) pp. 27–97.

Climate Action Network (1997) *ECO*, vol. 98, no. 8, 9 December.

Daniel, V. (1987) [1984] *Fluid Signs: Being a Person the Tamil Way* (Berkeley: University of California Press).

Dirks, N. (1996) 'Recasting Tamil Society: The Politics of Caste and Race in Contemporary Southern India', in Fuller, C. (ed.) *Caste Today* (Delhi and Oxford: Oxford University Press) pp. 263–95.

Douglas, M. (1992) *Risk and Blame: Essays in Cultural Theory* (London and New York: Routledge).

Hart III, G. (1973) 'Woman and the Sacred in Ancient Tamilnad', *Journal of Asian Studies*, vol. 32, no. 2.

Hunter-Wilson, M. (1951) 'Witch-Beliefs and Social Structure', *American Journal of Sociology*, vol. 56.

Illich, I. (1971) *Celebration of Awareness* (London: Marion Boyars).

Inden, R. and Nicholas, R. (1977) *Kinship in Bengali Culture* (Chicago: University of Chicago Press).

Jones, P. M. and Reece, G. (1990) *British Public Attitudes to Nuclear Defence* (Basingstoke: Macmillan).

Lakshmi, C. S. (1990) 'Mother, Mother-Community and Mother-Politics in Tamil Nadu', *Economic & Political Weekly*, Vol. 20 October.

Lakshmi, C. S. (1995) 'Seduction, Speeches and Lullaby', *Economic & Political Weekly*, Vol. 11 February.

Nair, J. (1996) *Women and the Law in Colonial India* (New Delhi: Kali for Women).

Nabokov, I., (1997) 'Expel the Lover, Recover the Wife: Symbolic Analysis of South Indian Exorcism', *Journal of the Royal Anthropological Institute*, vol. 3, no. 2.

Osella, C., and Osella, F. (1998) 'Friendship and Flirting: Micro-Politics in Kerala, South India', *Journal of the Royal Anthropological Institute*, vol. 4, no. 2.

Raheja, G. G. and Gold, A. G. (1994) *Listen to the Heron's Words: Reimagining Gender and Kinship in North India* (Berkeley and London: University of California Press).

Ramaswamy, S. (1992) 'Daughters of Tamil: Language and Poetics of Womanhood in Tamilnad', *South Asia Research*, vol. 12, no. 1.

Sahlins, M. (1972) *Stone-Age Economics* (Chicago: Aldine).

Said, E. (1978) *Orientalism* (London: Routledge & Kegan Paul).

Sangari, K. and Vaid, S. (1989) *Recasting Women: Essays in Colonial History* (New Delhi: Kali for Women).

Swaminathan, P. (1989) 'Legislation for the Improvement of the Socio-Economic Conditions of Women: The Indian Case', in Kanesalingam, V. (ed.) *Women in Development in South Asia* (Delhi: Macmillan) pp. 122–40.

Vera-Sanso, P. (1995) 'Community, seclusion and female labour force participation in Madras, India', *Third World Planning Review*, vol. 17, no. 2, pp. 155–68.

5 A RISKY CEASE-FIRE: BRITISH INFANTRY SOLDIERS AND NORTHERN IRELAND

Paul Killworth

PRELUDE

The incident comes from a moment with an infantry platoon, in the middle of a training exercise. The platoon sergeant, the corporal and I were walking across a field. We had been on exercise for several days, and the initial effects of a lack of sleep had begun to show. I do not remember precisely how the topic came up, but Corporal Heighton began to talk about an incident in Ulster, when the Land-rover ahead of them, containing two RUC officers, had encountered an explosive device.

The device had gone off, and had killed the first RUC officer instantly. As Heighton and others had approached, however, the second RUC officer had staggered forward. Heighton described it: 'He'd lost his face, half of it had been just blown away.' The RUC man was in some confusion, and said, over and over again, 'I can't see, I can't see.' He had no eyes. Heighton told how he took the man, and said to him 'It's just dirt, you've just got dirt in your eyes, that's why you can't see ...' He then added 'Of course he died a few hours later.' The narrative stopped, and the conversation between the three of us halted for a moment or two, before the sergeant started again on a different topic.

INTRODUCTION

This chapter is about the British Army in Northern Ireland, in particular the training processes that infantry units undergo before deployment to the province, and the ways in which soldiers have dealt with the risks involved in this conflict over the last three decades. It is based on fieldwork conducted in 1995–96, during the cease-fire; the researcher was involved in military training as part of participant-observation into Army culture and hierarchies. The primary unit of investigation was an infantry platoon in a regular battalion; a platoon contains around thirty soldiers, normally commanded by a lieutenant, with a sergeant as a second-in-command. British soldiers are volunteers, usually from lower-middle class or upper-working class backgrounds; most join the Army, however, with relatively little idea of the actualities of military service.[1]

Risk is in many ways a problematic concept to deal with. This was brought home to me in fieldwork, when, after many weeks of training to deal with potential paramilitary threats, a sergeant-major gave a talk on road safety in Northern Ireland. He noted that many present would be concerned about deploying to the province, because of the threat posed by the Provisional Irish Republican Army (PIRA); he then pointed out that in recent years, more Army personnel had died in road traffic accidents than in terrorist attacks.

I became curious about the way in which the soldiers within the platoon that I studied began to develop a discourse that stressed the risks involved in the cease-fire. It became clear that many of them considered the cease-fire, in its then current form, as more risky than the low-intensity conflict that had preceded it. For my own part, whilst analysing the casualty figures for the Army in Northern Ireland, which show a relatively low risk of fatality or injury in the province, I became interested in how the elaborate tactical procedures enacted by the Army had affected these risks. In other words, what were the *real* risks involved in patrolling the streets of Londonderry or West Belfast, and how did the Army's actions affect them?

In this article, I use Frank Knight's 1921 distinction between risk and uncertainty to explore why the scientific calculations of risk were relatively unimportant to the soldiers concerned. I argue that the relationship of risk to agency encouraged the soldiers to internalise the external threat through personal responsibilities and social relations, and by configuring, through internal discourses, organisations such as the PIRA as qualitatively very similar to the British Army. Simultaneously, however, historical accounts and paradigms used to explain the conflict were distanced from the Army, providing the possibility to lay moral blame on actors other than those in the Army. This combination of internalisation and externalisation, I suggest, goes some way to explaining the ambivalence felt by many soldiers about the cease-fire process, and the risks involved.

TRAINING AND THREATS

The regular unit with which I conducted fieldwork was a platoon in an infantry battalion. The unit was preparing for a six-month deployment to Northern Ireland. Units deploying to the province go through a prolonged period of training in their own barracks and various training areas, culminating in a two-week package at the Northern Ireland Training Advisory Team's centre, normally called NITAT, a word also used to refer to the team members themselves. This training has evolved and adapted during the period of the conflict, becoming increasingly specialised over time.

Infantry units are frequently deployed to Ulster, and experience there has become part of the process of becoming a senior infantry soldier. Unfortunately for 2 Platoon, which I studied, the battalion had not visited Ireland for several years, with the result that out of the platoon, only two private soldiers had been with the unit on its previous tour. As the platoon commander was also new to the unit, the result was that only the lance-corporals and corporals had experience of Northern Ireland operations. As shown in Figure 5.1, a platoon in a Northern Ireland role is divided into two multiples of twelve men each, and in turn into three teams of four soldiers. The team is the basic operating unit for most Northern Ireland tactics, and considerable stress is put on their often junior team leaders (see Dodd, 1976, on 'The Corporal's War').

Training is run primarily by the battalion itself, with help from external experts from NITAT. A range of topics are covered during training, including specialised patrolling techniques, observational skills to deal with the hazards of explosive devices, riot training and special weapons such as baton guns and shields, and an array of legal knowledge, including arrest techniques, the provisions of the Emergency Powers Act and other technical details. Most of this is quite distinct from the normal tactics used by the Army, and takes a considerable time to learn and to acquire.

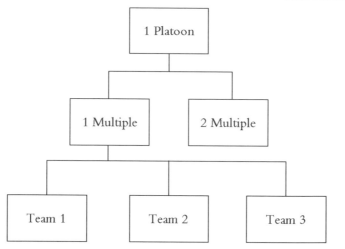

Figure 5.1 A Unit in a Northern Ireland 'Orbat' (Order of battle).

Risk in the context of Northern Ireland comes from the threat of paramilitary attack.[2] In the early days of the conflict, these attacks centred around mass riots; as the conflict progressed, a large array of tactics have been deployed against the British Army. Most of these, however, fell into two broad categories: explosive devices and sniper fire. Explosive devices have been used since the early days of the conflict, and have three main forms. Some are attached with timers: while early on, clocks were built into the mechanisms, nowadays electronic timers, such as those found in video machines, are used. The problem with these is that it is hard for the bomber to guarantee to hit his particular target; such devices are therefore normally used to strike at fixed targets, such as buildings, or as simple delaying mechanisms to keep the Army occupied.

Other explosive devices are radio-operated, and these were particularly popular during the early 1980s, as they allowed the bomber to set them off at the correct time and catch particular units or patrols. The difficulty with these is that they can be jammed, and thus made inoperative. A third way to use explosive devices is to attach them to a command wire, and detonate them with an electronic pulse. This is almost fail-safe, but does mean that a long wire, which can be noticed by soldiers, has to be attached to the device and requires that someone is at the other end of the wire to set it off, with the result that they are close to the scene of the explosion and thus more likely to be caught. Command wires remained one of the most popular current tools of PIRA at the time of fieldwork, especially in urban areas.[3]

Sniper fire from paramilitaries, called 'shoots', was very common early on in the Troubles as a method of attacking the Army. It was relatively easy to accomplish, but had significant drawbacks. First, actually hitting a soldier or policeman was quite difficult. Rifles were rarely 'zeroed', and so were likely to miss. Second, the firer was vulnerable to being caught in any follow-up by the Army. Despite the unpopularity of this method outside of the southern border areas, the Army still uses the shoot as the basic method of instruction in how to follow-up after an incident has occurred.

An illustration of the kind of problems faced by the British Army is given below. Figure 5.2 is a version of a diagram drawn by an informant, from an incident he was involved in during the late 1980s, in West Belfast.[4]

The buildings form part of a housing estate in the west of the city made up of houses and gardens, shown fully only in two of the blocks. The patrol, made up of four teams (1, 2, 3 and 4), each with four members, approached from the south; Team 2, lagging further behind than it ought to have done, was shot at from the building by a gunman, injuring one of the team. The remainder gave a target indication to the surrounding units and grouped around the injured man. Teams 1 and 3 ran up to the main road at the top of the diagram, ultimately setting up vehicle check points (VCPs) and assisting Team 4, when it caught up, in checking the firing point. This process is termed 'going into depth', a similar term to that used in conventional warfare.

It was believed that the gunman escaped through the back of the house to a waiting car; Team 1 thought that they must have seen the vehicle as they arrived at the main road but did not realise what it was at the time. Distinguishing 'civilians' from 'terrorists' is very difficult and contributes to the blurring of the categories in many conversations about Nationalist areas. After the event the patrol suspected that there were watchers keeping an eye on Teams 1 and 3, in communication with the gunman, who would have escaped around the

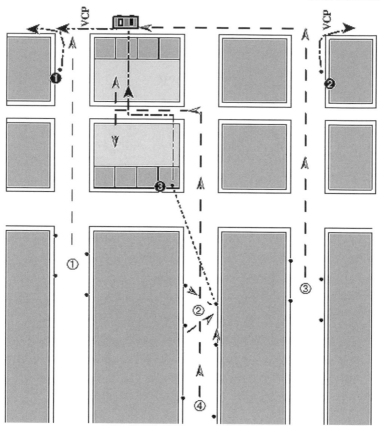

Figure 5.2 An incident in Northern Ireland, from a sketch by an informant

corners immediately after the shoot (marked on the map as 1 and 2). The injured soldier eventually recovered; the gunman was never identified or caught.

The closest the Army approaches to conventional attacks in Northern Ireland are these reaction drills to an enemy shoot. The various teams are supposed to close in on the firing point and adopt a defensive position around it as fast and as aggressively as possible; it is made clear that this is probably the only chance to take out the gunman that the units will have. The manner in which this is practised is very close to conventional section attacks, in that speed and a similar kind of aggressive spirit are encouraged; this is unsurprising, since the task that the soldiers are attempting to accomplish is very close to that of a conventional attack. Tension emerges, however, from the faceless nature of the encounters. In most shoots, the gunman will never be seen; the aim of killing a gunman, ideally in a legal manner, becomes an objective that is rarely achievable. After shootings and explosions, countless fruitless follow-ups and the experiences of injured, dead and crippled friends, this aim becomes an emotionally imbued desire that spans the history of the Army in the province.

Shoots have been somewhat rarer in recent years, but in training they continue as a key teaching tool. What this incident also illustrates well is the importance to the Army of deliberately injecting uncertainty into its own routines. The above attack depended upon the PIRA gunman having a clue as to where the Army might patrol, and where the surrounding patrols would be. The less certain he can be of this, the harder mounting such an attack becomes. Another way in which this is done is through the handling of the vehicle checkpoints. After a shoot or explosion, the area is sealed off, as shown in the example above. However the Army has become aware that PIRA take careful note of where checkpoints are usually set up, with the aim of placing secondary devices at those points. As a result, commanders now radio over their chosen positions, so that if they are registered on the computer as having been used before then the commander will be able to change them.

The cease-fire meant that soldiers were in less immediate danger. They were not likely to be shot at or hit by explosions so long as the cease-fire lasted. Unfortunately this state of affairs was marred by two problems. First, during the cease-fire, Army patrols in Catholic areas were strictly limited or banned altogether. Effective 'no-go' areas were set up where only RUC patrols could venture. Normal operations ceased to occur, with soldiers confined to their cramped barracks for long periods of time. Second, it was not believed that the cease-fire would hold. During fieldwork it became, as one commentator put it, 'a cease-fire by default' and the talk in the unit was of 'when the cease-fire ended'; the contemporary situation was seen as distinctively liminal.

In this sense, many soldiers in the unit, especially team leaders, began to talk about the cease-fire as containing a range of risks of its own. First, the reduction of Army patrols would mean that the platoon would not, when deployed, be able to get a feel for the streets in their area of responsibility (AOR). If anything did happen, and it must be stressed again that it was the almost universal opinion that something would, then they would not be ready. A lack of local knowledge could make follow-up operations extremely difficult. Second, the message continually repeated in lectures, discussions and literature was that PIRA was planning and practising new attacks. For PIRA, NITAT speakers would explain, the cease-fire was merely a time to acquire new weapons, regroup and plan. Their potential for action when they ended the cease-fire would be greater than when they began it. Furthermore, or so the word was circulated amongst private soldiers, they would begin it again in a major way, with the critical advantage of surprise. In this sense, the cease-fire was a 'risky' cease-fire, and the remainder of this chapter is concerned with explaining, in more detail, how the soldiers' approach to risk made it appear so.

CONCEPTUALISING RISK

The conflict in Northern Ireland has been what could be described in military parlance as a 'low-intensity' conflict. Definitions of the term vary (Bellamy, 1998, p. 26), but one common meaning assumes that the term refers to the pace and consumption of resources in a conflict. In Northern Ireland, except for a limited period in the early 1970s, attacks and actions have occurred infrequently. Much of the time, soldiers spend their days waiting to be attacked, so that they can respond. One soldier in my platoon suggested that the key role of patrolling was to 'draw fire'; once the paramilitary had shown his hand, then the security forces had a chance to take action.

The determination of when these attacks are likely to take place has been of obvious interest to the Army command, and it is here that scientific calculations of risk become most apparent. The Army created the Northern Ireland Bureau, whose job it is to keep track of the probabilities of different events occurring. They calculate, for example, the chances of being shot on a hot or a cold day, and when explosive devices are most likely to be used. These statistics and calculations are detailed, mathematically correct, and largely ignored by soldiers on the ground.[5]

The problem with these calculations of risk lies in a more fundamental difficulty within scientific notions of risk. Risk mechanics grew from a mathematical analysis of small, localised events and scenarios, around which probabilities could be calculated. As risk mechanics grew more sophisticated, these scenarios became more complex; however, all calculations of risk depend upon the construction of scenarios, whether they be as simple as flipping a coin, or as complex as a house fire or a nuclear plant meltdown. Constructing the scenario is essential to the trustworthiness of the calculations.

In his seminal book on the economics of risk, the economist Frank Knight (1921) argued that there was a difference between a chance such as that involved in the flipping of a coin, a measurable chance or *risk*, and that involved in an event such as a house fire, where the individual risk was effectively unknowable, which he termed *uncertainty*. For Knight, the latter case provided the possibility for firms to make profits, by offering to insure house-owners against the very small risks involved. The distinction lay in the difference between the unknown, almost unknowable chance of a *specific* house catching fire, and the possibility of *any* house catching fire. The first required a detailed knowledge and calculation of individual factors, the latter purely a volume of local government statistics. An insurer could turn an uncertainty into a risk, by pooling the individual uncertainties.

The insurance business increasingly tries to find ways to deal with individual details and circumstances, but the distinction expressed by Knight is a real one. A similar preoccupation underlies Beck's writing on environmental risk (1995), where the issue at stake is how scenarios of environmental catastrophe are designed in the first place. Beck's deep scepticism concerning the risks of nuclear power is centred on a belief that the risk scenarios used by plant managers are unrealistic, and fail to describe actual situations and behaviour.

For the soldiers in the platoon, the statistics produced by the Northern Ireland Bureau were unconvincing, mainly because the scenarios constructed by them, based around weather, the time of year and other factors, failed to take into account localised circum-stances. In effect, the Bureau produced risk assessments, whilst the soldiers were concerned about uncertainties. In particular, the Bureau excluded the role of personal agency, with the result that, initially, to look at the official figures, the risks involved in Northern Ireland service appear fairly low. Table 5.1 gives a breakdown of the number of incidents in Northern Ireland over the period.

Table 5.1 Paramilitary incidents in Northern Ireland, 1969–94

	Shooting Incidents	Bomb Explosions	Devices Neutralised
1969	73	9	1
1970–74	20,900	4,229	1,952
1975–79	6,275	2,408	1,151
1980–84	3,089	1,356	520
1985–89	2,398	1,033	698
1990–94	2,386	948	588
Total	35,121	9,983	4,910

Source: Northern Ireland Annual Abstract of Statistics, 1996

The central point to be made here is that although this marks a considerable problem for the security forces, the levels in recent times have fallen to the point where they do not form part of daily experience for the soldiers concerned. During 1990–94, shooting incidents occurred on a level of roughly nine per week, spread unevenly across the province; bomb explosions numbered just under four per week. Given the number of soldiers and units in Northern Ireland, this means that an individual soldier is very unlikely to be shot at, or directly involved in a bomb explosion. Indeed, as the RUC officer stated during the lecture, a soldier is more likely to die in a road traffic accident than at the hands of a paramilitary. The very low chance of death, and relatively low chance of injury, for the individual, especially within the regular Army, is illustrated in Table 5.2, showing the deaths and injuries during the same period.

Effectively, on one level, the conflict creates risks that are as hard to engage with as other low-level risks in civilian life. Several points must however be made here. First, although the individual risks may be low, the cumulative effect is still serious. To lose 23 regular soldiers during 1990–94 may be a low number in relation to the overall military presence in the province, but this is still a terrible human cost to the families and units concerned. Second, the reduction in these figures is in large part attributable to the changes in procedures and tactics discussed above; in other words, it is only through acting as if there is a constant, severe risk of death or injury that the risk is in fact reduced to the current levels.

Table 5.2 Security force casualties in Northern Ireland, 1969–94

| | Deaths | | | Injuries | | |
	RUC	Regular Army	UDR/RIR	RUC	Regular Army	UDR/RIR
1969	1	–	–	711	54	–
1970–74	58	236	46	1,517	2,521	98
1975–79	72	95	52	1,216	824	82
1980–84	69	53	49	1,034	381	114
1985–89	66	42	34	1,664	543	68
1990–94	30	23	22	818	955	131
Total	296	449	203	6,960	5,278	493

Source: *Northern Ireland Annual Abstract of Statistics*, 1996

The 'true' risk of patrolling, if soldiers walked about casually, as opposed to taking cover, following the earlier tactical procedures, and staying constantly alert, is effectively unknowable, as infantry soldiers almost never do so. The official statistics, therefore, show only the results of several decades of improving tactics, and ever tighter military procedures. The actual risks (whether or not someone is pointing a rifle at you, waiting for you to make an error) are unknown. Soldiers are aware of that, and approach the problem of risk accordingly. It is very difficult, if not impossible, to generate a risk scenario that takes these concerns into account.

So, a low-intensity conflict, knowing that there is an extremely low chance of being shot at, or targeted by a bomb, is not an effective way to conceptualise the problems around you. It tells you very little. It cannot easily be given material form, in the way that many other risks can be, and the risks concerned are largely attached to tasks that must be accomplished in any case. It may be useful to a senior commander to know that an attack is more or less likely on a sunny day, as he will have responsibilities for organising follow-up and reinforcements, but useless to the individual who will have to conduct the patrol in any case. The infantry soldiers that I studied were, unsurprisingly then, uninterested in official probabilities; instead, they conceived of, and understood, risk primarily through a process of internalisation.

INTERNALISING THE ENEMY

I have argued above that the soldiers deployed to Northern Ireland found the official, mathematical calculation of risks unsatisfactory as a mechanism for understanding and conceiving of the dangers that presented themselves. Indeed, so distanced from personal under-standing were these risks, that to say that soldiers perceived risks in this sense at all would be questionable. To the individual soldier, at the platoon level, dangers were instead effectively internalised. By inter-nalisation, I mean to imply the contrast between attributing risk and agency to individuals or the personal group around an actor, and attributing those elements to an outside world. In some ways, a parallel example might be the contrast Paul Farmer draws between Haitians blaming AIDS cases on local sorcery, and perceiving them as the impact of US policies (1992). In one case, agency and responsi-bility are modelled around internal social processes; in the other, external 'others' are taking actions and responsibilities.

   In the context of the Army, two major processes of internalising uncertainties were occurring. On the one hand, daily risks were linked closely to social action, such as good patrolling skills; on the other, the conception of the enemy facing the unit – PIRA – was modelled closely on the Army itself. In effect, a low-intensity conflict, difficult to measure or conceive of on a daily basis in terms of formal 'risk', became a conflict in which agency was contained primarily within the Army itself, and could thus be controlled and understood by its constituent members.

Internalisation through social responsibility

A large part of the training concerned the perfection of urban patrolling techniques, the methods by which small units of men could move through urban areas, covering one another, watching for potential devices, looking for snipers, searching for 'command wires', watching for the faces of paramilitary suspects. The training staff would watch carefully, monitoring individual performance, looking for mistakes and weak points. Hour after hour was spent honing the skills of the soldiers.

According to the NITAT team and the opinions of the NCOs in the platoon, experience had shown that PIRA also observed Army units whilst they were in the province. This observation was conducted at levels as low as that of the team, and individual soldiers could be identified as having poor drills and sloppy procedures. PIRA was *always* in Ulster, soldiers were told, and so had a better idea of Army procedures than the Army did itself, given the way in which Army units rotated through the province every few years. The result of this was that PIRA would identify and target patrols which had poor drills, and attack at the moment when they were weakest. If a patrol was conducting itself well, and an attack seemed likely to be unsuccessful, or the paramilitary was likely to be caught afterwards, it would be postponed until another time. A soldier who was careless was thus positioned as endangering his entire unit.

This logic provided a strong tool for enforcing care and attention during training, and eventually in Northern Ireland itself. Soldiers, especially junior NCOs, team leaders and those private soldiers claiming an element of seniority or prestige in the unit, would enforce judgements on those soldiers who seemed to be careless or error-prone. As a group of private soldiers said about one of their number, who seemed to 'flap' whenever matters became tense: 'If you think he's bad now, imagine what he'll be like when we get over there.' Another example of this sort of judgement was the OC of the company commenting on the radio communications from one of the corporals during an exercise, in which the former stated darkly how the latter seemed to 'get very excited' under pressure; the CSM added that this had been mentioned in previous annual reports. Such a commentary overshadowed the corporal's subsequent success in tracking down a fleeing gunman. This kind of discussion has a long history in Northern Ireland itself; there were constant resonances of the conversation recorded by Hockey (1986, p. 128), in which soldiers berated a newcomer to the unit who was taking cover during attacks, but failing to understand the importance of being able to fire back at the same time.

The problems of 'flapping' under pressure were a factor for concern. Some of the worst casualties have been suffered by the Army in follow-up attacks, such as at Warrenpoint in 1979, and the possibility for soldier error is at its greatest during the chaotic minutes that follow an attack. Soldiers were constantly warned about this kind of situation. An example is a private soldier, Handley, referring to an incident when, on an earlier tour, an over-eager platoon commander led a patrol into a shoot across a playing field; Handley and Deane came under fire although neither was injured:

Handley: Could I add something there, Howlett? I don't want to go against anything you've said, like, but when you're actually there it'll all be different. I mean you won't be going through it all like this, you'll just be saying whatever comes into your head. When me and Deane got shot at, it was like twenty minutes or so before we got on the net, we were shitting ourselves.

Howlett: Yeah, when I was out there we'd get people on the net and they'd just be saying 'I'm on the Falls Road, we need some help,' or something. You'd spend ages just trying to calm them down a bit until you could get the agencies out there. But you need to know where you are so we can get them out there quickly. You could be on your own for quite a while otherwise.

Norden: Are you trying to tell us this is a bluff lesson then?

Howlett: No, you'll need this for NITAT, they'll expect you to do it all this way down there.

Handley: Anyway, it'll be your team commander who does this normally and if he gets slotted you'll be crapping yourself. But someone needs to take the initiative, get on the net.

The consequences of losing control of a situation entirely could be severe. Many soldiers who had served in the province had experiences in which they had been lost, or boxed in by angry crowds. On several occasions during exercises, inexperienced platoon commanders found themselves separated from their units as they tried to control the confused mass of soldiers on the ground. As the OC commented on one: 'He's all alone now, in the middle of a Nationalist area: well, he's not going to last long, is he?' One private soldier in the platoon described the following situation whilst on guard duty with a younger soldier and myself, trying to get across the feelings involved:

He set an IED [an explosive device] off, lost both his legs. I wasn't a commander back then, just a member of the team. The IED had gone off and his legs were just everywhere, in pieces. The crowd had gathered round and they were shouting 'one-nil, one-nil'; the lads were just so angry. Then a dog started, like, biting some of the pieces. One of the guys he went over and pointed his rifle at it and put two rounds in it. I thought then, 'This has gone to pieces completely.'

In summary, there was a strong sense that being attacked was in all likelihood a response to personal carelessness or poor tactics, normally by private soldiers, but occasionally due to the commander of a patrol. When Handley was describing the shoot across the playing field, one of the points he was trying to make was that the commander, not the sniper, caused the incident by his foolishness. Flapping under pressure, too, could lead to follow-up attacks being more serious, or crowds getting out of control. Only by good patrolling, and tightly controlling the situation after an attack, could risks be minimised. Frequently the logic being expressed was that the agency for risks was the Army itself, even though the soldiers concerned were of course simultaneously aware of the agency involved in the nature of the PIRA threat facing them.

Internalisation through 'the Enemy'

Indeed, PIRA itself, as perceived by the Army, was in some ways the result of a process of internalisation. On the surface, beyond the few military trappings seen at funerals or on propaganda films, PIRA appears very little like a regular military force. The primary tool of a paramilitary insurgency is, after all, secrecy and unpredictability, and contemporary PIRA uses small active cells and fluid organisation to achieve this. The use of 'supergrasses' and British agents in the late 1970s and early 1980s ensured that PIRA members who did not accommodate to this new reality were rapidly caught and imprisoned (Taylor, 1980).

The model that the platoon used to describe and analyse PIRA was somewhat different however, and stressed the role of PIRA as 'the Enemy'. 'The Enemy' is a phrase used by the British Army, in a variety of contexts, to label an opposing enemy force. It frequently appears in training, to label an unidentified force: the British Army does not train against 'Iraqis', or 'Argentinians', for example, but against 'the Enemy'. 'The Enemy' in such training effectively resembles the British Army, in that it is almost always organised, disciplined, follows military procedures, and – on exercise – invariably looks like the British Army, as British soldiers play out the part of the opposition. The central point is that 'the Enemy' is traditionally another army, much like the British Army itself.[6]

PIRA, in training, was reconstructed in much the same way. Aspects of it which resembled a military force were played up, those that did not resemble 'the Enemy' were played down. PIRA, it was stressed, was trying to kill members of the Army, just like an enemy force would. Other political objectives or aims were downplayed, although it was noted that PIRA targeted the RUC more frequently than the Army. PIRA had organisation and ranks, and during suspect identification, when soldiers were taught the faces, names and addresses of PIRA suspects, ranks and organisational roles were stressed, giving a feeling of solid organisation within PIRA, not a fluid, changing, covert organisation. When the soldiers were taught about PIRA weapons, the mortars and bombs presented by the NITAT team were all labelled, grouped and classified, just as if they were mass-produced weaponry of an enemy army, and not homemade devices.

Throughout, the emphasis was on PIRA as 'the Enemy': an organised paramilitary army, with fixed goals and aims which it would try to carry out by known means, even if the exact moment of an attack would be unpredictable. PIRA resembled, in such accounts, the British Army itself, and, just like 'the Enemy' in regular training, the Army's aim was to defeat it. Principally, this made the unknowable risk posed by PIRA knowable. Instead of a confusing and chaotic threat, thinking in this way allowed the construction of knowable risk. The entire discourse above, on the importance of maintaining good drills and techniques, was dependent on the idea that PIRA acted logically, in targeting weak units, and that they planned attacks just as the British Army might when on exercise. In some ways this no doubt reflects the considerable internal organisation of PIRA, although it ignores issues of recruitment or kinship networks for example,[7] but in other ways it illustrates an innovative response to the problems of fighting a low-intensity war.

It might seem that this form of internalisation would make the Army perceive itself as the focus of explaining the conflict. In fact, the explanation for the conflict itself was almost entirely externalised, focusing on external actors and agency to explain the form and continuation of the war. For the soldiers, the conflict in Northern Ireland had nothing to do with them, and the history of the province was one in which the Army played only a marginal role, as a peace-keeper and a neutral party.

EXTERNALISING THE CONFLICT

At the time of fieldwork, the British Army was reacting to the process of the cease-fire in Northern Ireland. Although there had been brief cease-fires before, there was a renewed attempt by the British government and senior military officials to improve the image of the Army in the province, as part of a method of maintaining the halt in hostilities. As part of this process, the Army was to instil in the soldiers being deployed to the province a new sense of mission, based around respect for, and an understanding of, the Nationalist and Republican communities they would be patrolling.

As a result of this, numerous history lectures were given by the platoon commander, and the walls of the platoon barracks were in part lined with displays describing the various attitudes to the conflict, from both Loyalist and Nationalist perspectives. I describe more fully elsewhere the combination of historical narratives that emerged through this training (Killworth, 1997); what is of interest here is the manner in which both the 'official' portrait of Northern Ireland history, and most of the accounts given by soldiers amongst themselves, blotted out the Army as an historical actor.

Official accounts portrayed the conflict as starting in 1969, when the British Army was called in to protect Catholics from Protestant extremists; it then moved swiftly to a situation in which, in an ill-defined fashion, the conflict became one between the Republican paramilitary groups and the British Army, a conflict which continued throughout the intervening three decades. A central theme of this account was that the essential problem was a tribalistic conflict between Protestants and Catholics in the province, a conflict that had always existed. The Army's involvement was explained as one of separating the two sides, as an effectively neutral observer-participant.

Individual variations on this model existed, normally revolving around the dichotomy, also seen in civilian British narratives, between perceiving the history of the province as one of a society entirely obsessed with internal feuding and obscure symbolic displays, and perceiving the history of the province as one of a society exploited by quasi-criminal paramilitary extremists. In either case, the Army was still represented as distinct from the conflict.

Soldiers' own narratives stressed, above all, the timeless nature of the conflict. The cyclical nature of units' deployment to Ulster, and the long histories of senior soldiers' involvement with the situation, encouraged a sense of detachment and disengagement from political processes. The Army would deploy to Northern Ireland, come back, and would expect to return in a year or so: the idea that the conflict might cease was rarely voiced. Such actors did not include the Army within the conflict, which was fuelled by Northern Irish communities and politicians. The cyclical element to these histories is illustrated in the following quote from a corporal, from the end of a talk to the assembled unit: 'The thing is you've got to be aiming to kill the terrorist, not capture him. A dead terrorist won't do anything again. That's what my Dad taught me in Londonderry in '72, that's what I'm teaching you now and that's probably what I'll teach my kids in 20-fucking-10 or whatever.'

This was in stark contrast to Nationalist accounts of the Troubles, which place the British Army and the British government as central actors in historical accounts going back to the war of the 1920s. In many ways, the discussion at the unit level mirrored that occurring at Stormont, as the British government continued to play out a diplomatic line that divorced it from political initiatives: the British government portrayed itself as neutral, and with that it emphasised the notion that only Northern Ireland parties could provide a solution, as it was only Northern Ireland politicians who were causing or maintaining the conflict.

The consequence of these narratives was to externalise the conflict in Northern Ireland. Whilst daily risks might be internalised, through social responsibilities and the construction of PIRA along the model of the British Army itself, agency for the conflict itself was simultaneously distanced and externalised. In many ways, this ran counter to the official aim of training, which was to involve the Army in the peace process through changes to patrolling and attitudes, but it was implicated in the official policy regarding the history of the province. This contradiction underlies much of the Army's attitude towards Ulster, and, as I discuss in the conclusion, is crucial to understanding how total institutions can effectively operate in a plural political environment.

CONCLUSION

One of the reasons that I opened this chapter with the recollections of Corporal Heighton was to emphasise the contrast between such personal experiences, and the highly organised, tightly disciplined and refined counter-insurgency methods that have built up in Northern Ireland. Corporal Heighton was speaking about a particular moment in the middle of another year in the history of that involvement; he was also speaking during a cease-fire that many soldiers found deeply problematic. Although they were aware that the risk of injury or death was relatively low throughout the 1980s and 1990s, these risks masked what Knight would have termed the uncertainties of life in the province. The apparently low risk was the result of careful, disciplined patrolling and rapid responses to attacks. The combination made it relatively difficult to attack Army patrols, and made the risks of being caught higher, so that paramilitaries could make fewer attacks on Army units, with a consequent lowering of the risk of injury and death. It was only so long as soldiers behaved as if there was a risk, that the risk would in fact be low.

In addition, soldiers constructed their own unique risk scenarios around the proposition that the enemy would be most likely to attack units that showed poor drills and procedures. By this, the attitudes and actions of individual soldiers within a team could dramatically increase the risk of the whole team being attacked. Inevitably, this led to an internalisation of the potential risk within the military units, as soldiers began to attribute the agency behind attacks less to the individual decision of a paramilitary, and more to the effect of their own actions. This process of thinking was matched by the construction of PIRA as an almost reflected version of the Army, making the prediction of their actions easier. In the context of the cease-fire, with patrolling and the constant learning processes that it required limited by the necessity to avoid antagonising locals, this sense of risk saw the cease-fire as dangerous. It prevented soldiers from learning how to control situations, how to patrol safely, how to discourage attacks from happening at all.

If some approaches to risk saw a process of internalisation, another approach to the agency behind the risks was associated with a dramatic externalisation of the threat. The construction of the history of the conflict, through official lectures and internal debate, distanced the British Army from the conflict, writing it out as a political actor, and emphasising the internal nature of the conflict to Northern Ireland. The idea that PIRA was operating as a military entity not unlike the British Army itself, constantly preparing for a renewed attack, combined with the feeling that a resumption of violence was almost guaranteed by the nature of the Irish conflict, meant that the cease-fire, with all its restrictions, seemed more dangerous than 'business as usual'.

This combination of internalising and externalising the risks and dangers to the individual, although in some ways contradictory, is almost certainly linked to the problems of a total, bounded institution, and probably to many other situations in which dangers are combined with social divides, traversed by few relationships. In such a situation, practical agency clearly includes external social actors, whilst the individual is rarely capable of influencing any but those actually around him within the internal unit. Finding some way of mediating this practical contradiction can often be problematic, especially given the strong emotions that traumatic experiences generate.[8]

In the process of a cease-fire, discourse on risk is not purely academic. As has been mentioned above, the British Army was keen, during the period of fieldwork, to encourage a new attitude of tolerance and openness amongst the Army units in the province. Higher command felt that although the patrolling patterns and stance of the soldiers in the past had been appropriate to the situation as it then stood, they were unlikely to assist in maintaining a fragile cease-fire in Nationalist areas. Although the soldiers I worked with were perfectly happy to see a peace process in Northern Ireland, based around the above tactical concepts and discourses, they generally regarded the blandishments of their commanders as likely to increase risks to the Army and as unlikely to be successful, given indigenous interpretations of PIRA's motivations and the history of the province.

Ironically, such feelings, with different social actors, no doubt were mirrored by many politicians and citizens in Northern Ireland during the cease-fire, and it was perhaps unfortunate that the Army's contribution to taking risks in favour of peace was not better publicised.

To conclude, the statement of many of the soldiers in the platoon I studied – that the cease-fire was especially 'risky' – makes sense once it is understood how the enforced restraint from patrolling, resulting in less skilled soldiers and a poorer knowledge of the terrain, combined with a strong model of probable PIRA activity, the planning of new attacks, and a deep pessimism concerning a conflict perceived as external and tribal in nature, led to the opinion that a cease-fire would end in more bloodshed than the protracted, low-intensity, conflict seen in the early 1990s. Corporal Heighton at the beginning of this chapter was talking about the past, but I remember writing down the remarks of the longest serving private soldier in 2 Platoon, as we discussed the cease-fire one afternoon: 'If it does all start up again, we won't all be coming back. (Turns to another soldier) ... We're going to be one of the first to be hit – us or Crossmaglen. (Turns to me again) You know, I couldn't face that [again], losing mates ...'

NOTES

1. This fieldwork was conducted in uniform, with an effectively honorary rank, although the researcher was identified within the unit as an anthropologist at all times. Participant-observation involved participating in physical and military training. Permission for research was given on the understanding that certain classified materials and information used in training were not to be reproduced. Changes that have been made to comply with this, or to protect the identity of individuals, are not noted in the text. Names used in this article are fictional. I should like to thank all those soldiers who assisted in this research during 1995–96, and members of the British Army who have subsequently commented on manuscripts.

2. I use the label of paramilitaries here in preference to either 'insurgents' or 'terrorists'; the critical literature on the term

'terrorist' makes its deployment perhaps controversial (Fisk, 1992). This article attempts, probably unsuccessfully, a moral neutrality.

3. See Hamill (1985) for a detailed history of this.
4. Feldman (1991, p. 44) has a diagram drawn from the opposite perspective that complements this nicely.
5. It might be added that it is doubtful that the NI Bureau has them in mind as clients; these statistics are primarily aimed for higher command.
6. For a contrast see Falla (1994) on the Guatemalan security forces' images of local Indians, or Jeffords (1989) or Eisenhart (1975) on the US military's conceptions of the enemy in Vietnam.
7. Feldman (1991) and Zulaika (1995) highlight the relevance of these, for example.
8. Another example of this can be seen in the issue of 'fragging', well documented within the US military. Fragging involves the killing of a superior officer, normally in response to their actions in exposing a unit to combat. Particularly prevalent in the Vietnam War, commanders who insisted upon engaging with the North Vietnamese, who undertook an active defensive position or who volunteered their units for patrols, instead of maintaining a passive defence and minimising immediate risks, were not infrequently killed, either openly or by 'friendly fire' during an engagement. Important here is the way in which the more literal agents of the risks to the US soldiers, the NVA, were supplanted by an internal agent, a given commander, in a way that underlines both the objective and the subjective nature of constructions of risk.

REFERENCES

Annual Abstract of Northern Ireland Statistics (1996) No. 16 (London: HMSO).
Beck, U. (1995) *Ecological Politics in an Age of Risk* (Cambridge: Polity Press).
Bellamy, C. (1998) 'If You Can't Stand the Heat ... new concepts of conflict intensity', *Royal United Services Institute Journal*, vol. 143, no. 1. pp. 25–31.
Dodd, N. L. (1976) 'The Corporal's War: Internal Security Operations in Northern Ireland', *Military Review*, vol. 56, no. 7.

Eisenhart, R. (1975) 'You Can't Hack It Little Girl: A Discussion of the Covert Psychological Agenda of Modern Combat Training', *Journal of Social Issues*, vol. 31, no. 4, pp. 13–23.

Falla, Ricardo (1994) *Massacres in the Jungle: Ixcán, Guatemala, 1975–1982* (Boulder, CO: Westview Press).

Farmer, P. (1992) *AIDS and Accusation: Haiti and the geography of blame* (Berkeley: University of California Press).

Feldman, A. (1991) *Formations of Violence: The Narrative of the Body and Political Terror in Northern Ireland* (London: University of Chicago Press).

Fisk, R. (1992) *Pity the Nation: Lebanon at War* (Oxford: Oxford University Press).

Hamill, D. (1985) *Pig in the Middle: The Army in Northern Ireland* (London: Methuen).

Hockey, J. (1986) *Squaddies: Portrait of a Subculture* (Exeter: University of Exeter).

Jeffords, S. (1989) *The Remasculinization of America* (Indianapolis: Indiana University Press).

Killworth, P. (1997) 'The Contemporary Uses of Military History', *Royal United Services Institute Journal*, vol. 142, no. 4, pp. 58–63.

Knight, F. (1921) *Risk, Uncertainty and Profit* (Boston, MA.: Houghton Mifflin).

Taylor, P. (1980) *Beating the Terrorists? Interrogation in Omagh, Gouch and Castlereagh* (Harmondsworth: Penguin Books).

Zulaika, J. (1995) 'The Anthropologist as Terrorist', in Nordstrom, C. and Martin, J. (eds) *The Paths to Domination, Resistance, and Terror* (Oxford: University of California Press).

6 THE ERUPTION OF CHANCES PEAK, MONTSERRAT, AND THE NARRATIVE CONTAINMENT OF RISK

Jonathan Skinner

First-person narrators can't die, so long as we keep telling the story of our own lives we're safe. (Barker, 1997, pp. 497–8)

INTRODUCTION

This chapter considers the presence and consequence of risk.[1] It begins with the assumption that '[i]n ordinary life we make frequent risk-benefit analyses of various sorts where life and limb are concerned, usually informal and without bringing in numbers' (Dowie and Pym, 1980, p. 49). Or, as Holmes Jnr. puts it, 'people reason dramatically, not quantitatively' (Dowie, 1980, p. 108). In other words, risk – understood to be 'a chance or possibility of danger, loss, or other adverse consequences' (Thompson, 1996, p. 1189) – is apprehended, perceived, understood, assessed and acted upon by rational man and rational woman; to which we might add that such rational reasoning is based upon the actors' social and cultural experiences and premises. Our everyday encounter with risk, then, I am stating, appears to be socio-cultural and phenomenological: it takes place in a 'perceptual world organised through language and symbolic forms, as well as through social and institutional relations and practical activities in that world' (Good, 1996, p. 139).

My second purpose is to highlight the ubiquitous nature of narrative and to connect it with risk: '[n]arrative discourse dominates the way we relate to each other and to the world' cries Christopher Nash (1994, back cover). Narrative, declares Roland Barthes, 'is present in every age, in every place, in every society' (cited in Rapport, 1997, p. 43). Narrative, which is 'the telling (in whatever medium, though especially language) of a series of temporal events so that a meaningful sequence is portrayed' (Kerby, cited in Rapport, 1997, p. 74), even organises social life for the medical anthropologist Byron Good and the occupational therapist Cheryl Mattingly: both illness and therapy 'are presented as having a meaningful and coherent order' (Good, 1996, p. 139), 'a short story in the patient's longer life story' (Mattingly, 1991, p. 1000). Indeed, according to Mattingly, 'narrative makes sense of reality by linking the outward world of actions and events to the inner world of human intention and motivation' (1991, p. 999). Thus, in this way, narrative – an organised sequence of events – is inextricably bound up in the experience and portrayal of risk.

In our everyday world the management of risk and the assessment of risk have become big business, quite literally. The invention of the risk calculus has been a great boon to the insurance and industrial worlds in particular. Yet such inventions are not without their critics, such as the sociologist Ulrich Beck who argues that risk calculations are about 'making the incalculable calculable' (1992a, p. 100) by allowing 'institutions of developed industrial society ... with their ability to calculate hazards, to "spin" risk figures by under-estimation, [and] comparison out of existence' (p. 105). The social anthropologist Mary Douglas concurs, arguing against 'the pretensions of a risk analysis that is supposed to be a politically neutral analysis of culture-free individuals' (1994, p. 44), the 'bogus objectivity' of our risks coded in a mathematics of probability (p. 16). 'Risk' and 'narrative' would appear, then, to be concepts under investigation in the social and economic sciences.

A commercial example of risk assessment and insurance might be that renowned institution of insurance underwriters, Lloyd's of London, where, because of all the financial problems associated with unauthorised trading at banks such as Barings, with their notorious bad boys such as Nick Leeson, one particular Lloyd's insurance syndicate – SVB Syndicates – established insurance cover in October 1997 to protect banks from 'rogue traders' (Becket, 1997). These insurance underwriters expect to provide cover for around $250 million at a price of between $2 and $10 million. It appears that their only stipulation is that the bank applying for cover fill in a risk management form, and that they allow SVB to send in their own risk assessment experts before the policy is written.

Despite such insurance developments, just a few months earlier and four thousand miles away from London, insurance companies such as United Insurance and NEM West Indies had cancelled all their policies on the Caribbean island of Montserrat, severing all financial connections with the island because of the increasing levels of risk; even Royal Sun Alliance had put their insurance policies on Montserrat under review (Carr, 1997). Apparently, the risk insurance analysts no longer considered it worth underwriting investments on this island. These financial institutions – these 'risk-shifters' as Kenneth Arrow labels them (1971, p. 135) – thought that it was no longer viable for them to assume the risk of damage to properties and businesses on Montserrat. But whilst the insurance syndicates, the international banks, a social anthropologist and many Montserratians and expatriates were all pulling out of Montserrat, a proportion of the population on Montserrat had decided that they were staying put on the island, holding on despite the high levels of risk which they were told had entered their lives.

The intention of this chapter is not to study risk assessments and risk management strategies worked out by the likes of Royal Sun Alliance or SVB Syndicates. Here, I wish to examine the largely sociological and social anthropological debate about the nature of risk, and to proffer some narrative insights into an intriguing personal ethnography of risk on Montserrat which only recently have I been able to reread and revisit. To do this I will outline some of the sociological and social anthropological approaches to risk which seem to have been made in response to management and economic approaches to risk. From this debate I will then draw comparison, contrast and connection between risk critics, the intention being to erect a tentative gangway between the risk debate and the current prominence of narratology in the social sciences – the study of the construction, use and reception of 'texts', (whether strictly lexical (see Goody and Watt, 1981) or loosely cultural (see Geertz, 1993, p. 448)). Finally, I will illustrate such connections with a presentation of an ethnography of risk as perceived by a social anthropologist. These connections should support my thesis that narrative has a place in our theoretical approaches to risk, not least our noteworthy reactions to risk.

RISK AND NARRATIVE AS RESEARCH TOPICS

Whether deliberately or not, many social scientists, especially social anthropologists, court the '*crise revelatrice*' (Oliver-Smith, 1996, p. 304, emphasis added). They conduct fieldwork in hazardous environments, using '[d]isaster situations ... as an ideal medium to spawn and test a medley of social theories' (Torry, 1979, p. 529), 'natural laboratories' where social system performance can be examined under conditions of chronic and acute stress (Oliver-Smith, 1996, p. 304). These hazardous environments range from famine in Uganda (Turnbull, 1989) and disease in Haiti (Brodwin, 1996), to ethnic warring in the Sudan (Evans-Pritchard, 1969 [1940]), earthquake in Peru (Oliver-Smith, 1992), and radioactive pollution in Norway (Paine, 1992). In such extreme conditions – in times of trouble, loss and change – people are often confronted with existential questions which are answered by delving into their personal or group social and cosmic belief systems for explanation and meaning (Oliver-Smith, 1996, p. 309).

As expected, there is considerable disagreement as to what constitutes a disaster: they can be classified as events which culminate in severe damage to basic services (Torry, 1979, p. 518, note 4), or as natural/technologically destructive agent(s) combining with a population to produce social and technical 'environmental vulnerability' (Oliver-Smith, 1996, p. 305). Similarly, no academic consensus exists as to what causes a disaster: for the human ecologist, natural (meteorological or geophysical) events cause natural disasters such as hurricanes, droughts, floods and earthquakes (Torry, 1979, p. 518); but for the political economist, either the iniquities of the predominant social order, or the failure of a society to adapt are the cause of a disaster (Mossler, 1996, p. 87).

With their human focus, the social sciences, then, rather than the natural sciences, are best placed to investigate just how these disasters, hazards and extreme situations are defined and understood, and how different individuals and groups might respond to them.[2] The study of people's thoughts, fears, anticipations and perceptions of the occurrence of an extreme situation reveals remarkable social and cultural diversity and includes the following: ethnographic risk-perception mapping of community radiation fears from waste storage facilities (Stoffle et al., 1991), investigations into homeowners' narrative understandings of groundwater pollution (Fitchen, 1989), and 'vision quest' poison gas detection by Indians (Riddington, 1982). It is from my reading of such risk and narrative literature – where cultural and temporal concerns predominate – that I have identified the underlying issue of control which I would like to also push to the fore.

Handling risk – culture

According to *Zeitgeist* sociologists Ulrich Beck and Anthony Giddens, we are currently living through the new paradigm of risk: ours is a new 'risk society' (*Risikogesellschaft*) as Beck puts it; and our '[m]odernity is a risk culture', so Giddens declares (1991, p. 3). Both authors believe that we now live in a modern risk culture with new risk parameters with which we organise our social world. This modern risk society, or risk culture, has reflexive characteristics: by this they mean that in this post-traditional order of modernity we are able to structure, choose, create and revise our own self-identity; we are capable of writing biographical narratives of and for ourselves (Giddens, 1991, p. 5; Beck, 1992b, p. 19). Free of traditional social networks and relationships, we are, nevertheless, now subject to the global nature of the risk society since the danger of nuclear disaster (Chernobyl) or the hazard of forest fire (South-east Asia) have grave international implications for us all. Concomitant with Beck's and Giddens' universal democratisation of risk is a crisis over account-ability and responsibility (Beck, 1992a; 1996) which perhaps echoes the recent specific crisis of representation in the humanities and the social sciences – notably in social anthropology (Marcus and Fischer, 1986; Clifford and Marcus, 1986; James et al., 1997) – and the general ontological uncertainty as to the nature, form and context of knowledge (Lash and Wynne in Beck, 1992b, pp. 4–5; Paine, undated, p. 6).

With references to 'World Risk Society' (Beck, 1996) and 'Ecological Enlightenment' (Beck, 1992a; see also Giddens, 1991,

p. 4), the environmentally friendly authors – Beck more so than Giddens – hoist risk aloft as a universal controlling determinant of our global culture. Yet, *contra* Beck, the social anthropologist Robert Paine argues that our modern world has not been homogenised in the face of risk. According to Paine, the great social and cultural diversification of modernity, which Beck and Giddens are so keen to point out, ironically indicates that the *meaning* of living with risk cannot be quite as universal as they make it out to be, nor can the responses or abilities for coping with that risk be quite the same (Paine, undated, pp. 7–8). Far better, then, to turn towards the more dynamic cultural approach to risk taken by the social anthropologist Mary Douglas, one which – both as a language (1994, p. 14) and as a forensic tool (1990, p. 1) – pays more attention to the native speaker.

In keeping with her long-term interest in 'the social control of cognition' as she describes her work (Douglas, 1986, p. ix), or 'the sociology of perception' as Adam Kuper refers to it (1991, p. 183), Douglas translated her 1960s argument about danger and defilement from *Purity and Danger* (1996 [1966]) into 'terms of risk' (1992, p. 4) in the 1980s in her joint essay with Aaron Wildavsky, *Risk and Culture: An Essay in the Selection of Technical and Environmental Dangers* (1982). Together, Douglas and Wildavsky proposed a 'cultural theory of risk perception' (p. 8) which would make sense of risk-taking and risk aversion and in so doing help us to understand why there seems to be a growing sense of urgency to ward off risk amongst the general American population (p. 16), and how and why people ignore certain potential dangers around them and concentrate only on selected potential dangers. They were working on the premise that 'risks are socially accepted' (p. 14) and that different cultures highlight or downplay different risks: lightning rather than leprosy for the Lele of Zaire, industrial disease more than the endemic cardiovascular diseases or automobile accidents for the American (pp. 6–7). Douglas, now accompanied by Wildavsky, was merely reiterating her stance from *Purity and Danger:* no matter where we live, or in what society, we all choose our terrors and nightmares, selecting some and ignoring others, and such choice is culturally informed.

Apparently, each society needs its risk schemas just as each society needs its 'pollution ideas which are used by people as controls on themselves and on each other' (Douglas, 1975, p. 243). And so, it is the task of the social scientist to fathom just 'which kinds of risks are

acceptable to what sorts of people' (Douglas, 1982, p. 4). Risk –
'danger from future damage' (Douglas, 1994, p. 30), 'a joint product
of *knowledge* about the future and *consent* about the most desired
prospects' (Douglas and Wildavsky, 1982, p. 5, original emphasis) –
is also about the kind of social consensus intersubjectively shared and
affirmed by members of a community (Douglas, 1994, pp. 30, 12).
More likely to narrate risk from within than without a society or
collection of individuals, Douglas and Wildavsky's cultural approach
is not, however, unproblematic as Miriam Kaprow points out with
her observation that an overly culture-dependent approach to risk can
'trivialise real hazards and end up ... eliminating danger altogether'
(1985, p. 347).

In response to such criticisms, Douglas saves herself by pointing out
that the risk or danger may be very real, despite the cultural diversity
of the responses and reactions to it (1990, p. 8). But she still falls foul
of Paine's observation (undated, p. 10) that she charts a poor course
between the individual and society, between individual risk perceiver
and collective risk society. In *Risk and Blame* (1994), for example,
Douglas attempts to focus upon institutions and individuals, despite
typologising the individuals according to a number of culturally
informed grid/group environments ('egalitarians', 'hierarchists', 'individualists', 'fatalists' and 'autonomists' (1986, p. 54; 1987; 1994)).
According to Paine, such an approach really gives precedence to
society, thereby reiterating Durkheim's general proposition in *Suicide*
that 'what appears to be a phenomenon relating to the individual is
actually explicable aetiologically with reference to the social structure
and its ramifying functions' (undated, p. 12). In other words,
Douglas's cultural theory of risk slyly 'construes individuals as socially
constrained' (Boholm, 1996, p. 70).

In reality, the cultural approach to risk and risk perception goes
only halfway towards meeting the individual risk perceiver; it still
aspires to be a general theory of risk with universal classifications but
is in actuality merely a constraining construction. Avoiding such
'stodgy Durkheimian conservatism' (Beidelman, 1993, p. 1066), the
social anthropologist Åsa Boholm points out how useful it might be
to treat risk as a polyseme, a polythetic category sharing a family of
resemblances and meanings but lacking any essential feature (1996, p.
80 after Rayner and Cantor, 1987, p. 4). Such an approach is less
conceptually ambiguous and far more attentive and open to the

cultural diversity of risk perception, particularly in how it is shared intersubjectively. Though there are many incisive 'cultural' ethnographic studies of risk which work at the levels of group, culture and international policy and practice (see especially Jasanoff, 1987), the introduction of this concept rightly draws attention to the determination and justification of the level of the investigation taken in risk research, a concern which is already apparent in narrative studies of written material such as collective national tales (Bruner and Gorfain, 1984) and individual children's stories (Sutton-Smith, 1984).

Capturing change – time

Risk shares other similarities with narrative when we turn to the nature of time(-scale), rather than to the customary investigation of magnitude. A disaster is a time of change, a temporary or permanent change of routine (Paine, 1992, pp. 263, 275) which can be for good or for bad (Oliver-Smith, 1996). As far as risk and its perception go, they too incorporate temporal aspects as part of a dynamic process of interpretation and reinterpretation (Fitchen et al., 1987, p. 49), and as the final arbiters of judgement (Douglas, 1975, pp. 230–48; see also Giddens, 1991, pp. 109–43). Time is an important criterion for the risk calculations of Lloyd's, United Insurance, NEM West Indies and other organisations involved with the stock markets, places which, for Giddens, 'use risk actively to create the "future" that is then colonised' (1991, p. 118). The control of this time dimension – the 'colonisation of the future' (p. 111) in insurance in this instance – is paralleled in the field of literature where the past, present and the future can be imaginatively and creatively remembered, described and predicted in narrative sequences which either order, disorder or subjunctivise reality (Good, 1996, p. 144).

Checking texts – control

Finally, I would like to add that risk and narrative are both subject to individual and group control by institutions that attempt to manage risk and by writers who 'plot' their stories. Comparing risk perceptions by experts and lay people, Ray Kemp (1993, pp. 107,

114) determined that control – along with 'dread' – is a key element of risk perception. The personal control of consequences affects risk perception and subsequent behaviour in such a way that people may willingly expose themselves and others to high levels of risk on the roads or on the high seas if they feel that they are exercising some personal choice in driving too fast or sailing too close to the wind. Such a control perspective might go some way towards explaining Douglas's observation about Americans' fear of industrial disease rather than automobile accidents, as well as Giddens' comment that automobile accidents do not perhaps evoke the same degree of dread as the scenario of an air crash (1991, p. 130).

Writing, the predominant form of narrative construction that I am considering in this chapter, is 'the orderly inscription of words or forms *per se*' (Rapport, 1997, p. 45). As such, Rapport's *orderly* process is also Lamarque's *ordering* process – 'narrative imposes structure' (1994, p. 131) – an activity of routine composition whereby the writer can take charge of self, social world and literary world by creating, destroying, or amending; or by simply pinning these worlds down by definition, delineation and description. Thus, writing narratives can be used as a defence mechanism as much as a way of attacking a threatened change of routine for example. Writing down narrative sequences can disengage the author from the world around as much as they can engage him or her; public plays and political satires differ markedly from private poetry and personal diary entry in more than authorial intent. In the next section of this chapter, I go on to write about one such narrative sequence. In terms of risk, let me borrow and amend the title to the first part of Beck's book – 'Living on the Volcano of Civilisation' (1992b, pp. 17–84) – for this ethnographic account that leads up to my departure from the island of Montserrat by way of my reasons, decisions, risk perceptions and interpretations of risk, and – significantly – of those who influenced me; risk revisited indeed.

LIVING ON THE VOLCANO OF MONTSERRAT

Montserrat is a British Dependent Territory in the West Indies, a pear-shaped island in the Leeward group of the Lesser Antilles. The island is overseen by a British Governor (His Excellency) appointed by the Foreign and Commonwealth Office, and a locally-elected Chief Minister. Up until a few years ago, Montserrat *was* approximately 11 miles long and 7 miles wide, with a total area of 39½ square miles. It was home to some 11,519 residents divided between 'belongers', those born on Montserrat, the majority of the population, and 'non-belongers', those who travelled to the island and settled permanently, for a season, for a short vacation, or until their business was completed. A quiet island, since the 1960s Montserrat had embraced a form of luxury low-key residential tourism for wealthy 'snowbirds' – those who spend their winter on the island. In addition, there was on the island a small American University of the Caribbean (AUC) campus of several hundred American medical students. There was also a cluster of approximately a dozen Technical Co-operation Officers (TCOs) – British development workers under the responsibility of the Governor – engaged on long-term port jetty, hospital, government building and runway projects, necessary work following the devastation of much of the island by hurricane Hugo in 1989.

On Montserrat, 'the Emerald Isle of the Caribbean', there are three mountain ranges around which the local population used to cluster in small villages with St Patricks in the south, Long Ground in the east and the capital, Plymouth, on the west coast. In the arid north, the Silver Hills jut out to form an imposing cliff headland. Slightly north of the centre of the island are the Centre Hills which are softer and covered in thick tropical vegetation. And in the south of Montserrat are the Soufriere Hills, a chain of hills with gaseous springs which bubbled and deposited rich layers of sulphur; this mountain rainforest range is dominated by Mount Chance, an aptly-named part of the range which culminates in Chances Peak, 3,002 feet above sea level. It is the eruption of Chances Peak that is ending insurance policies on the island, dispersing the local population, and attracting international teams of seismologists.

July 1995: one hot and dry summer's evening I came home to my small rented apartment on top of 'Chef' Ted's 'The Shamrock Cafe' in Wapping, the south of Plymouth, directly beneath the AUC campus which was on the slopes of Chances Peak. I was nearing the end of my year on the island. I had spent my time working with Coaster and other local calypsonians at ZJB, the Government-controlled island radio station, courtesy of Jane Irish, its director; *liming* (hanging-out) with some fire-fighters around the island, or with George Weekes at Mrs Cassell's bar in Plymouth; socialising with the

Governor and the expatriate community such as Jerry, TCO Geoff and his wife, Georgina, and TCO Tom and his tennis-playing wife, Kath; playing endless games of Scrabble with my local landlady, Shirley, and her elderly sister, 'old Mary', and writing poetry with the Maroons Creative Writing Group (Skinner, 1997b).

Tuesday 18 July 1995, tired of note-taking and interviewing, I had hitched a ride around the island to build up a slide record of the whole place. Though I saw little out of the ordinary that morning and afternoon, when I returned home I switched on the radio and found that the world of Montserrat had changed forever for myself and for many others. News broadcasts were discussing an emergency on Montserrat, earthquake activity somewhere around Chances Peak, rumblings felt in villages close to Chances Peak, ash falling from the skies and a sulphur smell in the south of the island, all suggesting the formation of a new soufriere and explaining the earthquakes we had been having prior to July.

Trained to write daily comprehensive ethnographic notes to myself in large ledgers, all that I found myself able to do in this situation was to write an unusual letter to my girlfriend, one which was not necessarily to be sent to her. What passes next is an excerpted account of this unsent 28-page letter which I use as both fieldnotes and narrative example. Both the letter and excerpts constitute narrative sequences, the result of a compulsive chronological activity for the next two and a bit days on Montserrat, and the slow reconstructive activity between October 1997 and August 1998 whilst I wrote this chapter: the former a virtual dialogue, the latter an academic discourse. I would like to suggest that for me, as for others, the perceived risk of eruption, the dread that stemmed from the uncertainty of the situation, was contained during this time by the performance of everyday activities which people continued doing and which constituted narrative responses.

Montserrat volcanics – a risk narrative

Tuesday 18 July 1995, evening

8.45 p.m. My dearest,

... The radio has just mobilised the Defence Force [MDF] as there's volcanic activity in the south. Evacuations in Kinsale, Trials; pungent smells in the air; occasional tremors and ash on houses ... I can't catch up on my diary for listening to the radio announcements.

8.55 p.m. ... Don't panic those on the Emerald Isle! There's no eruption but a new soufriere forming around Runaway Ghaut; those in Kinsale, Trials are advised to pack an overnight bag and leave for relatives. Those further south in St Patricks are advised *not* to panic but they could pack a bag just in case. Please don't worry, leave it to the professionals at the Disaster Centre headed by H.E. All MDF are ordered onto the sides of the roads with their equipment where they will be picked up.

So what's to be done now? Sit and write!

8.57 p.m. ... Jane Irish is trying to calm people – 'not an eruption but a new volcano!' Isn't that great? Contact your relatives. Wapping phones not working. Listen to the nation-station. We na sleep tonight ya know.

10.15 p.m. '*Too young to die*' on the radio; ... jammed telephone circuits ... ; radios blaring all over town. Mrs Cassell 'sells'/gives drinks to take to soldiers and says London will have it on the news; cars everywhere and people with bundles and bags, evacuees; George Weekes mentions hearing activity in Gages where the ash is coming from ... and that you can't swim [from the island because of the] volcanic springs in the sea; mud/ash on cars and stinging a few faces; Coaster goes to take two kids to parents up north; ... AND THERE'S NOTHING TO DO ... . A man buys a tank of gasoline for his boat – all stations being open. The best to do is sit at home and listen to '*It's Alright*', wait, wonder and 'chill'.

11.15 p.m. ... [My neighbour] Sarah says she usually stores water at times like these. Shirley is asleep ... .

Wednesday 19 July 1995

12.30 a.m. [The] Governor tells all he's going to bed and recommends all to relax.

6.45 a.m. [Wake up to] Jane on the radio. A man shouts outside – 'Daylight!'

9.45 a.m. Ash rain spits down covering people in speckles.

10.15 a.m. Shirley and scrambled eggs covered (and wedding cake) in ash. She's optimistic, saying there's no pressure build-up with [the earth] tremors and she remembers living for three months in the garden following the 1935 earthquake ... . She thinks an evacuation would be easy – helicopter.

10.55 a.m. ... Home – ash in hair and all along bed covers. The neighbours' TVs have 'Volcano Alert': stay calm and keep the TV on. People are going home from work.

5.30 p.m. Sorry for the delay, I was in town almost suffocating from ash falling onto my body and getting into my lungs. Eerily quiet, a Wednesday morning like a half-day afternoon. ... No face masks left on the island: – at the Printery all wear them; Rasta at Texaco topless with a white filter mask and people driving/walking by with surgical masks or bandannas.

Some people work, some stay home, some drink. I get a bag together – toilet paper and tuna and money. ... Shirley is in her dining room sporting a bandanna, she's icing a wedding cake for Saturday whilst desperately trying to keep the ash off it. ... Also, at last, phone contact with parents who are cool; it doesn't sound so bad when I speak to people or describe what's happening. But what of my diary?? And how can I possibly speak to people about dialect/calypso with all this hanging over us?!

At 2 p.m. Geoff (and TCOs) met H.E. for briefing.

7 p.m. ... H.E. asks for Guard Ship by tomorrow – the experts here reassured them with at least 24/36 hrs of warning [before an eruption]. Lots of colonialism and independence rhetoric on the radio.

And I'm desperate to work!!!

10.30 p.m. Now I'm ready with my pack like everyone else, torch by bed, radio on, doors ready, bike outside, rooms tidied and one box of special notes/tapes packed if there's time to take them, water stored and cool. I can't tell the difference between cars passing/volcano rumbling. Ash has stopped falling – Ted's car is clean at last; it's left print marks on toilet/desk/bed where patches were covered. At 8.50 p.m. in Shirley's room with the radio/TV on there was an intermediate 3–4 sec. earthquake (volcano building pressure?) ... An RAF Nimrod took pictures earlier in the day. Gospel music on all the airwaves. There's nothing else to do now. At least the rooms are in order. Ideally tomorrow there will be a ring of boats around the island?! Apparently in Jamaica rumours [about here] are of fire and explosions. No one knows here – Margaret is tucked up with a good book, her mother up the hill [near the AUC campus]. Ted's is open and empty ... I cancelled tennis tomorrow despite Tom urging Kath to go – dust on the courts?! She's not been affected, watching [the south of the island] with other wives with binoculars. Though the TCOs' meeting recommended all to pack bags she doesn't sense any trouble (nobody really does too much, they're trusting in God/being ready). I mention the AUC students' departure – she replies, 'Typical Americans, get a ship or planes for them, not like the British' who are staying with Montserratians to leave with them (or be humbled ever after). Also Shirley and Mary expect this 'over reaction' from US people, Shirley says she'll be on the warship with the British. ... Many people in Churches, C.M. etc. ... Margaret hopes to collect the dust as fertiliser.

11 p.m. EOC [Emergency Operations Centre] are meant to have come on the air at 10.30 p.m. Jane tells all in Long Ground to listen in for their news after an important meeting – '*Don't worry about a thing*' is played for them by Marley followed by '*Living in a World of Uncertainty*' [by Jamiroquai]! ... There's a sort of detached, voyeuristic quality surrounding me.

11.30 p.m. 'We're preparing information for you ...'

11.50 p.m. [A]ll this time to get a ... man saying he really didn't see much and quibbles over 'extinct/dormant' words. 'We can monitor the magma'... can predict ... can change ... there are 'pre-cursor'

phenomena ... there are uncertainties before drawing conclusions ...
'I don't want to answer that' re significance of ash ... 'Do we need to
evacuate?' – 'Um, er, we, I think we can get more data and generally
look at things.'

– 'listen to your radio to find out what happens should a full-scale
eruption take place' i.e. 'wait and see?' 'YES.'

'What competence do you have?' ...

'The only thing I can say is, er ... the situation is being monitored.'
'Those believing in luck – fingers crossed: if God – pray.'

Thursday 20 July 1995

4.15 a.m. From 11.30 p.m. to 12 a.m. they faffed about saying they
knew nothing and could predict nothing. Shirley dozes and isn't
concerned. Jerry's out; 12.30 a.m. I phone Georgina – AUC closed,
two students there and no Brits to leave unless a general Montserratian evacuation. Never mind the US [Americans]; their house
cracking [because of] earthquakes; lava in the east and some
mudflows. All TCOs are ready with their bags. I play a radio
broadcast recording to Shirley and we talk till 1.40 a.m. about how
here's home so she'll sit out her time (or get rid of Mary) and how
hard it is for her to leave, but I don't have the ties ... I pack, write,
wait with cockerels and crickets.

The final entry on Wednesday evening was a collection of comments
which I transcribed from the radio as a long-awaited vulcanologist
from Trinidad – who turned out to be a student – fended off some
local reporters' anxious questions. According to him, volcanoes could
be monitored, but not really predicted. He elaborated upon his
fatalistic risk assessment of Chances Peak made before his seismolog-
ical equipment had arrived: he had climbed the Peak and tested the
ash thrown out around him by tasting it; soft muddy pyroplastic
material suggested that surface material was being thrown up and that
the volcano was still in its early stages whereas gritty debris indicated
dangerous new material being ejaculated. Sampling only an ashy,
muddy material, he had deemed the volcano safe for the night and
had returned to Plymouth without setting up his basic equipment.
Interpreting this information from the radio, Shirley and the

expatriates – whom I mentioned earlier – were relaxed by this; more at ease than before, they went to sleep.

I interpreted the situation and information very differently, my attention drawn to the contradictions which I perceived based upon my previous experiences: I had been in earthquakes before; I had studied volcanoes at school, and I had an unhealthy lay scepticism of many of science's dogmas. I made sense of these temporal actions and events of the outward world, linking them together to produce a cognitive narrative full of foreboding. For me, the end of the time waiting for the scientists brought a loss of confidence rather than relief. Not so for the others who had more faith in the radio broadcast than I and stayed on after I left Montserrat the following morning.

NARRATIVE, RADIO AND THE CONTAINMENT OF RISK ON MONTSERRAT

Whilst I had been aware of social anthropological fieldwork conducted in extreme situations and reflexive accounts by social anthropologists of their ordeals and sufferings (Nash, 1979; Moreno, 1995; Rosaldo, 1993), it was only recently, with hindsight, that I realised that my narrating activities constituted autobiography as social anthropology (Okely and Callaway, 1992), as 'auto/ethnography' (Reed-Danahay, 1997). As such, it is with caution that I present and use this data; writing about writing social anthropology is fraught with difficulty. It is a potentially tautological exercise, but profitable, I hope, in this instance for highlighting what social scientists can find in themselves and other subjects through careful reflexivity.

This is not an attempt to displace or marginalise events on Montserrat and Montserratian tragedies for my own: both should be accounted for, and will be elsewhere. Here, the above excerpts from a narrative sequence have themselves been selected – and edited – to work as yet another narrative sequence for the reader of this chapter. The gist of this part of the letter, its 'integrity' for want of a better word, I have sought to maintain. The impetus to write is maintained for another twelve pages as the letter develops into a travelogue commentary of my sudden physical return to Britain and my slow, resentful and turbulent psychological coming to terms with my arrival in what had now become an alien environment full of sounds and smells, place names and people names which caused me to 'return' to the like on Montserrat: cold sweats and palpitations from the earthquaking of the floor by a washing machine in spin-dry mode, for example. 'Back home', the ordering, sense-making impulse still continues through Internet and newspaper media items collected and sequenced, and hence narrated:

July 1995 – Chances Peak erupts after 350 quiet years

August 1995 – Two thirds of the population are evacuated to the north of the island to live in temporary accommodation

23 August 1995 – 5,000 people have left Montserrat; Plymouth is evacuated at close of business each night

April 1996 – Plymouth is evacuated permanently

27 June 1997 – Violent eruptions spill over villages in the east (Trants, Harris, Streatham), 6 bodies are found, the first 'direct' victims of the eruption; the count quickly rises to 23

6 August 1997 – Several days of eruptions land on Plymouth, destroying the former capital

30 August 1997 – Royal Sun Alliance withdraws insurance cover for homes in the south of the island but continues to insure in the north

Figure 6.1 Chances Peak

Reactions to risk

The reactions to the initial eruption of Chances Peak were varied, dependent upon place and proximity to the Peak, levels of information or lack of, and vested interests on the island such as family ties and landownership. On Tuesday night, Mrs Cassell kept The Emerald Isle Bar open in the centre of Plymouth, going about her usual business of supplying drinks: however, her routine was slightly altered in that she gave out many soft drinks to soldiers instead of charging civilians for alcohol. Married to a Montserratian, and thus more 'belonger' than most, Mrs Cassell continued to work at her bar just as, the next day, my landlady determinedly tried to ice a wedding cake for the weekend, against all odds. Shirley, like Mrs Cassell, had vested interests on the island such as her elderly sister, her apartment and a house that had been occupied by her family for several generations. Unlike many of the young on the island such as George, Coaster and his two kids, Shirley has a memory stretching back far further than hurricane Hugo in 1989, to previous bad years, back even to the 1935 earthquake; so Shirley was more experienced and more confident of her chances and more assured of her fate than many younger than her. Like other older and more experienced Montser-

Figure 6.2 Shirley icing a wedding cake

ratians, Shirley was able to joke and turn her back on the events as they unfolded, though she did move to sleep in the concrete part of her house that night.

Ted, who always parked his shiny Mercedes outside the front of The Shamrock Cafe, responded to the situation by keeping his restaurant open and by quixotically ordering the car to be cleaned of ash whenever possible. Opposite Ted's, Sarah went about her disaster preparedness routine, storing water and battening down the shutters as if she were facing one of the hurricanes during hurricane season. Diverse reactions and responses to uncertain times, Shirley's, Ted's, Sarah's and Mrs Cassell's activities constitute narratives which are performative and dramatic rather than literate and compositional. So too for those to the north of Plymouth where the disaster scenario was one of remove: Margaret, one of the island's librarians, took the opportunity to curl up and read a book; Kath and other TCO wives watched the Peak and Plymouth from their balconies with their binoculars. A visual spectacle for these non–belongers with fewer ties and interests bound up on the island compared with belongers and Montserratians, the expatriates' reactions and responses were just as varied – again, dependent upon criteria such as economic means, social, cultural and personal experience, proximity to Chances Peak, access to radio, television and government information.

The AUC students' immediate departure from their campus under the Peak was seen by some expatriates (Kath and Georgina) and Montserratians (Shirley and Margaret) as an example of the cultural difference between the Americans and the British/Montserratians. In this way, despite the diversity of individual reactions and responses to the eruption, there were moments of intersubjectivity – of shared perspectives, opinions and responses, when, usually, there would be far less commensurability or common ground between these people. The majority on the island were thrown together in this crisis: few on the island completely turned their backs on the volcano, and if they did so, it was out of mental obduracy (retired British soldier Peter Lake – see Laurence, 1995, p. 1) or agricultural necessity (villagers in the east – see Rhodes, 1997, p. 14), stubborn refusal to change their living area or bold resistance to the potential loss of their crops.

Radio as narrative

As evinced in my narrative above, the radio, always a popular local source of news and information on Montserrat, became the central communication medium right from the start of the crisis of the eruption of Chances Peak. Just as though we were in a hurricane, everyone on Montserrat was requested to tune in and heed the advice, messages and bulletins broadcast. Certainly, those on Montserrat without access to television, such as myself, were all able to get within earshot of a portable radio. The radio broadcasts were of especial use to the Montserratian government and British representatives in their attempts to maintain calm and order on the island, and to quash rumour and scaremongering. Throughout the initial stages of the eruption it was news and information that was craved. The uncertainty of not knowing what was going on around us, coupled with the reluctance of the government to make information announcements until they too were sure of the situation, led to a lack of trust in their abilities. Their announcements provide us with other narrative sequences to complement those contained in my letter.

During the graveyard shift on Tuesday evening, Jane Irish invited geography teachers to phone in and share their expertise by talking to the listeners about volcanoes. G.H. White talked about the signs we would see before an eruption but, similar to the Governor, he then qualified (or undermined) his words by saying that he was no expert on the subject; 'vulcanology is not a refined science', he added. The following morning (Wednesday 7 a.m.) Jane brought us the official version of the event to date, the official and authoritative narrative of government responses to the eruption:

Now the national news. And this first release from the Emergency Operations Centre. It provides the following update which I'll read as prepared: 'Reports reaching the Emergency Operations Centre in Plymouth on the afternoon of Tuesday 18 July indicate unusual volcanic activities centred around the Soufriere Hills of Montserrat. Residents of the surrounding villages reported that there were unusually loud rumbling noises coming from the Soufriere areas. Villages also reported light ashfall and a strong sulphur smell. The National Disaster Co-ordinator immediately took steps to verify these reports. The Emergency Operations Centre was activated and the reports were confirmed. By 6.30 p.m. of the same evening the Emergency Operations Centre (EOC) was fully operational. Contact was made with the Seismic Research Unit of the University of the West Indies, based in Trinidad. The unit indicated that while there was no evidence of peculiar earthquake activity, it would nevertheless advance plans to have its Technical Officer visit Montserrat. The Caribbean Disaster Emergency Response Agency (CDERA) was also informed and CDERA brought its own plans into action. Residents of Montserrat were advised via mass media of the nature of the reports and the actions which had been undertaken by the EOC management team. These reports were delivered by His Excellency The Governor and The Honourable Chief Minister. Three such reports were delivered during the course of the night ... A further media release will be available as soon as that report has been presented to the appropriate officials and cleared for release.'

This account was supplemented throughout Wednesday by shorter updates as the government used the mass media, constructing and disseminating press releases, to regulate, legitimate and govern information and its flow, and hence the activities of the population on the island. Other radio programmes adapted to the situation, assisting the population with going about their everyday activities. 'Drivetime', a radio programme about car maintenance, turned to the topic of how to ensure that windscreen wipers managed the great quantities of ash building up on windscreens. Surprisingly, other discussion programmes tackled the hoary issue of political independence from Britain, and an end to colonialism. Yet, despite such feelings, it was the Governor rather than the Chief Minister who addressed the island in the evening, just as after the hurricane Hugo natural disaster it had been the Governor who had assumed control of the island, leaving public relations and morale building to the Chief Minister. Late Wednesday evening (6.30 p.m. approximately), after a résumé of recent events, the Governor said the following:

Um, we have, I, I've spoken to er, er, the Foreign and Commonwealth Office today, um, I've informed them that we have a situation which none of us can predict what is going to happen, but as a precaution, I've asked whether the West Indies Guardship can divert to our area. Um, not because I believe that it is, is going to be needed, but because um, I would like the assurance that we would have professional assistance on hand should it be needed.

The content and manner of this sample from an official broadcast, followed by that of the scientist's interview later on, were so disconcerting for me that I resolved to leave the next morning and await developments from Antigua. Unfortunately, the situation continued to deteriorate to such an extent that I never managed to return. Risk-wise, I had far less to risk in going than many Montserratians: I was near the end of my period of fieldwork and had little invested on the island apart from a lot of close relationships. Shirley tried, valiantly, to continue with her daily routine – though with a standby flight ticket in her back pocket. However, just after my departure I heard that many of those I had known on the island had left for friends and relations on neighbouring islands, and in North America and Britain – Shirley included.

CONCLUSION

I do not intend this chapter to be a comprehensive account of the initial eruption of Chances Peak, nor just a personal account of my departure from the island: responses to and rationalisations of risk are its subject, and the importance of narrative in our dramatic calculations is its argument. The various reactions to risk portrayed above show great diversity, both individual (such as for myself, Shirley, Georgina, the Chief Minister and Margaret) and collective as people came together in loose groups (American, British, Montserratian) and individual aggregations (such as Shirley and Georgina). Our reactions, I would like to suggest, were influenced by social, political, cultural, economic and spatial contexts, past experiences and present vested interests all impinging upon our various and varied qualitative risk assessments. Therein lies the diversity upon which I have touched.

There are many other narratives which I could have mentioned besides my letter and radio samples, but hopefully there is enough here to have shown that risk cannot be universally, objectively quantified for it is subjective, polysemic and dramatic – to return us to Paine, Boholm and Holmes Jnr. On Montserrat we were all trying to cope with disturbing and disrupting events which we sought to order, structure and sequence. We each attempted to preserve our activities of routine: composition for myself (compare with Lamarque, 1994), cooking for Shirley, radio coverage for Jane. And, as we can see, both 'time' and 'control' feature heavily in these socio-cultural activities.

For me, writing was a way of distancing myself from being helplessly tossed about by events beyond my control, evidence of the significance of time and control in my social anthropological risk response to the eruption of Chances Peak. Furthermore, this writing impulse is not an uncommon response; in building a world of words, the narrator cocoons himself from its potential harm. And so long as the narration continues, so too will the narrator – omniscient and invulnerable, detached from the proceedings, a voyeur and escape artist, or invulnerable soldier such as those frantic diarists and letter writers of the First World War before they were sent 'over the top' (Barker, 1997; see opening quote).

In this chapter I have thus sought to resist what Rapport criticises as the 'objective impulse' (Rapport, 1997, p. 13), which conforms to Giddens' ideal worldview that there is an 'impersonal, informal social reality above and beyond the actions, subjectivities, motives and intentions of individuals' (Rapport, 1997, p. 13). Instead of turning towards quantitative, holistic or cultural approaches to risk, my experience of the eruption of Chances Peak on Montserrat, my reaction to that risk event and my observations and records of others' reactions convinced me of the legitimacy of the subjective and dramatic 'narrative' impulse. Here, I have intended to establish a link between risk and narrative studies by identifying their shared cultural, temporal and control components. With these features and some dramatic illustrations from my letter and from the ZJB radio broadcasts, I hope to have added a narrative note to the risk debate in the social sciences. Risk, so I conclude, can be contained by culture, nature – and narrative.

NOTES

1. This chapter has benefited from general comments made during research seminars at the Universities of London (Goldsmiths College), St Andrews, Hull and Keele, and specific advice and constructive criticism given by Pat Caplan, Nigel Rapport, David Riches, Judith Okely, Jean Besson, Pnina Werbner, Gordon Fyfe and Mils Hills. I have chosen to disguise the names and identities of those mentioned in this chapter.
2. The traditional analytical distinction in risk research has been between 'objective risk' (defined according to statistical calculations of the probabilities of 'adverse' events) and 'perceived risk' (how people understand the likelihood of such adverse

events)' (Boholm, 1996, pp. 64–5); between 'prescriptive' quantitative risk assessments (what we should do) and 'descriptive' qualitative risk evaluations (what individuals actually do) (Cashdan, 1990, p. 3); between etic risk and emic perceptions of risk. These distinctions have been exploited by '[s]pecialists who ... use "perceived risk" to refer to what they view as an irrationally fearful response to risk' – 'the fallacy of dismissing the layperson' according to Stoffle et al. (1991, p. 612). For Ray Kemp, such distinctions should be collapsed as opposing camps mutually enlighten each other, and as the former learn from the rich lay conceptualisations of risk, and the latter gain specialist risk assessments (1993, p. 108).

REFERENCES

Arrow, K. (1971) *Essays in the Theory of Risk-Bearing* (Chicago: Markham Publishing Company).

Barker, P. (1997) *The Ghost Road* (London: BCA with Penguin Books Ltd).

Beck, U. (1992a) 'From Industrial Society to the Risk Society: Questions of Survival, Social Structure and Ecological Enlightenment', *Theory, Culture and Society*, vol. 9, no. 1, pp. 97–123.

Beck, U. (1992b) *Risk Society – Towards a New Modernity* (London: Sage Publications).

Beck, U. (1996) 'World Risk Society as Cosmopolitan Society?: Ecological Questions in a Framework of Manufactured Uncertainties', *Theory, Culture and Society*, vol. 13, no. 4, pp. 1–32.

Becket, M. (1997) 'Lloyd's offers cover over "rogue traders"', *Daily Telegraph*, 4 October 1997, Business Section, B1.

Beidelman, T. (1993) review of *Risk and Blame* by Douglas, M., *American Anthropologist*, vol. 95, no. 4, pp. 1065–1066.

Boholm, Å. (1996) 'Risk Perception and Social Anthropology: Critique of Cultural Theory', *Ethnos*, vol. 61, nos. 1–2, pp. 64–84.

Brodwin, P. (1996) *Medicine and Morality in Haiti: The contest for healing power* (Cambridge: Cambridge University Press).

Bruner, E. and Gorfain, P. (1984) 'Dialogic Narration and the Paradoxes of Masada', in Bruner, E. (ed.) *Text, Play and Story: the construction and reconstruction of self and society* (Prospect Heights, IL: Waveland Press, Inc.), pp. 56–79.

Carr, M. (1997) 'Left high and dry by the volcano', *Daily Telegraph*, 31 August 1997, p. 14.

Cashdan, E. (1990) 'Introduction', in Cashdan, E. (ed.) *Risk and Uncertainty in Tribal and Peasant Economies* (London: Westview Press), pp. 1–16.

Clark, W. (1977) 'Managing the unknown', in Kates, R. (ed.) *Managing Technological Hazard: research needs and opportunities* (University of Colorado: Institute of Behavioural Science), pp. 111–42.

Clifford, J. and Marcus, G. (eds) (1986) *Writing Culture: The Poetics and Politics of Ethnography* (London: University of California Press).

Douglas, M. (1975) 'Environments at Risk', in *Implicit Meanings* (London: Routledge and Kegan Paul), pp. 230–248.

Douglas, M. (ed.) (1982) *Essays in the Sociology of Perception* (London and New York: Routledge).

Douglas, M. (1986) *Risk Acceptability According to the Social Sciences* (London and New York: Routledge).

Douglas, M. (1990) 'Risk as a Forensic Resource', *Daedalus*, vol. 199, part 4, pp. 1–16.

Douglas, M. (1994) [1992]) *Risk and Blame: Essays in cultural theory* (London and New York: Routledge).

Douglas, M. (1996) [1966] *Purity and Danger: An analysis of the concepts of pollution and taboo* (London and New York: Routledge).

Douglas, M. and Wildavsky, A. (1982) *Risk and Culture: An Essay on the Selection of Technical and Environmental Dangers* (London: University of California Press).

Dowie, J. (1980) 'Bounds and biases', in Wooldridge, C., Draper, N. and Hunter, T. (eds) *Risk and Rationality* (Milton Keynes: The Open University), pp. 99–156.

Dowie, J. and Pym, C. (1980) 'Risk to life and limb', in Wooldridge, C., Draper, N. and Taylor, T. (eds) *The World of Physical Risk* (Milton Keynes: The Open University Press), pp. 7–54.

Ebanks, G. (date unknown) *The Population of Montserrat: A Demographic Study*, Caricom Secretariat document (no other references available).

Evans-Pritchard, E. (1969) [1940] *The Nuer: A description of the modes of livelihood and political institutions of a Nilotic people* (Oxford: Oxford University Press).

Fitchen, J., Heath, J. and Fessenden-Raden, J. (1987) 'Risk Perception in Community Context: A Case Study', in Johnson, B. and Covello, V. (eds) *The Social and Cultural Construction of Risk* (Dordrecht: D. Reidel Publishing Company), pp. 31–54.

Fitchen, J. (1989) 'When Toxic Chemicals Pollute Residential Environments: The Cultural Meanings of Home and Homeownership', *Human Organisation*, vol. 48, no. 4, pp. 313–24.

Geertz, C. (1993) *The Interpretation of Cultures: Selected Essays* (London: Fontana Press).

Giddens, A. (1991) *Modernity and Self-Identity: Self and Society in the Late Modern Age* (Cambridge: Cambridge University Press).

Good, B. (1996) *Medicine, rationality, and experience: An anthropological perspective* (Cambridge: Polity Press).

Goody, J. and Watt, I. (1981) 'The Consequences of Literacy', in Goody, J. (ed.) *Literacy in Traditional Societies* (Cambridge: Cambridge University Press), pp. 27–68.

James, A., Hockey, J. and Dawson, A. (eds) (1997) *After Writing Culture: Epistemology and Praxis in Contemporary Anthropology* (London and New York: Routledge).

Jasanoff, S. (1987) 'Cultural Aspects of Risk Assessment in Britain and the United States', in Johnson, B. and Covello, V. (eds) *The Social and Cultural Construction of Risk* (Dordrecht: D. Reidel Publishing Company), pp. 359–97.

Kaprow, M. (1985) 'Manufacturing Danger: Fear and Pollution in Industrial Society', *American Anthropologist*, vol. 87, no. 2, June, pp. 342–56.

Kemp, R. (1993) 'Risk Perception: The Assessment of Risks by Experts and by Lay People – a Rational Comparison?', in Ruck, B. (ed.) *Risk Is A Construct: Perceptions of Risk Perception* (Munich: Knesebeck), pp. 103–118.

Kuper, A. (1991) *Anthropology and Anthropologists: The Modern British School* (London: Routledge).

Lamarque, P. (1994) 'Narrative and Invention: The Limits of Fictionality', in Nash, C. (ed.) *Narrative in Culture – The uses of Storytelling in the Sciences, Philosophy, and Literature* (London and New York: Routledge), pp. 131–53.

Lash, S. and Wynne, B. (1992) 'Introduction', in Beck, U.(ed.), *Risk Society: Towards a New Modernity* (London: Sage Publications), pp. 1–8.

Laurence, C. (1995) 'Montserrat exodus gets under way as volcano smoulders on', *Daily Telegraph*, 25 August 1995, p. 1.

Marcus, G. and Fischer, M. (1986) *Anthropology as Cultural Critique: An Experimental Moment in the Human Sciences* (London: University of Chicago Press).

Mattingly, C. (1991) 'The Narrative Nature of Clinical Reasoning', *American Journal of Occupational Therapy*, vol. 45, no. 11, pp. 998–1005.

Moreno, E. (1995) 'Rape in the field: Reflections from a survivor', in Kulick, D. and Wilson, M. (eds) *Taboo: sex, identity and erotic subjectivity in anthropological fieldwork* (London: Routledge), pp. 219–50.

Mossler, M. (1996) 'Environmental Hazard Analysis and Small Island States: Rethinking Academic Approaches', *Geographische Zeitschrift*, vol. 84, no. 2, pp. 86–93.

Nash, C. (ed.) (1994) *Narrative in Culture: The uses of Storytelling in the Sciences, Philosophy, and Literature* (London: Routledge).

Nash, J. (1979) 'Ethnology in a Revolutionary Setting', in Huizer, G. and Mannheim, B. (eds) *The Politics of Anthropology: From Colonialism and Sexism Toward a View from Below* (Paris: Mouton Publishers), pp. 353–70.

Okely, J. and Callaway, H. (eds) (1992) *Anthropology and Autobiography* (London: Routledge), pp. 134–46.

Oliver-Smith, A. (1992) *The Martyred City: Death and Rebirth in the Peruvian Andes* (Prospect Heights, IL: Waveland Press).

Oliver-Smith, A. (1996) 'Anthropological Research on Hazards and Disasters', *Annual Review of Anthropology*, vol. 25, pp. 303–28.

Paine, R. (unpublished, 1998) 'Social Theory of Risk and The case of Israel', Catastrophe and Culture: The Anthropology of Disasters Seminar, The School of American Research Advanced Seminar, Santa Fe.

Paine, R. (1992) '"Chernobyl" reaches Norway: the accident, science, and the threat to cultural knowledge', *Public Understanding of Science*, vol. 1, part 3, pp. 261–80.

Rapport, N. (1994) *The Prose and the Passion: Anthropology, literature and the writing of E.M. Forster* (Manchester: Manchester University Press).

Rapport, N. (1997) *Transcendent Individual: Towards a literary and liberal anthropology* (London: Routledge).

Rayner, S. and Cantor, R. (1987) 'How Fair Is Safe Enough? The Cultural Approach to Societal Technology Choice', *Risk Analysis*, vol. 7, no. 1, pp. 3–9.

Reed-Danahay, D. (ed.) (1997) *Auto/ethnography* (Oxford: Berg).

Rhodes, T. (1997) 'Irritable volcano turns island paradise into hell', *The Times*, 2 July 1997, p. 14.

Riddington, R. (1982) 'When Poison Gas Come Down Like a Fog: A Native Community's Response to Cultural Disaster', *Human Organization*, vol. 41, no. 1, pp. 36–42.

Rosaldo, R. (1993) *Culture and Truth: The Remaking of Social Analysis* (London and New York: Routledge).

Skinner, J. (1997a) '"Doing Ethnography" as action and in-action', *Anthropology in Action*, vol. 4, no. 2, pp. 13–16.

Skinner, J. (1997b) *Impressions of Montserrat: a partial account of contesting realities on a British Dependent Territory*, PhD thesis, St Andrews University.

Stoffle, R. et al. (1991) 'Risk Perception Mapping: Using Ethnography to Define the Locally Affected Population for a Low-Level Radioactive Waste Storage Facility in Michigan', *American Anthropologist*, vol. 93, no. 3, pp. 611–35.

Sutton-Smith, B. (1984) 'The Origins of Fiction and the Fictions of Origin', in Bruner, E. (ed.) *Text, Play and Story: the construction and reconstruction of self and society* (Prospect Heights, IL: Waveland Press), pp. 117–34.

Thompson, D. (ed.) (1996) *The Concise Oxford Dictionary of Current English* (London: BCA).

Torry, W. (1979) 'Anthropological Studies in Hazardous Environments: Past Trends and New Horizons', *Current Anthropology*, vol. 20, no. 3, pp. 517–40.

Turnbull, C. (1989) *The Mountain People* (London: Triad/Paladin Books).

7 'EATING BRITISH BEEF WITH CONFIDENCE': A CONSIDERATION OF CONSUMERS' RESPONSES TO BSE IN BRITAIN

Pat Caplan

In their work on risk published in 1982, Douglas and Wildavsky note that 'Fear of risk, coupled with the confidence to face it, has something to do with knowledge and something to do with the kind of people we are' (p. 2). In that book, and in Douglas' subsequent work on risk (1986, 1992), the focus is upon difference both between and within societies in terms of risk perception: 'Thus the choice of risks and the choice of how to live are taken together and each form of life has its own typical risk portfolio. Common values lead to common fears ... Risk taking and risk aversion, shared confidence and shared fears, are part of the dialogue on how best to organize social relations' (Douglas and Wildavsky 1982, p. 8).

For Douglas, the key question is how do people decide which risks to take and which to ignore? In the work of Beck (1992) and Giddens (1991, 1994), on the other hand, high or late modernity is seen universally as a risk society: 'The risk climate of modernity is thus unsetttling for everyone; no one escapes' (Giddens 1991, p. 124). Beck too contends that 'risk society in this sense is a world risk society' (1992, p. 23, see also 1994, 1995).

All of these authors write against a background of globalisation, a process to which they continually refer. The flip side of globalisation is, of course, localisation, a term which is not mentioned by any of our authors, although its use by other social scientists has been proliferating in recent years, particularly by anthropologists whose interests, historically, have lain in the local rather than the global domain. These are not either/or but both/and processes, as will be discussed.

One of the questions raised in this chapter is whether risk is differently perceived according to social location, as Douglas and Wildavsky have suggested, or whether perception of risks, such as those around the consumption of beef, is universalised, and thus transcends social distinctions such as gender, class and ethnicity, as is implied in the work of Beck and Giddens. For Beck, in risk society, knowledge of risk gains a new saliency, and brings about a major change: whereas in class and stratification societies, position determines consciousness, in risk societies, *consciousness determines being* (1992, p. 36).

This brings us to the second question, which all of the main writers on risk identify as crucial, namely how knowledge of risk is constructed. The extent to which people are endangered by the risks Beck discusses is to some extent dependent upon knowledge, a knowledge which frequently the victims themselves do not have. For this reason, Beck suggests that 'quality of life and the production of knowledge are locked together' (1992, p. 55). For Giddens, knowledge alone is insufficient, trust is also needed: 'Trust and security, risk and danger: these exist in various historically unique conjunctions in conditions of modernity' (Giddens, 1991, p. 19). As will be shown in this chapter, knowledge and trust are indeed intimately linked in the context of the BSE crisis, which is the subject of this chapter.

The discussion begins by considering the symbolic significance of beef in British society. It then analyses responses to the first BSE 'scare' by a range of informants in two areas of Britain, an inner-city borough of London and a village and surrounding area of west Wales, and seeks to explain the differences between them. The third part of the chapter compares media coverage at local Welsh and national levels during the second BSE scare, demonstrating that their coverage was very different and discussing the reasons for this. In the fourth part of the chapter, I seek to show how national campaigns to 'rebuild confidence' in British beef utilised two sets of ideas already highlighted in the chapter. The first is the way in which it symbolises national, gender and class identity; the second is the way in which it was sought to build knowledge and trust not only through *what* people know, but *who* they know, thus campaigns, especially in Wales, became increasingly localised.

BRITISH BEEF AND ITS MEANINGS

In Britain, beef carries a peculiarly heavy symbolic load. First, it is seen as something quintessentially British (as in roast beef and Yorkshire pudding), or English (as in 'the roast beef of old England'), or Beefeaters in the Tower of London. In other words, beef is bound up with national identity. Second, in British society, and indeed in other parts of the West more generally, including North America, beef epitomises masculinity and virility (Adams, 1990; Fiddes, 1991). Further, beef is viewed as food for 'real men' – masculine food *par excellence*: men are thought to need meat, and especially red meat, and to need more meat than do women (Delphy, 1979; Bourdieu, 1984; Murcott, 1982). Small wonder then that 'beefing something up' in common parlance means strengthening or improving it.

Beef has also been considered a special, indeed luxury, food. Until recently, steak and chips ('French fries') was the most popular dish when eating out, and beef constituted the traditional Sunday joint for the main meal of the week (Douglas, 1975). Only the more recent advent of McDonald's and other fast food chains has made beef, in the form of the burger, an everyday food, especially for the young.

In spite of these factors, the consumption of red meat in Britain had been declining somewhat in the 1980s (see, for example, Realeat Surveys, 1990 and 1993; also Fine et al., 1996), a factor largely attributed to health warnings about the risks of coronary heart disease associated with the consumption of food high in fat. This trend was considerably accelerated during and after the two major BSE 'scares' in the late 1980s, and again in the 1990s.

FOOD AND FOOD SCARES

In the last few years, there has been a series of so-called food 'scares' or 'panics', each of which has revolved around a particular item such as listeria in cheese or salmonella in eggs (see Davison, 1989; Miller and Reilly, 1994, 1995; Smith, 1991). Such scares have been the focus of intense media interest, and the result has generally been a considerable, but temporary, drop in the consumption of the product concerned. The contrast between public reaction to such scares, and that to a constant stream of public health nutritional advice to eat foods containing less fat, sugar and salt, is striking (Davison et al., 1991). Whereas, for example, at the height of the 'salmonella in eggs' scare in 1988, millions of hens were slaughtered, and purchase and consumption of eggs dropped dramatically, public responses to campaigns to eat healthier food have had only moderate success (Davison, 1989). It has been suggested that reasons for this include a greater concern for short-term effects (for example, salmonella) than for long-term effects which are, in any case, only potential risks (such as coronary heart disease). It has also been suggested that the public is more concerned with poisons and contaminants in food, than with the alleged effects of known ingredients (Davison et al., 1992). Nonetheless, it is clear that at the latter end of the twentieth century, there is a heightened concern in the West with issues of food and its safety. Eating has become a risky business.

THE CONCEPTS OF HEALTHY EATING RESEARCH PROJECTS

Between 1992 and 1995, anthropological research focusing on people's ideas about the relationship between the food they ate and their health was carried out in two locations in Britain.[1] Through a mixture of semi-structured interviews, food frequency questionnaires, food diaries and participant observation, a large data-set was assembled on all aspects – social, cultural, economic and political – of food and eating.[2]

The first location was the borough of Lewisham in SE London. In this densely populated, economically and ethnically diverse area, a mixture of respondents – white and black (mostly of African-Caribbean origin), males and females, middle and working class – talked at length about what they ate and why. The second location was in south-west Wales, in a large village, locally termed a 'town', and its surrounding rural hinterland. This area is Welsh-speaking, although with the recent in-migration of English speakers, some of them seeking alternative life-styles, the balance of languages in the town is now more or less equal. In the hinterland, however, Welsh speakers predominate, especially among farmers.

Reports from informants in London

The fieldwork in London was carried out in 1993–94, which was some time after the original BSE 'scare', and prior to the second and more significant scare which developed in 1996. Respondents were asked about their reactions to BSE or 'mad cow disease' and whether it had had any effect on their eating habits. Responses fell into four categories.

The first were those who stopped eating beef long-term. Some informants had plainly been extremely concerned about this issue: one woman said 'I even stopped feeding the cats cat food.' Those with children were particularly likely to express high levels of concern: 'My son was living at home and I cut out beef'; 'I told my daughter she can't eat any more hamburgers.'

Second were those who stopped consuming beef temporarily but later went back to it, giving a variety of reasons for their decision. One was that it was too much bother to cut it out: 'I followed that one [the BSE scare] and the one for hormones in milk in cows[3] and fallout [from Chernobyl] in Welsh lamb. The reason I'm trying to forget is I want to go on living.' Another was an assumption that if it was no longer headline news, the danger must have passed: 'I take a lot of notice of the media. When something like mad cow disease dies down, I started eating beef again.'

Several supermarket managers in the area noted the effects of the BSE scare on their sales and one commented: 'When you had the beef scare, it was a nightmare. It took about three months to build up the beef market after that. It has built up again, but it has never got back to what it was.' He went on to note how the supermarkets had coped with this situation: 'The supermarkets were clever at regenerating interest in products after scares, so after BSE they said "Their meat comes from reputable suppliers."' Such a claim might have helped sales in the early 1990s, but, as we shall see, much more drastic measures would prove necessary after the second BSE scare.

A third category of informants had responded by switching to organic beef: 'I never buy [meat] from Tesco's [supermarket] – only organic'. 'I won't touch beef with [because of] BSE ... when we buy meat we don't buy it from Tesco's any more, we only buy it from this particular butcher that has a very closely controlled stock ... I do worry about BSE – terrifying.' In London and other urban areas, there has been a boom in the organic butcher trade. A report in the (north London) Times Group of newspapers in April 1996 at the inception of the second BSE scare is headlined 'Organic butcher cuts in on beef scare' and he is quoted as saying that business for him has never been so good (*The Times*, 25 April 1996, p. 15).

While buying organic meat or buying from a trusted source might help, some informants were concerned about the quality of the meat when they ate out and would be more selective than previously: 'I think it's more worrying if you go out to dinner now because if you go out to a restaurant you don't know what's in the meal then. So that's actually more worrying, so I tend to sort of stick to things that you know, or dishes that you know what's gone into them ...You're more careful about where you go out to eat these days than we did [you were] before.'

Finally, there were those on whom BSE had no effect. Some stated that the assumed risks associated with eating beef were only one of many such issues around food: 'If you listen to everything you hear ...'. Others were sceptical of what was often termed 'media hype'; as one woman said, 'BSE didn't worry me. I thought "I expect there's something bogus here".' One elderly couple had even welcomed the scare for economic reasons: 'All of a sudden the beef in Tesco's went down to half price and we lived on beef.' Indeed, several older informants sometimes noted that they did not worry about BSE because by the time it developed in their bodies, they would be dead anyway; some noted that if they had been younger, they might have acted differently. As a 53-year-old woman said: 'I think most probably at my age it wouldn't matter. It's got a very sort of long gestation ... I think I'd possibly give it up if I were 20.'

In the Lewisham study, then, reactions to the BSE scare were varied. Correlations between social factors such as ethnicity, gender, age, class and household composition were difficult to establish. Although women were somewhat more likely than men to report that BSE had had an effect on their consumption of beef, older people tended to think it not worth worrying about themselves (although they were often concerned about their children or grandchildren and the presence of children or young people in the household was significant), while only the middle classes could contemplate switching to much more expensive organic meat. But in many respects, it proved difficult to predict which way people would react to food scares such as BSE. In this regard, then, risk appears, as Beck and Giddens suggest, to be 'universalised'.

Informants in West Wales and BSE

In this area of Wales, there were also varied reactions to the BSE scare, but they were somewhat different to those in Lewisham. First of all, there were those who had stopped eating beef. Unsurprisingly, people who defined themselves as 'alternatives', of whom there is a significant minority in this area of Wales, tended to be much more concerned about BSE, as in the following example of a complementary medical practitioner: 'This mad cow business, well I just think it's a sympton of the way cows are treated. I think cows are treated abominably ... I think the amount of chemicals that goes into a cow, even if it's just a milking cow, is so horrendous I don't feel like having anything from it.' Another woman from an alternative community commented: 'BSE? I am surprised it hasn't been a lot worse. How long can we treat animals [in the way we do] without the repercussions? I am amazed animals can exist in the conditions we give them. Amazed the meat industry can exist.'

For both of these women, BSE symbolised industrialised farming and intensive rearing of animals: a male alternative informant noted that he had stopped eating beef not only because of concern about health but also to 'protest about this country being so crass in relation to cows and land and everything'. He went on to comment 'I think a lot of people are on protest. They see it as "Aha, we told you so". We are sorry for all the farmers, but it's like they need to stop and think what they are doing.' Another male informant, who also defined himself as alternative, noted that, while he had been trying to eat more healthily for some time and had been reducing his meat intake, the first BSE scare was 'the final piece in the jigsaw' and he became a vegetarian.

On the whole, however, apart from some members of the alternative community, there were few people in this area who gave up eating beef as a result of the BSE scare.

The second category of respondents, which included some alternatives, were those who continued to eat beef under certain conditions: 'I do feel insecure about the food produced in society. [But] I am happy to know that I know how the animals [I eat] are fed. I'll eat [meat] when I can. I'll eat when I know where it comes from … It is a bit of a responsibility killing an animal [but] animals die anyway and the way that we kill is less painful. Life feeds on life.'

Many alternative informants felt that their attitudes came from 'knowing' how meat was produced, whereas they felt that, as one put it: 'There is a problem with [other] people not knowing how meat is produced.' The implication was clearly that if they did, they would behave differently; once people realised how dreadful were the conditions under which meat was produced, they would either become vegetarian, or else turn to eating organic ('happy') meat.

The third group were those who continued to eat beef as before, which was a high proportion of our respondents, both Welsh and English-speaking, although Welsh speakers generally were less likely than English speakers to cut out beef. They used a variety of arguments. One was that they 'knew where the meat had come from', which was true, given that some of the farmers would have one of their own beasts slaughtered, and that otherwise, they bought their meat from the local Welsh-speaking butcher, whose business had been in existence for many years, and whom they trusted. Another frequently used argument was that their parents and grandparents had eaten such meat, and 'it never did them any harm'.[4] A third reason given was that those in power, as well as the urban consumers, had 'got it wrong'. It was frequently pointed out to me that BSE is associated primarily with intensively reared dairy cattle and not with beef herds, who are usually raised mainly on grass. Why, then, was beef being targeted? Some, like a Welsh-speaking farming woman, felt it was part of a general trend: 'the country as a whole, they're going against farming, against meat.' A similar view was expressed by an English-speaking farming woman:

You know farming just now is in the doldrums. Nobody wants to eat beef. BSE has just about devastated everything and this week particularly we've got the ban on the exports of live animals[5] and trade has just gone … Nobody wants to buy beef because they're worried about BSE. In fact if you go into the beef herd itself there's no BSE. It's only the dairy herds that have got BSE, because they're fed intensively, possibly to produce the milk. The beef herd has only grass and there's no contamination … It's just [risky] when the butchers buy barren cows [from dairy herds] and try to get rich quick on poor beef. If people bought proper beef there's no BSE. No one seems to be supporting that [line] yet but perhaps they will, but at the moment, no, beef full stop is a dirty word.

It is scarcely surprising then, that farmers never contemplated giving up beef. As another Welsh-speaking farming woman said: 'I haven't thought about not eating it. We haven't had one [a case of BSE] since the thing has come about and we hope we won't have it but no, I haven't thought about it at all really, about the meat or anything really.'

This theme of 'knowing where it comes from' was a very important one which recurred in many interviews. But as important as knowing *where* it comes from is knowing from *whom* one buys it, in other words knowledge comes from personal relations, as is shown in the following extract from an interview with a Welsh-speaking townswoman who had, unusually, stopped eating meat some time earlier because of her numerous health problems: 'The BSE issue is serious and I think people should listen and be fairly balanced. I think there are plenty of farms who supply butchers who are totally free of BSE. If I was eating beef, I would happily buy from X [the local butcher] because I'm sure he would be very conscious of where he buys his beef from.'

A similar argument was put forward by a Welsh male informant: 'Beef with X [the local butcher] in the shop with us I know it's first class beef. It's all BSE free and it's all under a year old and things like that ... it [the BSE issue] would affect me if I was eating out, but if I knew it was our meat, I wouldn't [worry] about it.' Both of these informants trusted their local butcher. They 'knew' him, and they were sure that he would know where he got his meat from and ensure that it was only from safe sources. Indeed, the last respondent emphasises the extent to which he identifies with the butcher: 'in the shop with us' and 'if I knew it was *our* meat'.

Similarly, a caterer, who ran an up-market country guest house in the area, on being asked if the BSE scare was affecting her customers, replied 'No, not at all, absolutely not. No. I think people just think that here we use local [meat] which we do, we do use local produce.' This response resonates with those of local residents who bought their beef from the local butcher and thus 'knew where it came from'.

In London, however, it was much more difficult to be sure of the sources of the meat on sale at the supermarket, and a frequent remark by informants there was 'You don't know where it's come from';

under such conditions, confidence had to come from other sources, such as the certainty that it was organic.

Trust, then, came from knowledge, 'knowing' where the meat had come from, under what conditions it had been produced, and, above all, knowing the person who sold it. In the process of constructing a series of dichotomies between knowledge (confidence) and lack of knowledge (risk), people used oppositions such as organic/non-organic, local/non-local, and small butchers/supermarkets. Scarcely surprising that with the advent of the second BSE scare, by now more generally termed a 'crisis', use was made by the industry of these themes, as we will see later.

What is very clear from the interviews in both Lewisham and Wales is how little people trusted either the media or the government when it came to issues of food safety, and this regardless of other social factors: as a working-class African-Caribbean woman in Lewisham said 'I don't believe half of what I hear because they're politicians at the end of the day. For me if there is a doubt, there is a doubt.' Such views were to be magnified many times over during the second half of the 1990s.

THE SECOND BSE SCARE

After the government's statement in March 1996 that BSE could be linked with new variant Creuzfeldt Jakob's Disease (nvCJD), beef consumption, which had begun to pick up somewhat again after the first scare, declined steeply. Although further interviews could not be carried out in Lewisham, a re-study in 1996 of Glasgow informants originally interviewed in 1992 by Eldridge et al. as part of their study 'The role of the media in the emergence of food panics' found that 'A number of respondents had clearly redefined their beliefs in quite a radical way' (1998, p. 6) and that the proportion which had stopped eating beef altogether was considerably higher than had been the case after the previous scare. While their work, like the present research, suggests that having children is a very significant factor, as is the age of informants, it also notes that 'In 1996, they [respondents] were clearly more aware of the scientific and political issues being discussed in the media' (p. 8). Indeed, Eldridge et al. suggest that the BSE issue has ceased to be a food scare, with a clearly defined beginning and end, and now constitutes a major ongoing issue.

I have been able, however, to continue monitoring the situation in west Wales, through both the local press and occasional interviews, and it is clear that for many people in this area, BSE now epitomises a defining moment in the decline of their agricultural community. Farmers and others in west Wales have vigorously supported campaigns to increase the consumption of beef: most farmers' cars sport stickers proclaiming 'We support British beef' or 'We eat British beef with confidence', even as the industry has continued to decline. They bracket out food risks, since other risks to livelihood and community are much greater and more immediate.

Media coverage of the second BSE crisis

There has been considerable analysis of the media coverage of the BSE crises (see Miller and Reilly, 1995; Reilly and Miller, 1997) and I do not propose to discuss this issue comprehensively. Rather in this section I compare two sets of newspaper reports during 1996, the year in which the second, and much more serious, BSE crisis dominated the headlines for many months. The first set is from national newspapers, particularly the broadsheets, and the second is from local Welsh newspapers serving the area studied in west Wales.

In March 1996, the government announced that there was a strong likelihood that a link existed between BSE in cattle, and new variant Creutzfeld Jakob's Disease (nvCJD). There were two responses: Europe banned the export of cattle from Britain, and the national consumption of British beef dropped considerably, indeed the Secretary of State for Agriculture, Fisheries and Food reported on 16 April in Parliament that the consumption of beef was down to 85 per cent of what it had been before the BSE crisis. A number of food processors, including Birds Eye and, most notably, McDonald's, banned the use of British beef in their products. In May, the Prime Minister John Major threatened the European Community with a British 'work to rule' unless the ban was lifted, thus precipitating the so-called 'beef war' with Europe. Eventually, however, the government was forced to do a U-turn and began introducing a whole raft of measures, including a huge cull of cattle.

Newspapers such as the *Guardian* and *Independent* carried lengthy articles not only on the BSE crisis and its political outfall, but also on why BSE epitomised all that was wrong with modern farming methods. For example, an article in the *Guardian* by John Gray was headlined 'Nature bites back: we will pay an even higher price for technological hubris unless we mend our ways' (27 March 1996). Another article in the same edition was headlined as follows: 'Lies of the land: intensive farming is on trial following the BSE crisis. Worse than we think? Guardian writers report on how the first law of nature is being ignored in the dangerous dash for quick profits.'

The *Independent* also drew wider lessons from the BSE crisis: 'Crisis in a sesame seed bun: the burger is an icon for our times: it has been a symbol of rebellion, technology, even Thatcherism ... And, argues Paul Vallel, BSE is its crowning glory' (27 March 1996, pp. 2–3).

A second theme taken up in some articles in the national press was the role of the scientific advisers: 'Once the men in white coats held the promise of a better future: why have we lost our trust in them?' (John Durant, *Independent*, 1 April 1996, reprinted in Franklin, 1998). Such a view reflected that frequently voiced by informants interviewed earlier in Lewisham and Wales, which was one of acute scepticism about experts of every ilk, including scientists and politicians, whom they castigated for having broken such a fundamental law of nature as feeding animal remains to herbivores, as well as for 'always changing their minds'.

However, views expressed in local Welsh newspapers contrasted sharply with those in the national press: 'As politicians fiddle, livestock industry burns' (*Tivyside Advertiser*, July 1996). Considerable coverage was given to the attempts of farmers to improve their lot in a variety of ways. One such was through putting pressure on politicians ('New [Welsh Office] Minister grilled by farmers within hours of his appointment', *Western Telegraph* 12 June 1998) or on the local council ('Council told of farmers' plight', *Western Telegraph* 12 June 1996).

Another tactic widely reported was direct action in the form of blockades and demonstrations at ports where Irish beef was being imported into Britain (*Tivyside Advertiser*, 23 April 1996). There were also reports of protests and demonstrations by farming women about the continued high price charged for beef in supermarkets at a time when prices paid to farmers were at rock bottom ('Tesco beef price protest at [agricultural] show by delegation of farmers' wives and ordinary housewives', *Tivyside Advertiser*, 1 August 1996). Such demonstrations were always sympathetically reported, usually with pictures.

A third tactic used by farmers which also received wide coverage in the local press was the holding of a series of events at which beef products were served or given away, often for free. The National Farmers' Union organised a day in October 1996 at which beef was widely and publicly served throughout the country, including west Wales, as the local press reported: 'Beef Saturday cooks up prime support for farmers' (*Western Telegraph*, 30 October 1996), complete with a picture: 'Little Emily-Jane Warlow enjoys a beef roll with butcher Mark Purnell to celebrate National Beef Saturday in Castle Square, Haverfordwest.' The following year, one local farmer gave five 'prime beef animals' to a local secondary school 'for the children to enjoy Welsh beef' (*Tivyside Advertiser*, 10 August 1997), a gift publicly welcomed by the headmaster. The tone of such reports contrasts sharply with the derision heaped by the national press on John Selwyn Gummer, the government Minister who was pictured on television feeding a hamburger to his daughter to 'prove' that British beef was safe to consume, and with the widely reported decisions by many local councils in Britain to ban beef in school dinners.

In the *Tivyside Advertiser*'s month-by-month review of the year 1996, published in December, the major story for four months was BSE. March had 'Mass bankruptcies in farming and its allied trades are a certainty the longer the beef crisis rumbles on', complete with a picture: 'Market forces: a lone cow at Cardigan Mart in the height of the BSE scare'. April headlined the farmers' wives' beef protest, with a picture. May's review had a picture of cattle in a field with a large sign on the fence 'Eat Welsh beef or we burn', while that for October had a headline 'Beef farmers take on [William] Hague' with a photograph of a demonstration of farmers and a large sign 'Patience has run out'.

There was frequent mention in the local press of the very high suicide rate among farmers, said to be either 'twice the national average', or the highest rate by occupation. A local farmer's wife was reported as having recorded a compact disc to raise money for a charity dealing with stress and suicide in rural communities (*County Echo*, 15 August 1997).

In short, then, local Welsh newspapers were very sympathetic to the plight of farmers and others involved in the livestock industry, rarely questioning the basis of farming methods, while national newspapers took a very different view.

RESTORING PUBLIC CONFIDENCE

From 1996 to the present, there have been a number of campaigns – by the Meat and Livestock Commission, the National Farmers' Union (NFU) and the supermarkets – to 'restore confidence' in the consumer/housewife, and persuade her or him to buy British beef again. These high-profile campaigns have used two tactics. One is to play heavily on the symbolic meanings of meat already discussed at the beginning of this chapter: love/caring, as in 'home' and proper meals (see Murcott, 1982, 1998), and also in terms of sexuality, passion and virility, with the long-running 'Food of Love' campaigns. Numerous glossy recipe cards were distributed not only at supermarkets but more widely. These incorporated beef in a variety of ways: one used the idea of special foods in the seasonal cycle (including Christmas), another played upon the multiple uses of beef in the newly creolised British cuisine. Second, there was a new emphasis on the issue of knowledge ('knowing where it comes from') and hence safety and control; increasingly, this has been achieved by supermarkets signing deals with farmers whereby they gain complete control of the meat production process. Such beef can then be presented as coming from a known source: 'our farms'. In some supermarkets, the name of the store's butcher, and sometimes his photograph, is prominently displayed for customers to see, seeking to build trust through a personalised form of knowledge.

Another tactic to gain the trust of the consumer has been in terms of localisation. At an early stage, the response of Northern Irish and Scottish farmers to the ban on the export of beef to Europe had been to emphasise their beef's distinctive qualities. In Northern Ireland, a scheme for tracking cattle had been in operation for a relatively long period, and thus one tactic to allay consumer fears was to argue that beef from that area was safe because its antecedents were known. In the case of Scotland, there was no such guarantee; instead farmers argued that Scottish beef had always been raised on grass. The advertising for 'Scottish' beef played on the idea of a wholesome and natural regime for beef animals, as well as earlier ideas about the quality of steak from Scottish beef.

In Wales, there was initially no such 'localisation' of beef products. On the contrary, from 1996 to the present day, most of the advertising and car stickers seen in Wales have revolved around the notion of 'British beef'. As an observer, I found this somewhat surprising for several reasons. The first is that 'Welsh lamb' had long been localised as a distinctive product ('mountain-reared'), and continues to be so. The other is that over the period of the research, we had observed an increasing 'invention' of Welsh cuisine, both in conjunction with the tourist industry, and as a way of encouraging small-scale production of items such as cheese which could be marketed as 'locally produced' (see Williams, 1997). Furthermore, during the late 1990s, Welsh identity became an even more significant issue with the devolution debates and referendum, and the prospect of elections to the Welsh Assembly.

It is only very recently, however, that the marketing of beef seems finally to have become localised. As I was writing the first draft of this article in the summer of 1998, I paid a visit to Fishguard and observed the following sign, handwritten in chalk on a blackboard outside a butcher's shop:

Dinas beef
Preseli lamb
Pembrokeshire pork

What struck me was that each of these meats was 'localised' at a different level: pork was from Pembrokeshire, the county; lamb was from the Preseli Hills (the main sheep-rearing area in the county), while beef, potentially the most dangerous, was from the next village, three miles up the road.

Six months on, and the localisation process had been taken even further. Each piece of meat displayed in the window of the butcher's shop in Newport carried a large sign 'Welsh', while outside was a large blackboard, topped with a picture of a cow, on which was written 'This week's beef comes from ...' giving the name of the farmer, the farm and its location, a couple of miles away.

CONCLUSION: RISK KNOWLEDGE, TRUST AND LOCATION

I have argued in this chapter that there is a politics of location in relation to risk perception; in other words, to some degree at least, people do perceive risks according to their social location and this is likely to affect their behaviour. To put it another way, being still determines consciousness in some areas. The risk of eating beef looks very different to a rural-dweller in Pembrokeshire whose livelihood is under threat than it does to a middle-class family in London, for whom perhaps the argument that consciousness determines being is more appropriate. For the former, beef production and consumption are about not only making a living, but about a whole way of life, one which they 'know'. For the latter, BSE epitomises not only all that is wrong with modern food production methods, but also mistrust of both government and scientists – 'them', 'the experts' – who have been shown to be inadequate or worse, leaving the public 'not knowing'. Such constrasts are also, inevitably, reflected in media coverage of the BSE crisis in national and local papers.

In countering public fears about BSE, the beef industry, from supermarkets to butchers' shops, has sought not only to utilise long-standing symbols surrounding beef, but also to play upon ideas of confidence or trust as arising from knowledge, of ensuring that consumers do (potentially) 'know' how beef is produced and trust such a source. But knowing *where* it comes from and *who* produces and sells it is only really feasible in a small-scale society epitomised by the Welsh case study. London people and the national newspapers may know *what*, but the people in the small-scale communities (and their newspapers) know *who* produces the cattle, slaughters it, and is losing their livelihoods. Inevitably, then, risks around BSE are perceived very differently in the two areas.

NOTES

1. The research was funded by the ESRC, and formed part of its interdisciplinary Research Programme entitled 'The Nation's Diet: the social science of food choice'. The two projects were

based at Goldsmiths College, and directed by Pat Caplan; the researchers were Anne Keane and Anna Willetts (London) and Janice Williams (Wales).

2. See Keane and Willetts, 1995; Keane 1997, 1998; Willetts, 1997; Williams 1997; Caplan et al., 1998; Caplan and Keane, 1999.
3. This refers to BST – bovine somatotropin – a hormone which augments milk production in a cow by 10–15 per cent. Its proposed introduction in Europe in the early 1990s was highly controversial (see Pratt and Wynne, 1995)
4. In fact the eating of beef in this area on any general scale is relatively recent. As Williams' work demonstrates, until a generation or so ago, the major source of meat would have been the pig kept not only by farmers but by villagers and even some townsfolk (see Williams, 1996). The notion that 'we' have 'always' eaten beef is also discussed for North America by Ross, 1980 and Edelman, 1987.
5. She was referring to the widespread demonstrations in Britain at this time against the export of live calves to Europe.

REFERENCES

Adams, C. (1990) *The Sexual Politics of Meat: a Feminist-Vegetarian Critical Theory* (Cambridge: Polity Press).

Beck, U. (1992) [1986]. *Risk Society: towards a new modernity* (London: Sage Publications).

Beck, U. (1994) 'The Reinvention of Politics: Towards a theory of reflexive modernization' in Beck, U., Giddens, A. and Lash, S. (eds) *Reflexive Modernization: Politics, tradition and aesthetics in the modern social order* (Cambridge: Polity Press).

Beck, U. (1995) *Ecological Politics in an Age of Risk* (Cambridge: Polity Press).

Beck, U., Giddens, A. and Lash, S. (eds) (1994) *Reflexive Modernization: Politics, tradition and aesthetics in the modern social order* (Cambridge: Polity Press).

Bourdieu, P. (1984) [1979] *Distinction: a social critique of the judgement of taste* (London: Routledge).

Caplan, P. (ed.) (1997) *Food, Health and Identity* (London and New York: Routledge).

Caplan, P., Keane, A., Willetts, A. and Williams, J. (1998) 'Concepts of Healthy Eating: Approaches from a social science perspective', in Murcott, A. (ed.) *The Nation's Diet* (London, Longman).

Caplan, P. and Keane, A. (1999) 'Health Professionals' Views of Healthy Eating' in B.M. Koehler and E. Feichtinger (eds) *Public Health and Nutrition* (Berlin: Editions Sigma).

Davison, C. (1989) 'Eggs and the Sceptical Eater', *New Scientist*, 11 March, pp. 45–9.

Davison C., Smith, G.D. and Frankel, S. (1991) 'Lay epidemiology and the prevention paradox: the implications of coronary candidacy for health education', *Social Health and Illness*, vol. 13, no. 1, pp. 1–19.

Davison, C., Frankel, S. and Smith, G.D. (1992) 'The limits of life-style: reassessing "fatalism" in the popular culture of illness prevention' *Social Science and Medicine*, vol. 34, pp. 675–85.

Delphy, C. (1979) 'Sharing the same table: consumption and the family', in Harris, C. (ed.) *The Sociology of the Family* (Keele: Social Science Review Monographs no. 28).

Douglas, M. and Nicod, M. (1974) 'Taking the biscuit: the structure of British meals', *New Society*, vol. 34, pp. 744–7.

Douglas, M. (1975) 'Deciphering a Meal', in Douglas, M. (ed.) *Implicit Meanings* (London: Routledge and Kegan Paul).

Douglas, M. and Wildavsky, A. (1982) *Risk and Culture: an Essay on the Selection of Environmental and Technological Dangers* (Berkeley: University of California Press).

Douglas, M. (1992) *Risk and Blame: essays in cultural theory* (London and New York: Routledge).

Edelman, M. (1987) 'From Costa Rican Pasture to North American Hamburger' in Harris, M. and Ross, E.B. (eds) *Food and Evolution: towards a theory of human food habits*, (Philadelphia: Temple University Press).

Eldridge, J., Kitzinger, J., Philo, G., Reilly, J., Macintyre, S. and Miller, D. (1998) 'The re-emergence of BSE: the impact on public beliefs and behaviour', *Risk and Human Behaviour Newsletter*, issue 3 (London: Economic and Social Research Council).

Fiddes, N. (1991) *Meat: a Natural Symbol* (London and New York: Routledge).

Fine, B., Heasman, M. and Wright, J. (1996) *Consumption in the Age of Affluence: The world of food* (London and New York: Routledge).

Frankel, S., Davison, C. and Smith, G.D. (1991) 'Lay epidemiology and the rationality of responses to health education', *British Journal of General Practice*, vol. 41, pp. 428–30.

Giddens, A. (1991) *Modernity and Self-identity: self and society in the late modern age* (Cambridge: Polity Press).

Giddens, A. 1994. 'Living in a Post-Traditional Society' in Beck, U., Giddens, A. and Lash, S. (eds) (1994) *Reflexive Modernization: politics, tradition and aesthetics in the modern social order* (Cambridge: Polity Press).

Keane, A. (1997) 'Too hard to swallow? The palatability of healthy eating advice' in Caplan, P. (ed.) *Food, Health and Identity* (London and New York: Routledge).

Keane, A. (1998) 'Conceptualising Food and the Self: Normality and the Body as Potential', unpub. Ph.D. thesis, University of London.

Keane, A. and Willetts, A. (1995) 'Concepts of healthy eating: an anthropological investigation in South-East London', Working Paper, Goldsmiths College, London.

Miller, D. and Reilly, J. (1994) 'Food "Scares" in the Media', Working Paper, Glasgow University Media Group, Glasgow.

Miller, D. and Reilly, J. (1995) 'Making an Issue of Food Safety: the Media, Pressure Groups, and the Public Sphere', in Maurer, D. and Sobal, J. (eds) *Eating Agendas: Food and Nutrition as Social Problems* (New York: Aldine de Gruyter).

Murcott, A. (1982) 'On the social significance of the "cooked dinner" in south Wales', *Social Science Information*, vol. 21, nos 4/5.

Murcott, A. (1998) (ed.) *The Nation's Diet: the Social Science of Food Choice* (London and New York: Longman).

Pratt, J.H. and Wynne, A. (1995) 'The livestock industry – some controversial issues', *Nutrition and Food Science*, vol. 3, May/June, pp. 24–8.

The Realeat Survey (1990) *The Realeat Survey, 1984–90: Changing Attitudes to Meat Consumption* (London: Realeat Survey).

The Realeat Survey (1993) *The Realeat Survey, 1984–93: Changing Attitudes to Meat Consumption* (Newport Pagnell: Realeat Survey Office).

Reilly, J. and Miller, D. (1997) 'Scaremonger or scapegoat? The role of the media in the emergence of food as a social issue', in Caplan, P. (ed.) *Food, Health and Identity* (London and New York: Routledge).

Ross, E.B. (1980) 'Patterns of Diet and Forces of Production: an economic and ecological history of the ascendancy of beef in the United States', in E.B., Ross (ed.) *Beyond the Myths of Culture: Essays in Cultural Materialism* (New York: Academic Press).

The Royal Society (1997) 'Update on BSE', July, London.

Smith, M.J. (1991) 'From policy community to issue network: *salmonella* in eggs and the new politics of food', *Public Administration*, vol. 69, Summer, pp. 235–55.

Willetts, A. (1997) '"Bacon Sandwiches Got the Better of me": meat-eating and vegetarianism in South-East London.' in Caplan, P. (ed.) *Food, Health and Identity* (London and New York: Routledge).

Williams, J. (1996) 'Globalization in rural Wales: some dietary changes and continuities on Welsh farms', Working Paper, Goldsmiths College, London.

Williams, J. (1997) '"We never eat like this at home": food on holiday', in Caplan, P. (ed.) *Food, Health and Identity* (London and New York: Routledge).

8 RISK, AMBIGUITY AND THE LOSS OF CONTROL: HOW PEOPLE WITH A CHRONIC ILLNESS EXPERIENCE COMPLEX BIOMEDICAL CAUSAL MODELS

Simon Cohn

Much mischief has been wrought on weak minds by the craven plea that man is the creature of circumstances. It is time to fling that sinister aphorism to the winds ... Man is the master of circumstances! (Mortimer–Granville, 1880, p. 237)

INTRODUCTION

The above proclamation encapsulates the confidence and sense of mastery that infused much of biomedicine at the beginning of the twentieth century, the triumph of the technical and rational over disorder and chaos. But at the end of the century we are witnessing a growth of a paradox in this narrative of Western modernity: though it has promised so much in the way of control and certainty it continues to reveal greater and greater chaos. Increasing scientific knowledge is presenting the possibilities of danger and risk not merely appearing at the gaps of knowledge, but as its inevitable consequence.

According to some, the proliferation of discourses of risk may be but one contribution to a social impetus towards self-reflection, in which every person is encouraged to place her or himself at the centre of a vast landscape of influences, events and strangers (see, for example, the debates in Franklin, 1998). It is said individuals are invited to strive to find understanding through assessing every relationship with an external world of other people, other things and other selves; they must build defences and adopt strategies, analyse every action and calculate every ramification. Authors such as Beck and Giddens, now synonymous with debates about risk, propound scepticism and doubt as worthy successors to lay ignorance and compliance, and suggest that the status of the expert is becoming so fluid as to challenge traditional hierarchies of knowledge and generate a new kind of democratic participation (see, for example, Beck et al., 1994).

Though a positive dimension of risk, that is as providing the possibility of prediction for manipulation and gain, underpins its usage in spheres of commerce such as those celebrated by Bernstein (1996), beyond the world of economic conjecture risk has largely become synonymous with the possibility of loss (Douglas, 1986). Nevertheless, it has retained its association with individual choice, decision and agency. For example, in health promotion, where risk is employed to discuss the possible dangers or hazards that may occur, an underlying theme is that, given the right kind and quantity of information, risks can either be avoided or their possibility reduced. Taking its cue from the 1960s literature on the Health Belief Model (Becker et al., 1972), health promotion has employed cost-benefit analyses of health-seeking behaviour based on individuals' beliefs and expectations of possible benefit (Bloor, 1995). Thus, in a US Congress report, the logic is presented in the following way: 'We estimate risks every day, every time we cross the street, every time we drive. Before making a left turn, we examine the hazard ... we consider the consequences of exposure to the hazard ... and we estimate the probability of occurrence ...' (Environmental Protection Agency, 1994, p. 45). The presentation of knowledge of risk as a source of action is thereby closely allied to a rational model of human behaviour, in which all decisions are expected to be subject to a continual process of computation. The central motif cast is that all individuals calculate by themselves, and ultimately for themselves. Consequently, discourses of health risk may be seen as much a part of a more pervasive and historically rooted process of individualisation as a new source of empowerment; by conceptualising risks as pertaining to individuals rather than groups, health narratives emphasise that their perception and understanding can only be gained from an essentially personal, rather than cultural, perspective (Frankenberg, 1993).

Douglas has presented an influential model[1] that suggests a direct relationship between risk perception and the degree of social inclusion/exclusion within four different sub-cultural categories (Douglas, 1992). Though an attractively simple schema, the notion that individuals belong to such groups in any stable way is itself at best out of date and anthropologically problematic. What is influential about this work is its insistence that risk is socially constructed, and that the perception of risk is a result of cultural factors as well as individual psychological processes. The claim of 'objective' or 'real' risks, independent of their perception, attempts to locate the discourse within a scientific and technical neutrality that is often compounded by legal rationalisation (see, for example, Kemshall and Kingsley, 1995). However, since *all* calculations to establish at what point something may be considered a substantive risk require diverse judgements, even the most arithmetical principles must be weighed up in non-mathematical ways. From the social sciences, therefore, one central message is that risk must be seen as a social construct (Green, 1997). Previous literature tended not to discriminate between risk assessment, risk perception and ideas of 'objective' risk. Not only was this confusing but it tended to curtail an anthropological analysis by implying it is only legitimate for the social sciences to study the (mis)perception of risks by specific groups (Pidgeon et al., 1992).

This chapter will draw chiefly from unstructured interviews conducted with people in south-east London suffering from Type II diabetes mellitus carried out as a follow-up study to ethnographic fieldwork originally conducted for a PhD thesis at a Diabetes Day Centre. Talking to people about illness is a revealing process. It forces them to reflect on their own vulnerability, on the fragility of their daily lives. Chronic illness is a particularly important catalyst of these feelings. As acute infectious diseases have declined in Western societies, so chronic illnesses, especially those associated with an ageing population, have increased (Kuh and Ben-Shlomo, 1997). Danger to health is thereby no longer solely associated with a simple narrative of hostile attack, or about clear distinctions between being healthy and having disease. Preceding diagnosis of a chronic illness, ideas of its cause and recollections of everyday life are clearly going to be imbued with a rich set of beliefs and values. The experience of chronic illness changes not merely ideas about what illness is, but also how people view themselves. But a crucial additional feature for diabetes, as with other chronic conditions, is that diagnosis does not displace concerns for health risks in the future, but actually heightens them, since the condition is chiefly presented as a status of vulnerability. People with diabetes are neither healthy nor unwell, caught within a biomedical discourse that stipulates they have already suffered at the hand of fate, which may have more in store for them.

There can be many harrowing experiences when conducting fieldwork in a health setting. Harrowing, not because as an outside researcher one is unused to the appearance of physical trauma in the way that medics are, but harrowing because one is sometimes faced with a situation or behaviour which is impossible to trap in any semblance of understanding. One such case concerns a 54-year-old man who had been diagnosed with diabetes for over ten years. From the outset, he had adamantly refused to change his diet, his smoking or his heavy drinking, and was now confined to a wheelchair having lost one foot. A doctor, highly concerned with the man's apparent lack of concern for his condition despite the appalling effects that had already struck, was examining the remaining foot. With a rising stench the sock was peeled off, revealing a barely recognisable foot almost entirely black-red, damp with discharge, and with only three gangrenous toes remaining. Even the doctor looked shocked, and turned his gaze up to the man. Without prompting the man said, 'I'm just waiting till it drops off I know it's my own fault and that, but there you are. And I know you said it could happen and it has. I've got diabetes, and this is what it's done to me.'

In this chapter I hope to show how the social meaning of complex health risks and the responses of people with diabetes to them can only be understood in parallel with people's existing beliefs. There is an inevitable disjunction if these risks are presented as such without attempting to modify simple mechanical understandings of disease. What is clear is that the complexity of etiological models in current medical discourse can serve to sever them from lay perceptions, and consequently can actually reduce or suppress a sense of controllable danger for sufferers. Finally, this study will show how risk messages effectively challenge the underlying temporal dimension of people's lives. At first, people already suffering from a chronic illness may seem an unusual case, but, though already diagnosed, they are nevertheless subject to repeated warnings and concern for the risks of complications. What is crucial is to begin questioning the processes that appear to be confrontational resistances to such messages, and whether these really reflect an inability to accept that there are different possible futures, especially once labelled as 'ill'.

RISK AND CAUSALITY

Clearly if risk is to be associated with behaviour modification of any kind, in order for any subjective reckoning and any decision for action to be made, one must have some belief not only in the probability of adverse events and their severity, but also the means by which they might occur. And, since ideas about how things can happen are firmly based on beliefs about how they have happened in the past, risk perception must be examined in conjunction with theories of causation. Kelman (1976) has suggested that there has been an important shift in biomedicine from thinking of the body as a machine to a conception of the bio-individual within an ecological model that stresses lifestyle and social epidemiology. In parallel to changes in other arenas of scientific explanation, causal complexity is replacing the simple linear and mechanistic causal explanations (Hempel and Oppenheim, 1948) so championed in the previous century by Laplace (1951). Many scientific facts can no longer all be reduced to definitive causes, but must incorporate causal conjunctions, bifurcations and uncertainties to such a degree that explanation can only ever exist at a statistical level (Salmon, 1984).

The shift towards acknowledging statistical patterns as explanation has been a feature of many areas of science and has been proclaimed as the dawn of a new holistic and indeterminist cosmology (Griffin, 1988). Certainly it is no longer valid to characterise biomedicine as solely operating only from an unassailable mechanistic paradigm as some critics continue to claim (see, for example, Romanucci-Ross and Moerman, 1997). In biomedicine, the rise of models of complexity has its roots in epidemiology, the study of disease distribution in a population. Often regarded as a branch of medicine that precedes detailed understanding of concrete biological mechanisms, epidemiology serves to implement action based merely on the patterns, rather than fully known causation, of diseases. Ever since Snow's discovery of a clear association between a cholera epidemic with a particular water source in Soho, epidemiological models have had to modify simple causal germ theories of contagion and adopt a more Humean approach to the association of possible causal elements (Pelling, 1993). In order to progress from observing a statistical association to making any kind of biological inference, epidemiologists increasingly have had to resort to standards that served only as approximations to strict causality. For example, one of the most well-known criteria proposed, known as the Henle-Koch set, developed at the turn of the last century, outlined nine points that only in combination suggest a disease narrative based on exposure to a causal agent (Ashton, 1994).

The twentieth century has consequently seen a continual drift from the deductive criteria of 'sufficient and necessary', as ideas of causation themselves have drifted further from a linear model (Casti, 1995). In particular, attempts to chart the distribution of chronic illness led Hill, famous for his partnership with Doll on the association between smoking and lung cancer, to list a range of concepts that should be used flexibly in making causal inference (Beaglehole et al., 1993). Hill concluded that ultimately causation must be a matter of 'common sense'. Aspects of current epidemiology therefore illustrate clearly the growing untidiness that accompanies the recognition of detail in causal processes. For example, in accounts of contemporary health hazard controversies (from sick building syndrome and VDU radiation, to electric pylon magnetic fields), Foster et al., seeking science to provide a bedrock for legal certainty, are determined to identify 'phantom risks' as those 'unproven and perhaps unprovable' (1993). Yet it is the rise of scientific knowledge itself, increasingly producing these 'theoretical' possibilities of unrecognised confounding factors, that has led to a more widespread acceptance by epidemiologists that causality, and therefore risk, can in practice only be considered an *assessment* (Lilienfeld and Stolley, 1994, p. 62).

In scientific metaphors of how diseases develop the skin is no longer seen as an impermeable boundary between the self and a hostile, unhygienic environment; instead the body's outer-most surface is now conceived as in a dynamic constant interrelationship with other matter (Martin, 1995). Similarly, descriptions of the human immune system and allergies describe a fluid process of constant recognition, checking, feedback, information processing and learning (Haraway, 1989), and the role of the genome as potential rather than prescription (Rabinow, 1996). Arguably, more than acute illness, the chronic illness forcefully illustrates how biomedical concepts of causality and risk are imbued with a broader theme of uncertainty. In a study by Davison et al. (1991), for example, informants described how the lack of clear causality of coronary heart disease meant they tended to reject or dismiss health prevention messages. In fact, the greater the number of risks included in the medical model the more it appeared to contradict people's own experience and knowledge of who actually suffered from heart attacks. The point well illustrated by this study is that the lack of specific causality allows for a greater flexibility of interpretations and this can actually nullify health promotion messages.

From within psychology, attributional theorists have tended to characterise people's causal beliefs along various dimensions: stable or unstable, internal or external, controllable or uncontrollable. Pioneering work by Heider (1944) that divided people's perceptions into those within or beyond individual command led Rotter (1966) and Starr (1969) to maintain that people make sense of their social world and attribute cause according to how they view themselves in it.[2] Later, Kelley (1973) postulated a further development based on whether people have access to repeated events, which promotes a computational modelling of causation, or whether an event is observed only once. Slovic (1992) has since stressed how any such calculation of risk is also shaped by the degree of dread. The point that all these authors stress is that the interpretation of past experience accordingly provides the source for the subjective perception of risk and any predictions of the future.

In this vein, it has been suggested that chronically ill patients attribute success to internal, stable, and controllable factors while they attribute failure to external, or unstable, uncontrollable factors (Affleck, 1984). Though in any life-threatening situation, the search for a cause of the misfortune is both acute and personal, causal explanations become less clear-cut and more complex (Lowery and Jacobsen, 1984). It is therefore not surprising that in one such study on the culture and diversity of beliefs concerning six chronic illnesses, the researchers found no association between these beliefs and either gender or ethnicity, and concluded that 'people's beliefs about the causes of illness may be far more complex than the current literature suggests' (Klonoff and Landrine, 1994). The point is that chronic illness, though demanding meaningful explanations for patients, often appears to deny a clear moral framework and route for action. The neat dimensions of psychological attribution theory are, in this instance at least, too simplistic.

Williams, from a medical sociology perspective, has argued that ideas of cause often serve as a narrative construction of a changing relationship with the world (1984). He goes on to suggest that a person who is already afflicted by a condition is likely to have a more complex set of explanations, since they have 'both causal and purposive or functional components', and this theme is explored further in Scott and Williams (1992). Similarly, in *The Illness Narratives*, Kleinman, a practising psychiatrist as well as anthropologist, has argued that the illness experience is profoundly shaped by the entangled narratives that patients construct, reproduce and adopt. These tend to be ignored or dismissed by biomedical professionals. In one short passage he contrasts the patients' perception of risk and vulnerability with the complex concepts and findings of science (1988, p. 241). He consequently argues that such differences must be appreciated in order that the chosen therapy addresses the entire experience and not solely the clinical reality. Though his general argument suggests that anthropology be employed for a more successful application of biomedicine, and therefore resembles a more sophisticated version of earlier compliance studies (Fox, 1993, p. 113), what is highlighted is the different function that illness beliefs have, and it is likely that this disparity has crucial effects on the understanding of health risks.

TYPE II DIABETES AND PATIENTS' PERCEPTIONS OF RISK

A key theme in diabetes therapy centres around management and monitoring (Drucquer and McNally, 1998), reflecting how at the heart of many biomedical etiological theories are ideas of control and certainty (Strauss and Corbin, 1985). The condition effectively means that sufferers will, for the rest of their lives, have constantly to be aware of their internal metabolism, and try to compensate for lacking the hormonal capacity that continually adjusts blood sugar levels. Thus, the drugs, whether they are oral tablets or injections of insulin, are deliberately not presented as medication but as methods of gaining and maintaining control as part of a lifestyle regimen that also includes diet and exercise, and, if relevant, giving up smoking and alcohol and losing weight.

There are some major and severe complications from having a poorly controlled level of blood sugars over time, in particular macro-vascular disease that can lead to amputations, and micro-vascular disease that can cause blindness (Sima, 1999). Nevertheless, these possibilities are not used by health care professionals to frighten sufferers into compliance and tend not to be part of lay associations with diabetes, often initially described it as a 'mild' condition. The ideology behind this reticence to stress explicitly the risk of complications, as described in the health promotion literature, is that successful control must be achieved through the motivation and autonomy of sufferers themselves, and not through the manipulation of fear (Goodman and Biggers, 1995). Therefore complications are 'merely' described as possibilities, while some staff refuse to mention them at all. In this way the concept of risk is not overtly used to warn against the possibility of future hazards, but rather as a way of trying to influence the state of the sufferer at the present – as rational, independent, and in sufficient control to be constantly trying to determine how the condition will progress.

These ideas promote a different type of health prevention to that of the past. Prevention is no longer simply a matter of using a prophylactic – it is about changing oneself so that strength is gained from the 'moral correctness' of one's body. The new-style stress on diet, exercise, and on refraining from smoking and drinking alcohol, for example, all are now incorporated into a wide spectrum of what is a healthy lifestyle. The moral weight is therefore not on a particular agent causally connected to a specific disease, but on the behaviour of the undivided individual (see, for example, Edwards, 1996). The issue of risk in current health education strategy no longer relies on a direct chain of knowledge-action-behaviour change, which has proved ineffective in the past (Tones, 1986). While information is still regarded as essential for a health behaviour change, it is now increasingly argued that it should be combined with a process of empowerment, in which rationality and free choice are viewed as providing the motivational force for people to alter how they live (see, for example, Libov, 1999).

Medical literature presents diabetes as having a number of particular difficulties of description. First, diabetes, like so many other chronic conditions, should not be considered a disease with a single overall etiology and prognosis, but rather as a syndrome, encapsulating a complex metabolic variation from normal functioning homeostatic balance, that is currently divided into at least three different 'types' (Bloom and Ireland, 1990). Type II diabetes tends to affect people over the age of 35 and often does not initially require insulin as part of the regimen. Second, the current medical position also largely rejects a single causal agent of Type II diabetes, and instead integrates a multi-factorial model aimed at placing the patient at the centre of a virtually infinite set of possible agents (Jones, 1989). The current clinical notion is essentially that there is a genetic predisposition that then may lead to the condition through one or more converging factors. This notion of 'predisposition' is not a cause, in the strictly mechanical sense, but rather suggests an 'environmental' context of possibility. And finally, it is described as a 'silent' disease referring to epidemiological evidence suggesting that up to 50 per cent of people with Type II diabetes do not realise they have it (Mann et al., 1983, p. 8).[3]

Patients have difficulty with all three of these aspects of diabetes: with the biomedical resistance to conceiving it as a singular entity, its lack of clear unequivocal cause and its silence. Below I wish to briefly describe not only how they make sense of these anomalies with their own notions of illness, but how this then shapes their notion of being vulnerable to further health risks. The overall effect is potentially to deny them a way of finding meaning as to what diabetes is, why they developed the condition, and how they may possibly deal with it in the future.

Relating to the first of these issues is a common distinction made between feeling 'unwell' and being 'ill'. Feeling unwell constitutes the subjective experience of not being 'all right in yourself', and is not explained as being the result of an external agent. This state does not necessarily mean that any illness-associated behaviours take place, but is simply a personal recognition of not feeling 'normal'. Illness, on the other hand, is defined by some means; either by another person or by themselves if the symptoms are interpreted as constituting a known category which is seen to have a particular origin. There is therefore a clear hierarchical distinction between the moral implications of a resultant sick role and causal model. When asked about 'disease', nearly all thought it was the cause of an illness, and not of feeling unwell which 'isn't really because of anything ... it's just feeling under the weather'. The general concept underpinning a 'disease' is the notion of contagion: 'No, the germs aren't really the disease, the disease is what you get from them. You can catch them from lots of things, like food and the air. For many diseases you can go to the doctor and he'll give you something, but for some there's no cure, like cancer.'

Diseases are conceived of as *things*, that cause definite, observable symptoms, and this is blurred with the agent of contagion such as bacteria or a virus. Initial patient accounts combine this idea of disease as a disrupting agent with an interpretation of the professional narratives explained to them. For example, the notion of predisposition may be used as a way of identifying an unambiguous origin: 'They asked me if my parents had diabetes. I said no. But then she said that they may have had and that nobody had spotted it. I suppose that could be so. My mother died during the war, so she might have had it, you know. Nurse also said that they might have had the gene for it but for some reason it didn't come to anything.'

However, in accounts by those who have had diabetes for some months, trigger events and stress assume greater importance. There is an apparent shift as the issue of causation is elaborated, after either having talked to friends and members of their family, or by reading or personal reflection. The majority list what would be classed as external factors as causing their condition and exploit the ambiguity, as they see it, of the medical model.

For any area of science that employs statistical relevance as a method of explanation and prediction, there are inevitably going to be contradictions, competing hypotheses and alternative accounts. The result is often an increasing lay frustration with the biomedical model. A single explanation becomes intangible not because of inadequacy in medical science *per se* but because the significance of a range of factors resists unequivocal determination. So it is that as biomedicine talks now of 'risk factors', of 'triggers', and of 'genetic predispositions' people experience this as the dissipation of cause, and thereby the disappearance of an elementary moral resource for thinking about the future. Moreover, in addition to a straightforward rejection of risk messages, the ambiguity of prediction and untidiness of meaning is often linked to a conceptualisation of 'competing' risks. The uncertainty of one thing happening is 'weighed' against the uncertainty of something else. As one man in his mid-thirties, who had just been diagnosed, explained to me: 'The thing is, they aren't certain, are they? I mean you hear on the news one day that things are bad for you, and the next that they're good. What's the good in that? I just get on with things, 'cause it seems doctors can't be sure of anything.'

Despite a widely-held expectation that medicine should provide definitive answers, the belief that scientific knowledge can stipulate with any certainty what is good for people and what is bad has been significantly eroded. Whilst causal factors not felt to be under individual jurisdiction, such as environmental or genetic ones, appear to present few difficulties for people to accept, in the case of those factors perceived to be within the scope of individual determinism the inescapable ambiguity of the account is emphasised. In such circumstances, the information is seen to be a threat and encroachment on individual liberty. As a woman reminded of the range of possible serious health risks associated with her obesity proclaimed: 'It seems to me that there's a hidden agenda. They seem to stress some things and not others. I'm convinced that it's to do with who funds them – so the government can argue for certain that we do this and that, and hide other threats to our health.'

Causation is thereby not merely a mental construction to enable people to cope in the physical world, but is also a moral one that serves to reassert how people view their own independence and authority in a social environment that to many appears to be increasingly stressful and dangerous. Isolating simple causes from health risk messages has become a necessary means of trying to assert autonomy in an increasingly chaotic world.

The permanence of diabetes is wrestled with in the telling of personal narrative. People presented their lives as a linear sequence punctuated, as would be expected, by events considered significant. In addition to this linear sequencing, cyclical or continual episodes are placed along the time-line, such as employment at the same place for many years, doing the housework, or having the same friends since childhood. Against this, the medical message is that diabetes not only is life-long, but could have existed prior to diagnosis for many years. The fact that diabetes is not presented by biomedicine as a discrete period in linear time raises anxieties. Some feel not only that their notion of their past is challenged but also that their sense of future is

now permanently also modified by the notion that they do not know
the state of their own body. The idea that they should somehow
nevertheless continue to perceive health risks seems alien – now that
they have a disease they feel prevention renders modifications of
lifestyle effectively irrelevant.

The emphasis on risk presents a new discourse of possibilities that
serves as a potential disjunction between people's past and their sense
of future. Suggesting that the line from past events to future ones is
not singular, and that there is always a range of causes and possible
conjunctions, denies a clear conceptual framework necessary to cope
with being ill. As one man said: 'Anything could happen – as they
always say, I could die tomorrow. So I just think to myself, well, do
the best you can, and I inject myself like they say to stop it getting
worse, but that's it. You can't control everything in life.'

People diagnosed with diabetes find themselves in a bewildering
position on their own timeline; their ideas of the past tend to adhere
to the following pattern: (i) they were once normal; (ii) at some time
or other they became diabetic; (iii) they then may have suffered from
certain problems; (iv) they were diagnosed. But their sense of future
is dominated by the notions that (i) they will always have diabetes;
(ii) it can be 'controlled' with the right combination of diet/exercise/
medication; (iii) but crucially, there is a possibility of complications,
in addition to the diabetes itself, that can never be entirely forecast.
A kind of fatalism is often begrudgingly adopted, an acceptance of
this indeterminacy, not because people don't listen or understand but
because these messages are not perceived to imply an overall sense of
chronology at all: 'I just get on with my life. I do listen to what people
say, but I don't usually do anything about it ... I probably listen to
some things, but I ignore most of it ... There's no point worrying
about things that probably won't ever happen.'

The notion of fate is one important way of reinterpreting the
complex models put forward by health professionals. For example,
one woman who continued to have sweet foods daily as a 'treat' to
herself said: 'If I'm going to get worse I will ... I got diabetes by living
a normal life, and so whether I'll suffer any more is already decided.
It's just something I believe in. I got diabetes in the first place from
nothing I've done, so what will be, will be.'

In the light of this, some patients are particularly sceptical of what
the professionals tell them since, if they define disease in terms of

symptoms, and if they had presenting symptoms that are no longer present, the apparent silence of diabetes when it is under control contradicts the permanence stressed by the health care professionals. As a recently diagnosed person said: 'What I can't understand is why I've got to carry on with the tablets when I'm cured ...' And another: 'I don't get it ... Why, if they don't really know what caused my diabetes, why am I meant to change what I eat and that just because they think it might affect me one day?'

Maines states that 'temporal processes are at the very heart of the diabetic experience ... these processes unite the physiological, emotional, social, interpersonal, technological, organisational, institutional and personal arenas ... In a fundamental sense diabetes itself is a temporally-defined disease' (1983, pp. 103–104).

Just as discussions of risk have revolved around attempts to distinguish between the 'real' and the 'subjective', so too have debates about time. For example, Gell (1992) is keen to distinguish the subjective experience of time, which he characterises through a phenomenological framework, from an objective conception of time, which he presents via a range of positivist philosophies. He claims, as is common with such an oppositional tactic, that the subjective experience should be considered a partial approximation of a reality that exists beyond the messy interpretations that we may make of it. Yet to reduce the phenomenological experience of time to a process of approximation fails to recognise the highly complex and rich construction of a past that seeks some kind of security. The past is the flotsam and jetsam of experience left bobbing on the surface that we invest in as signifiers not only of the present, but as markers of the future; the constructed past becomes a vital resource for people to establish a sense of identity, and from which to imagine a future.

For most people, most of the time, the past is always perceived to have a simpler causal structure than the possible. However, the new complex etiological model that is ongoing rather than simply a description of 'catching' a disease, defies any such easy distinction, potentially threatening the safe and familiar separation made between what has been and what may occur. The new emphasis on convergence of factors suggests that there are as many potential influences from the past as there are possibilities of the future. People are forced to ask how, if events are now presented as so complex and so potentially threatening to safety, one can do anything to prevent them. As making decisions and taking control are fastened to a particular sense of temporality, the new quandary of diabetes management also jeopardises how people relate to their past, their present and their future. Where they feel they stand, therefore, is in a new sense of bewilderment; the future is not only one of uncertainty but potentially of personal indeterminacy.

These perspectives on the subjective experience of placing oneself in the world suggest that there is a key contradiction set within the current biomedical messages of the risk of complications. The philosophy of health prevention, risk assessment and risk avoidance is increasingly designed to persuade people to project themselves into a future of possibility and act on it in the present. In contrast, for many of the people interviewed in this study, the function of biomedicine is perceived in terms of the past: diagnosis means establishing what led to an illness, and by this providing a potentially meaningful framework. The question of the extent to which people perceive that the future can be self-determined arises, and this question naturally raises others concerning the ways in which others might help or hinder this desire for control. As greater knowledge is being accumulated and communicated in greater and greater detail, the asymmetry between the past and the future, that may once have offered a bedrock for the construction of certainty in people's everyday lives, is becoming less distinct. Fewer and fewer things have those delineated elements that distinguish them as causes rather than effects, and so the message of having to incorporate and act on the possibility of risk is interpreted as directly contradicting the target of diabetic control.

RISK AND CONTROL

Though Hume argued that the imperative to construct tangible causes is a cognitive 'infirmity' of what it is to be human, anthropology has long argued that to classify is as much a moral as it is an intellectual process. The desire to establish clear causes is a way of keeping the past and the present reasonably tidy and a way of gaining some sense of control over what might occur. Attribution is a task of 'housekeeping' – of dusting surfaces, of putting things away, of placing things where they belong, and of trying to gain some stability with respect to predicting possible risks in the future. Such processes are therefore ways of trying to assert order, not only in a strictly cognitive sense, but in a moral sense as well. Consequently, the point is not that in the search for meaning and order risks become invested with moral and metaphorical meanings, but that cultural and symbolic dimensions determine just how risks are identified and constructed in the first place. It is therefore a moral, rather than cognitive, impetus that induces such statements as the following made by a 49-year-old woman with high blood pressure, tired of instructions made by medical professionals to alter her behaviour:

I just don't know what I should do. If what they say is correct then I should just give up smoking and drinking and all that right now. But I reckon you never know how you might die – it could be this or that. I know everyone says this kind of thing – but it's true – 'You've got to go sometime'. So I just think, 'Well, there's no point me changing this or that because I'll most probably die from something else anyway ...'

Concerns over risk, therefore, directly relate to ideas of individual control and freedom. The rational basis of behaviour modification, via education, is an attempt to transpose this statistical model of risk to the individual, who is directed to act independently and autonomously. Reception to these probabilities requires imagining a sense of membership, of being able to place oneself within a social world; to embrace risk equates with identifying with an abstract group over time and accepting a distributional spread of probability. Yet such risk, based on a principle of statistical patterning, exists only in terms of a given population and can never be fully calibrated for each individual because at a personal level people require specific and tangible items of threat and danger to themselves. Just as the cause of diabetes is shaped and composed into a definite narrative, so dangers are perceived and contextualised only with respect to the experience of the world that the person lives in. Emphasis on individual responsibility divorces action from the social world: 'I'm not saying that scientists don't know what they're talking about, but when they say "one in a hundred" I never think it might be me ... you can always think of someone you know who did all the wrong things and is fine. It's my choice what I do, nobody else's; if I choose to go drinking or whatever, I'll go.'

The lack of a straightforward future discloses threatening spaces between people and suggests illness cannot be averted by simple barriers or physical defences. Thus, just as many illnesses are no longer conceived of as enemy invasions but as the breakdown of internal stasis, so health hazards and risky behaviours are assessed in the context of how people view the integrity of interrelationships with others. Specific directives to change behaviour and abstract reference to probabilities are all placed by people within a framework of how they currently experience their social world. This argument suggests that certain areas of people's lives can serve as an enacted metaphor for control and security to counter emotions of helplessness and uncertainty. Yet, decisions to reduce risk are made precisely in relation to fear and dread, and therefore rather than offering an escape from uncertainty can reproduce it, as in the following contradictory account:

> I know it's a risk to smoke, but it's a different risk from breathing in the crap every morning on my way to work. I have no choice over that. And when I get home, I just want to relax, I want to feel more myself, and I can't really mind that having a cigarette might damage my health … I just think we should all take more care of ourselves. We have to … There's no reason to get fat or anything. And I reckon most diseases can be avoided if you eat the right thing, and exercise. For me, it's a way of achieving my potential, and of avoiding the consequences of living.

It has been assumed for many years that people will only feel responsible for those things they see as having been able to alter in the first instance But many sufferers feel a total inability to be in control of something that is as amorphous as the metabolic interactions of diet, exercise and medications. It is not so much being out of control, as being forever vulnerable to unexpected factors.

Medical knowledge increasingly presents particular problems for lay conceptualisation of risk. Initially, it would appear that the refusal of medical discourse to provide clear and definite causes is itself the difficulty for people to understand. However, people do not necessarily have cognitive difficulty with the concept of multi-factorial models; the difficulty is that the absence of a scientific discourse on simple causal agents challenges how people see themselves symbolically in the world – their degree of volition in the world – and so challenges assumptions of control and agency. Causal process tends to 'relegate' individual action to one of a range of factors generating a potentially irreconcilable contradiction with concerns of health risk. Risk discourse attempts to promote individual rational action within a world of increasing chaos. This reliance on a 'rational model' ignores the fact that individuals live in a complex world of competing aims and values that are neither felt nor classified in terms of outside and within.

The new forms of causal process that are at the heart of health discourses of risk are in effect interpreted as denying meaning. The diffusion of risk in health as a unifying language of negative possibilities effectively denies that this social world of the self and the apparently non-human world of objects are so intimately related. People require causes not because of 'infirmities' they have in the mind but because they have an imperative to know how objects relate, according to how they see themselves both materially and emotionally in the world around them. Attributing cause and imagining definitive hazards reflects ways in which people conceive of their own action and determinacy, and provides the material for their own subjective temporality. Risk is not a logical deduction but a cultural perception based on controllability and temporality.

NOTES

1. Gabe (1995, p. 7) points out that the Royal Society Study Group (1992), acknowledged the value of Douglas' 'cultural' perspective.
2. The dominance of this model is reflected in the much-used Health Locus of Control developed by Wallston and Wallston (1978).
3. It is also recognised that even mortality rates continue the silent nature of diabetes, since it is rarely recorded as a primary cause of death – other related conditions seeming more suitable for causal status, such as heart attacks and strokes (Harris, in Mann, Pyörälä and Teuscher, 1983, p. 40).

REFERENCES

Affleck, G. (1984) 'Causal and Control Cognitions in Parents' Coping With Chronically Ill Children', *Journal of Science and Clinical Psychology*, vol. 3, no. 3, pp. 367–77.

Ashton, J. R. (ed.) (1994) *The Epidemiological Imagination: a reader* (Buckingham: Open University Press).

Beaglehole, R., Bonita, R. and Kjellström, T, (1993) *Basic Epidemiology* (Geneva: World Health Organization).

Beck, U., Giddens, A. and Lash, S. (1994*) Reflexive Modernization: Politics, Tradition and Aesthetics in the Modern Social Order* (Cambridge: Polity Press).

Becker, M. et al. (1972) 'Motivations as predictors of health behavior', *Health Service Report*, vol. 87, pp. 852–61.

Bernstein, P. L. (1996) *Against the God: the remarkable story of risk* (New York: John Wiley and Sons).

Bloom, A. and Ireland, J. (1990) *Colour Atlas of Diabetes* (St. Louis: Mosby).

Bloor, M. (1995) 'A user's guide to contrasting theories of HIV-related risk behaviour', in Gabe, J. (ed.) *Medicine, Health and Risk* (Oxford: Blackwell).

Casti, J.L. (1995) *Searching for Certainty: What Scientists Can Know About The Future* (London: Abacus).

Davison, C. et al. (1991) *Private Risks and Public Dangers* (Aldershot: Avebury).

Douglas, M. (1986) *Risk Acceptability According to the Social Sciences* (London: Routledge and Kegan Paul).

Douglas, M. (1992) *Risk and blame: essays in cultural theory* (Routledge: London and New York).

Drucquer, M. and McNally, P. (1998) *Diabetes Management* (Oxford: Blackwell Science).

Edwards, M. (1996) *Screening for Complications in Diabetes* (Oxford: Blackwell Science).

Environmental Protection Agency, US Congress (1994) *Researching Health Risks* (USA: US Congress, Office of Technology).

Foster, K. R., Bernstein, D. E. and Huber, P. W. (1993) *Phantom Risk: Scientific Inference and the Law* (Cambridge, MA: The MIT Press).

Fox, N. (1993) *Postmodernism, Sociology and Health* (Buckingham and Philadelphia: Open University Press).

Frankenberg, R. (1993) 'Risk: Anthropological and Epidemiological Narratives of Prevention' in Lindenbaum, S. and Lock, M. (eds) *Knowledge, Power & Practice* (Berkeley: University of California Press).

Franklin, J. (ed.) (1998) *The Politics of Risk Society* (Cambridge: Polity Press in association with IPPR).

Gabe, J. (1995) 'Health, medicine and risk: the need for a sociological approach', in Gabe, J. (ed.) *Medicine, Health and Risk* (Oxford: Blackwell).

Gell, A. (1992) *The Anthropology of Time* (Oxford: Berg).

Goodman, J. I. and Biggers, W. W. (1995) *The New Diabetes Without Fear* (London: Avon Books).

Green, J. (1997) *Risk and Misfortune: a social construction of accidents* (London: UCL Press).

Griffin, D. R. (1988) *The Re-enchantment of Science* (Albany: State University of New York Press).

Haraway, D. (1989) 'The Biopolitics of Postmodern Bodies: Determinations of Self in Immune System Discourse', *Differences*, vol. 1 no. 1, pp. 3–43.

Heider, F. (1944) 'Social perception and phenomenal causality', *Psychological Review*, vol. 51, pp. 358–74.

Hempel, C. and Oppenheim, P. (1948) 'Studies in the Logic of Explanation', *Philosophy of Science*, vol. 15, pp. 135–75.

Jones, D. (1989) 'What is the cause of diabetes?', *Balance* (BDA), February/March.

Kelley, H. H. (1973) 'The process of causal attribution', *American Psychologist*, vol. 28, pp. 107–28.

Kelman, S. (1975) 'The Social Nature of the Definition Problem', *International Journal of Health Services*, vol. 5, no. 4, pp. 625–42.

Kemshall, H. and Kingsley, J. (eds) (1995) *Good practice in risk assessment and risk prevention* (Bristol, PA: Jessica Kingsley).

Kleinman, A. (1988) *The Illness Narratives: Suffering, Healing and the Human Condition* (USA: Basic Books).

Klonoff, E. and Landrine, H. (1994) 'Culture and Gender Diversity in Commonsense Beliefs About the Causes of Six Illnesses', *Journal of Behavioral Medecine*, vol. 17, no. 1, pp. 407–18.

Kuh, D. and Ben-Shlomo, Y. (1997) *A Life Course Approach to Chronic Disease* (Oxford: Oxford University Press).

Laplace, P. S. (1951) [1819] *Theorie Analytique des Probabilités*, trans. F.W. Truscott and F. L. Emroy (New York: Dover).

Libov, C. (1999) *Beat Your Risk Factors: A Woman's Guide to Reducing Her Risk for Cancer, Heart Disease, Stroke, Diabetes and Osteoporosis* (New York: Plume Books).

Lilienfeld, D. E. and Stolley, P. D. (1994) *Foundations of Epidemiology*, 3rd edn (New York and Oxford: Oxford University Press).

Lowery, B. and Jacobsen, B. (1984) 'Attributional Analysis of Chronic Illness Outcomes', *Nursing Research*, vol. 34, no. 2, pp. 82–8.

Maines, David R. (1983) 'Time and Biography in Diabetic Experience', *Mid-American Review of Diabetes*, vol. 2, pp. 23–38.

Mann, J., Pyörälä, K. and Teuscher, A. (1983) *Diabetes in Epidemiological Perspective*, (Edinburgh, London and New York: Churchill Livingstone).

Martin, E. (1995) *Flexible Bodies: Tracking Immunity in American Culture – From the Days of Polio to the Age of AIDS* (Boston: Beacon Press).

Mortimer-Granville, J. (1880) *Common Mind Troubles* (London: David Boyle).

Pelling, M. (1993) 'Contagion/germ theory/specificity', in Bynum, W. F. and Porter, R. (eds) *Companion Encyclopedia of the History of Medicine*, Vol. 1 (London: Routledge).

Pidgeon, N. et al. (1992) 'Risk Perception', in The Report of a Royal Society Study Group *Risk: Analysis, Perception and Management* (London: The Royal Society).

Rabinow, P. (1996) *Making PCR : a story of biotechnology* (Chicago: University of Chicago Press).

Romanucci-Ross, L. and Moerman, D. E. (1997) 'The Extraneous Factor in Western Medicine' in Romanucci-Ross, L., Moerman, D.E. and Trancredi, R. (eds) *The Anthropology of Medicine: from culture to method*, 3rd edn (Connecticut: Bergin & Garvey).

Rotter, J. (1966) 'Generalized Expectancies for Internal versus External Control of Reinforcement', *Psychological Monographs*, vol. 80:1.

Royal Society Study Group (1992) *Risk Analysis, Perception and Management* (London: Royal Society).

Salmon, W. C. (1984) *Scientific Explanation and the Causal Structure of the World* (Princeton, NJ: Princeton University Press).

Scott, S. and Williams, G. (1992) Introduction, in Scott, S. et al. (eds) *Private Risk and Public Dangers* (Aldershot: Avebury).

Sima, A.F. (1999) *Chronic Complications in Diabetes* (London: Harwood Academic).

Slovic, P. (1992) 'Perception of risk: reflections on the psychometric paradigm', in Krimsky, S. and Golding, D. (eds) *Social Theories of Risk* (Connecticut: Praeger).

Starr, C. (1969) 'Social benefit versus technological risk', *Science*, vol. 165, pp. 1232–8.

Strauss, A. and Corbin, J. (1985) 'Accompaniment of chronic illness: changes in body, self, biography and biographical time', in Roth, J.K. and Conrad, P. (eds) *Research in the Sociology of Health Care*, vol. 5 (Greenwich, CT: JAI Press).

Tones, B.K. (1986) 'Health Education and the Ideology of Health Promotion: a review of alternative approaches', *Health Education Research*, vol. 1, pp. 3–12.

Wallston, K.A. and Wallston, B.S. (1978) 'Development of the multidimensional health locus of control scales', *Health Education Monographs*, vol. 6, pp. 161–70.

Williams, G. (1984) 'The Genesis of Chronic Illness: Narrative Reconstruction', *Sociology of Health and Illness*, vol. 6, no. 2, pp. 175–200.

9 GOOD RISK, BAD RISK: REFLEXIVE MODERNISATION AND AMAZONIA
Stephen Nugent

Risk is a notion with many resonances in Amazonia and in the literature on Amazonia. It would not be pressing the issue too far to say that the notion of risk is overdetermined in Amazonia: the fact that the region is still presented as a frontier – an amplified risk metaphor par excellence – after almost 500 years of incorporation into the world system depends heavily on the idea that risk has succeeded in denying any sort of convincing regulatory discourse. Archaic 'green hell' symbols (bad animals, unfriendly plants, oppressive weather) stand side by side with detailed, largely speculative bio-genetic analyses and neo-liberal crystal ball musings, and risk flux prevails.

The types of risk long associated with Amazonia may usefully be contrasted with the kind of risk which serves as the guiding metaphor in the reflexive modernisation project put forward by Beck, Lash and Giddens. On the one hand, we have the notion of risk used to defer socio-historical explanation (Amazonia is a risk-laden natural domain which pre-empts neat categorisation), while on the other, we have a notion of risk which sets limits on, but doesn't preclude, the possibilities of sociological encapsulation and, possibly, explanation. One is recumbent, passive, naturally given; the other is dynamic, manipulable, open to negotiation.

In a comparison of the role of risk in portrayals of Amazonia and in the promotion of a postmodernist sociological innovation there is a striking irregularity. For analysts who identify 'risk society' as a significant marker of the postmodernist condition, risk is a novel outcome of the project of modernity, while for those at the periphery of that project of modernity, risk has a less exceptional status. In Amazonia, for example, risk could be said to represent less the

226

outcome of the project of modernity than a condition of its entry into the project, that is, it is 'discovered' as a risk domain and thereafter persists as 'the frontier'.

One contention of this chapter, then, is that the notion of reflexive modernisation propounded by Beck – and in sympathetic fashion by co-workers Giddens and Lash – makes assumptions about the maturing of old-fashioned modernity (that is, the phase following traditionalism and preceding reflexivity) which don't always stand up to scrutiny when one includes in the discussion of modernity regimes such as those in Amazonia. The kind of uncertainty which the risk discourse of Beck, Giddens and Lash addresses may represent a plausible stage in a European social theory of self-consciousness, yet a key historical feature in the development of such self-consciousness has been uneven development in global terms; this is, however, hardly acknowledged. In short form, the ambitious reflexive modernisation/risk analysis has seized upon a series of conditions – variously termed a 'legitimation crisis', 'postmodernism', 'Enlightenment ennui' – which are salient, but also parochial. The Eurocentric risk society which is the focus of Beck's attention is one shorn of the complications of the globe, even though it is that very globe (invoked not as a structure, but as a process – globalisation) which provides the restorative meta-narrative: ecologism.

This chapter has two main sections: the first concerns matters raised by Beck – and others – and his arguments concerning reflexive modernisation. The second concerns notions of risk as they pertain to Amazonia. Amazonia is conveniently apposite for a discussion of risk: actual (acquiring malaria, getting hit by a bus, enclosure), metaphorical ('green hell') and fabulous (Scythian women archers each with a breast removed for better control of bows). While authors both journalistic and scientific/ethnographic have long preyed on such Amazonian risks, in recent years there has been a significant convergence of 'risk' and 'Amazonia' in the domain of Western eco-politics and environmentalism. This convergence is neither trivial nor unproblematic: in the globalisation of environmental politics, the aforementioned iconic status of mythic Amazonia has been reproduced, although now through bio-diversity, sustainability or indigenous knowledge. Meanwhile, another Amazonia, that of complex colonial subject, has been put back on the shelf.

BECK'S RISK ANALYSIS

Let me first give a capsule account of Beck's central argument. I hope it is a fair and reasonably accurate, if necessarily truncated, reading. Historical and sociological accounts of the great transformation from traditionalism to modernity – regardless of their political leanings – have assumed a stages model of development, with each stage marked by macro, galvanizing ruptures. What is different, however, about the transition from modernity to reflexive modernisation (modernity) is that there is no unifying stage. Instead, there is a fragmentation, a multiplicity of cogent, but disarticulated tendencies which resist generic characterisation. A key term used here suggestively by Beck is 'surreptitious'. What is radical about reflexive modernisation is precisely that it defies encapsulation within the categories of social change to which sociology has become accustomed, hence the realities of social change remain beyond grasp. In short, if one takes the structure-agency contrast as a central concern of sociology-born-of-modernisation, in terms of reflexive modernisation the heuristic value of the pairing is lost because there is a superabundance of both agency and structure possibilities.

In contrast to nominally adjacent postmodernist accounts, Beck's characterisation of reflexive modernity resists a radical relativism and a fascination with nihilism, but there are still convergent notions of decay, and these are embraced by the concept of risk. The basis upon which agents ease their way through life is uncertain, not because the categories of agency and structure have been superseded (or have disappeared), but because they no longer serve a heuristic purpose. As guides for explanation within a science-oriented sociology, so the reflexive argument goes, agency and structure have exhausted themselves.

The dilemma outlined by Beck, Lash and Giddens has a number of prescriptive implications. A central one is that social theory is out of step with the predicament of the actors it addresses: once capable of presenting a plausible account of the structures which shape con-sciousness, social theory is now driven by a set of calculations – how to deal with risk – which seems to exceed its explanatory powers. At the same time, however, that risk theory relinquishes explanatory authority in favour of describing a condition – it still invokes the authority of a situated theory. But where is this theory situated?

One common answer to that question is that it is irrelevant given globalisation, but globalisation is hardly a precise term. It is as easily invoked by those claiming the end of history/victory of capitalism as it is by those claiming Gaia one-ness. Even within more carefully modulated arenas of technical debate, however, the connotations of globalisation present a wide range of incompatibility. Weiss, for example (1997), shows that the term is currently used by academic/policy insiders to cover at least four quite different concepts. Her article is of particular interest because it suggests that Beck's characterisation of reflexive modernisation does not even adequately address arguments about globalisation as conducted in the core, much less further afield. Instead of there being general subscription to the sequence traditionalism-modernisation (stages) followed by reflexive modernisation (non-stages), Weiss argues that reflexive modernisation appears now in four clearly different versions of globalisation (1997, p. 5):

1. strong globalisation with state power erosion (viz. Robert Reich)
2. strong globalisation; state power unchanged (viz. the *Economist*)
3. weak globalisation (strong internationalisation); state power reduced in scope (viz. Paul Hirst and Graham Thompson)
4. weak globalisation (strong internationalisation); state power adaptability and differentiation emphasized. (Weiss, 1997, p. 6)

In relation to the reflexive modernisation thesis, this set of tunings is instructive, for it not only calls attention to the status of 'risk' as 'the big factor' (and implicitly queries it), but also drags into the discussion a version of modernisation (or in this case, its globalisation gloss) which explicitly sets the issue outside the confines of Europe. If modernisation has any content, it is surely not limited in import to European social theory. Also underlined is a point which might have been thought obvious for some time: the modernisation of Europe has been neither unilineal nor unrelated to processes in the global realm. Can the proverbial 'other' which has formed or informed a significant portion of the social sciences (anthropology, post-colonial theory, multiculturalism, development studies) in the late twentieth century still be regarded as extraneous to 'modernisation'?

Zizek's wide-ranging article 'Multiculturalism, or, the cultural logic of multicultural capitalism' (1997), cannot be adequately summarised here, but the punch-line, 'leftist enlightenment demands struggle whose main form is reflective struggle' (p. 51), appears more than superficially allied with Beck's claims, yet it is preceded by a salutary discussion of ideology and appearances. Where Beck argues that the only certainty is uncertainty, Zizek reminds us that such claims are subject to the standard forms of scepticism. Perhaps, then, what appears to be uncertain is not so at all, but merely a passing moment, an accessible representation, or – as Weiss has suggested – one of several moments currently on offer, and one whose salience is exclusively informed by itself.

The development of financial markets in Asia, for example, has for some time been enthusiastically seized upon as a clear indication that at least some processes of globalisation (economic integration of the apparatus of investment and speculation) have overcome the obstructions of colonial/imperial legacy (for example, the sharp divide between North and South), yet the globalisation thesis – *grosso modo* – has hardly been abandoned following the recent, dramatic decline of key 'tiger' economies (not to mention that of Japan, long the beacon of capitalist otherness/reflexivity). That Singapore, much less dependent on external capital for its inclusion as a tiger, should have emerged as less risk-laden than, say Indonesia or Malaysia (heavily dependent on external capital), may not reflect as much the riskiness of the postmodern condition as much as it reflects well-established observations about the virtues of local development of productive forces.

If Weiss and Zizek query the propriety of assuming that the notion of reflexive modernisation (and its globalisation baggage) is an adequate starting point for diagnosing the postmodern condition, Giddens explicitly links reflexive modernisation/risk/uncertainty to a political programme which bridges the gap between academic theory and social policy. The profile of Giddens in the *New Yorker* (Boynton, 1997) may be slight, but it is hardly uninformative. Not least of its features is the citation of key concepts which, like 'reflexive modernisation', have been widely used to get around a central problem: how can you claim to offer a solution when your analysis of the situation is based on claims that the situation exceeds the explanatory limits of the tools at your disposal? Cited key concepts include 'radical centre' and 'utopian realism', both admitted oxymorons, but no less useful, it appears, for that failing. 'The radical centre', says Giddens, 'is an oxymoron only if you believe that the left and right still define all the worthwhile ideas and policies. I don't, and I don't think Blair does' (Boynton, 1997, p. 74). This begs the question: even if you don't believe that left and right still define all the worthwhile ideas, this doesn't really make the notion 'radical centre' any less oxymoronic. 'Utopian realism' aspires to join the company of such phrases as 'one size fits all', 'the cheque is in the post' and other discredited vernacular claims. The position which appears to be on offer here is that conceptual ambiguity is not an issue if one has political power.

The large metaphor lurking behind claims of indeterminacy and risk is 'the market', a notion which, reconsecrated at the altar of neo-liberalism, is casually used, even by those who might know better, as a euphemism for 'society'. As the economist Gary Mongiovi observes: 'The folklore of the market has so deeply penetrated our collective intuition that to doubt the rationality, desirability or inevitability of capitalism is to identify onself as a naive – or dangerous – eccentric' (1997, p. 29).

To the degree that many citizens are frankly baffled by the operations, say, of the stock market, the centrality of the notion of risk is perhaps not so misplaced. On the other hand, however, as Mongiovi points out, stock markets themselves (which dominate financial systems only in the US and UK, not Germany and Japan, where central banks play that role) are less centrally involved in the allocation of funds to productive investment in the larger social domain. Most productive investment is financed out of previously accumulated profits, over 90 per cent of stock market trades concern speculative reshuffling of corporation ownership and most corporate debt is used to underwrite mergers and acquisitions, not enter into new production.

A radical centre which pretends that the market – and by extension, society – consists of non-enumerable bits and pieces is relinquishing explanatory power. Uncertain things may be, but to suggest that the underpinnings of the social landscape are less structured than they were before reflexive modernisation is an empirical matter not effectively captured by oxymoronic soundbites.

To summarise: there is a disaffection with social theory's capacity to anticipate what happens in its domain of expertise, but the risk/reflexive modernisation claim is not a balanced reply. Risk affect may be persuasive, but risk structure looks like the same old same-old.

ECOLOGICAL PANACEA OR PANEGYRIC?

One of the most interesting aspects of the reflexive modernisation argument is the fact, especially as developed in Beck's essay 'The reinvention of politics' (Beck et al., 1994), that the solution is said to lie somewhere in the arena of ecology. This is interesting not necessarily because it is persuasive, but because it is contradictory: an analysis of the fragmentary consequences of reflexive modernisation is resolved by recourse to the most meta of meta-systemic options (putting aside Mike Davis' valiant attempt to introduce galactic catastrophism into the discussion (1996)).

This is interesting and contradictory (and, not insignificantly, ironic) because the ecological domain identified is a passive, descriptive one: the big, balanced, ideal type. While there is a big, dynamic version of this (Gaia), the system-ness of the ideal is crosscut by differential demands made on it by the social systems which occupy (and transform) it. Were the social demands on the ecosystem (Gaia, perhaps) to be made uniform, say in terms of energy consumption (Enzensberger, 1974), the consequences would be clear: core consumers would have to cut down enormously, and peripheral consumers would have vastly more energy at their disposal. Even if levels of energy consumption were equitable globally, it is not known whether such levels would be Gaia-tolerable. And more to the point, such recalibration would represent a significant decline in the standard of living of those long accustomed to preferential treatment. Those espousing a/the 'Third Way' which actually takes an accurate global view should be preparing their constituents to accept rather grim costs: no winter shoes for the kids this year or next.

I arrive, at last – almost – in Amazonia where I hope to locate two strands of the arguments sketched above. These concern the notion of risk and the characterisation of modernisation. With regard to the former, my argument is that the privileging of the notion of risk is actually retrogressive. In the case of the latter, my argument is that the versions of modern society depicted by Beck through the notion of reflexive modern society are parochial (Eurocentric) and not particularly modern in any useful sense.

Let me introduce the latter first. Anderson (1986), in a review of Berman's *All That Is Solid Melts into Air* (1982), made a set of observations about the ambiguities of the notion 'the modern'. One of these concerns the fact that the concept is obviously and significantly internally differentiated, certainly in the core, and to a greater degree on the periphery, and that what passes as 'the modern' is a deceptive shorthand. Three aspects of the modern are noted: modernity (attitude); modernisation (socio-economic effect); modernism (aesthetic). A central example is a comparison of 'the modern' in Britain and in southern Europe. In the former, 'modernisation' stands for 'the modern' (the industrial revolution, in short), while 'modernism' (the aesthetic moment) has relatively little visibility. In southern Europe, the modern was first expressed through 'modernism', and only latterly in 'modernisation' (mill towns versus Picasso). In the US, the configuration is different again, with a high degree of synchronicity between modernisation and modernism: tail fins and TV dinners. The point here is that the virtues of the reflexive modernisation arguments of Beck et al. appear parochial not only in terms of the offically modern world, but also in the outer reaches. One such example is Amazonia, which can be nothing other than modern even if singularly configured: eating *farinha de mandioca* off a Disney motif plate, or watching soap opera after a day of rubber tapping. Hence what is designated by Beck as the authentic marker of reflexive modernisation – uncertainty, risk – has a non-standard form, one which is intimately related to the European form explored by Beck, but which also challenges the idea that the locus of the exploration of reflexive modernisation is in Europe.

Using material from Amazonia, I want to look at two notions of risk: the heroic and the mundane. Later, I will suggest that the notion of risk is a distraction and that privileging it as a topic of discussion is symptomatic of a field which has lost its way. Just as the notion of *homo economicus* makes reductionist assumptions about society and human nature, so too does the tendency to highlight essentialist concepts such as risk subvert the possibility of a critical social science.

An early example of a critique or questioning of conventional assumptions about the trajectory of modernisation may illustrate the general thread. The discovery of the informal sector had at least three effects: it debunked a received view about the presumed disorder of petty producers trapped in the eddies of uneven development; it consolidated arguments concerning the structural relationship between development in the core and underdevelopment on the periphery, and it created a new anthropological object of analysis – a sector, literally – the agents of which could be scrutinised in terms of the adequacy of their coping. From the insight that such a domain was not in fact understandable without a broader appreciation of the structures and consequences of colonialism, we moved to an assessment of those factors which seemed to feature most highly: survival strategies, risk management, coping mechanisms, and so on. That is, risk appeared as an object of analysis, and the underlying causes – revealed in the course of valorising the very notion of informal sector – were left behind. The structure of the informal succumbed to the essence of the informal. Terms of trade and unequal exchange were overshadowed by the Rapid Rural Appraisal programme.

WORKING TOWARDS RISK IN AMAZONIA

The concept of risk – both heroic and mundane – has a long history in Amazonia. According to those of cultural ecological bent, the virtual absence of sociological complexity in Amazonian societies reflects the overwhelming need to minimise risk. As this story goes – one codified in Steward and Faron's *Native Peoples of South America* (1959) and pursued with vigour by generations of vulgar materialists – Amazonia presents such an impoverished set of natural resources that in order for society to exist at all, it has had to scale down its expectations. Poor soils, high heat, high rainfall, depauperate protein resources (and a host of other defects) made impossible the development of complex societies. When presented with evidence of complex societies – as on the island of Marajo – the conventional retort has been, *à la* Meggers and Evans, that such societies could not continue precisely because they exceeded the carrying capacity of the natural environment. They took a risk, and it didn't pay off. I shall return to these founding risk arguments later, but for the moment I want to say a bit about the way in which the generalised social field in Amazonia – from the Conquest to the present – has been dominated by other notions of risk.

Depending on cultural backdrop, risk assumes different connotations. In Frederick Jackson Turner's account of the conquest of North American frontiers (1920) risk is good. It makes demands on social actors which allow them to reveal their intrinsic mettle. Presented with the challenge, they rise to the occasion, ford rivers, climb mountains, kill Indians, build homesteads, and in doing so, institutionalise the virtues of risk. It is character-forming, and nation-forming.

There was no Brazilian or Portuguese analogue of Turner – not because of lack of candidates, but because Amazonia turned out to be a different kind of frontier. There, risk rendered the conquerors not a caste of heroes, but a class of failures. Few in Amazonia are held in such low regard as the Portuguese colonist and trader, despite the fact that if you look at a map of the world *c.* AD 1500, the reduction of risk factors in Portuguese terms looks pretty good: significant portions of Africa, Asia and the New World incorporated into the Empire.

Suggested here is the idea that even within the traditional/modern transition, there is already a significant degree of differentiation. Within the narrow category of white settler colonies between the sixteenth and eighteenth centuries, the varieties of modernising experience display radically different faces, yet risk as a central feature is easily retrievable, albeit in non-compatible readings.

Counterposed to the foregoing heroic mode is the mundane. A case in point is the argument mounted by Beck in *Risk Society: Towards a New Modernity* (1992), mundane not in the sense of ordinary – for Beck's book grapples with central issues concerning the role of sociology and social criticism in the late modern period – but mundane in the sense that the referential world is European, not to say Eurocentric. In the preface, Beck writes that:

The guiding theoretical idea which is developed to this end can once again be best elucidated in a historical analogy. Just as modernisation dissolved the structure of feudal society in the nineteenth century and produced the industrial society, modernisation today is dissolving industrial society and another modernity is coming into being (1992, p. 10).

He goes on to claim that the apparent modernisation which preceded the late modern period merely laid the groundwork for what is the actual occurrence of modernity: consciousness or recognition of what modernisation actually entails, what he refers to optimistically as 'reflexive modernisation'.

Part of this restatement of what the meaning of modernity/modernisation is constitutes a useful critique of the tendency to account for the late modern condition by attaching the prefix 'post' to all and sundry and the tendency to adopt a crude stages approach to the passage of time.

But there are several curiosities to this formulation. First, the official date of modernity – the nineteenth century – is unvalidated. One suspects, for example, that for the peoples of the humid neo-tropics, effective modernity began in the sixteenth century, if not earlier. It is significant that few lived to appreciate the dilemmas of the transition from tradition to modernity (and beyond), as is the fact that the transition from feudalism to capitalism has both parochial and global readings. For those parts of the world system for which the dilemmas of northern European feudalism were shared after the fact, the great transformation which began as that of someone else now appears to deny them membership.

It is thus ironic that Beck should ridicule the notion of 'the end of history' ('a mad joke': 1992, p. 11) when in fact the history to which he refers is only that which pertains to a European and Eurocentric rendering of the world.

Second, it is quite remarkable to encounter a critique of modernity which does not acknowledge those arguments which reasonably insist that the notion of Western modernisation cannot be detached from the developmental cycles of expansionary social systems. Is it conceivable that a discussion of modernity/modernisation produced in the late twentieth century could pay so little heed to the world system, especially in light of the post-colonial idioms of 'borderlands'/'hybridity'/'creolisation' which have such strong professional associations with the reflexive modernisation project?

Third, and to follow on from the point above, one could argue that one of the major examples of risk avoidance in living memory was the transfer to debtor nations of the accumulation crisis of the 1970s. Had that option not been available, the risk to which Beck refers as an overriding concern of European moderns might well have been bypassed in favour of a more ordinary preoccupation: again, no winter shoes for the kids.

Finally, in this section, one wonders about the assumptions of normalcy according to which Beck diagnoses the reflexive future and its possibilities. Beck writes that 'components of a traditionality inherent in industrialization are inscribed in varied ways within the architecture of industrial society – in the patterns of classes, nuclear family, professional work, [etc.]' (1992, p. 11).

Yet, where do we position those also inscribed within 'the architecture of industrial society' whose patterns defeat neat inclusion within the parameters of the archetypal European experience? It seems far-fetched to regard them as having pursued fully independent trajectories, yet the outcomes of their modernising experience are excluded from a formulation which assumes that the crucial features of debates about the consequences of modernisation rest fundamentally – if not exclusively – in Europe. The indigenous peoples of North and South America – most of whom had disappeared by the eighteenth century – and the millions of Africans transported to the New World can hardly be regarded as having been involved in a different modernisation.

To sum up: the version of mundane modernisation proposed by Beck pays insufficient heed to the global dimensions of the shift from traditionalism to modernism. In the next section, I propose to look at the notion of risk as it has appeared in Amazonianist discussions and suggest that some light may be shed on the reasons why the risk focus is both plausible and problematic. The general argument is this: reflexive modernisation is actually a local theory which depends for its authority on the fact that it is merely core culture common sense; the notion of risk society described and analysed by Beck is incomplete.

AMAZONIA AND THE DOCTRINE OF TROPICAL NASTINESS

Considering Amazonia in the light of the reflexive modernisation thesis, three things are immediately suggested. One of these is the convergence of eco-politics – a prominent feature of the Amazonian social landscape – and a contested modernisation somewhat different from that proposed by Beck et al. The second is the fact that the notion of risk has great historical depth in Amazonia, being represented in many different attempts to document and analyse what is, unfortunately, still depicted as the epitome of a 'green hell'. And the third is that a social and natural landscape long consigned to the risk bin has suddenly become valorised in the name of 'risk management': a region historically treated with a brutality rationalised on the grounds that it was an implacably risky domain has, in two decades, been transformed into a region treated with no less brutality, but now in the name of risk management. That which once justified exclusion with prejudice (risk) now justifies inclusion (risk is manageable and is, in fact, good). The indolent *caboclo* of two decades ago (tolerable, but suffering, riskologist) is now the 'wise forest manager' (exemplary riskologist).

This is horribly compressed, so let me raise a single example to make a general point. J.M. Blaut, in his book *The Colonizer's Model of the World* (1993), has drawn attention to 'the doctrine of tropical nastiness'. This doctrine has appeared twice: first when people perhaps didn't know any better (we were anthropologically and historically naive); second, when they not only knew better, but publicly declared that they knew better (we wore our reflexivity on our sleeves).

The elements of the doctrine of tropical nastiness (DTN) are:

1. Humans in the tropics can't work because they are physiologically ill-adapted.
2. Tropical soils are poor, therefore agricultural output is a limiting factor.
3. Evil diseases are prevalent in the tropics.

First, people can and do work in tropical climates and the effects of heat, humidity, etc., fall within the limits of human tolerance. Second, tropical soils are different, but not in any unequivocal sense poor, only in terms of the expectations of temperate-region farmers and markets. Third, the evil diseases associated with the tropics are hardly unknown in temperate regions. The fact that they are assigned 'tropicality' reflects social system provision as much if not more than it reflects a natural condition. The fact that malaria is no longer a major risk to the inhabitants of Cambridgeshire has little to do with tropical/non-tropical climate.

The point here is that even though the DTN is known to be fallacious, it has lost little of its force as an adequate rendition of the mechanical relationship between climate and social possibility. It prescribes the parameters within which risk appears as a dominant feature, despite the fact that there is little justification for privileging risk as a defining feature of the tropics.

INADVERTENT RISK

In focusing on Amazonian matters, there are two general guiding points in relation to modernisation and reflexive modernisation claims. The first of these concerns the complicity of Amazonia in what is claimed as modernisation by the core. The second concerns the reinvention of Amazonia as a particularly fraught domain of eco-politics in the late twentieth century.

First, to the degree that Amazonia is conventionally included within the modern brief, it is an exotic footnote consisting of the rubber boom, the opera house in Manaus and, for the attentive, Roger Casement and the curious amalgamation of the Congo, Putumayo, Irish nationalism and execution for treason. The so-called boom in the last quarter of the nineteenth century did occur, but was part of a much more extended relationship: until 1911, Amazonia was the only source of rubber (*hevea brasiliensis*), production of which was vital to industrial growth in Europe and North America from 1822 onwards. The boom period is that celebrated by remote observers, but was in fact little more than the end phase of a long-lived (hundred-year) industry which, with a boring steadiness not often seen in extractive 'booms', annually increased output and price in line with core demand, until felled by the introduction of plantation rubber in South-east Asia.

Amazonia may be exotic, but it is modern exotic, and represents less the transition from traditionalism to modernisation than it does the creation of modernisation on the basis of global integration.

The second point concerns reflexive modernisation: Beck argues that the consequences of modernisation result in a particular form of disarticulation: the possibilities afforded by modernisation do not lead to crisis/rupture/consolidation. Rather, they lead to uncertainty and risk. What happens to this thesis if it turns out that this risk phase has been anticipated? What if it is the case that the experience of modernisation for some has been precisely that of a risk society, and probably a significantly more exposed version? What if, in fact, the risk society identified by Beck and others is not – or not just – the next stage in European modernisation, but actually represents the Third World-isation of Europe?

OPERATIONALISING RISK IN AMAZONIA

Let me go on to discuss some blatant aspects of risk in Amazonia. I will deal with only three, two sketchily, one in somewhat more detail.

At the level of local societies, there are indeed such phenomena as Indians with blowpipes, floods, piranhas, snakes, jaguars, forest spirits, caboclos with chainsaws and so on. These are real, without question, and are treated as such, culturally codified, integrated into lifestyles and institutions. They pale into insignificance, however, in terms of life-threat when compared to public health issues, provision of education, struggles over land, militias, corrupt politicians and other social pathologies.

In terms of macro-level, synthetic risk, Amazonia is also generously supplied. The relative failure of state, religious and private colonisation during the first three hundred years of modernisation confirmed Amazonia as 'green hell' and a 'lost world'. The risk posed by Indians was hardly insignificant, but as most of them were rapidly decimated, their actual threat was minimal and incidental by the time of independence in the early nineteenth century. The detailed chronicles of Victorian naturalists no doubt enhanced Amazonia's reputation as a region literally crawling with risk. And the images of Amazonians represented two conclusively unappealing human responses to this climate of risk: on one hand, the atavistic Indian lurking behind palm frond, ready to snatch (*à la* Boorman's film *The Emerald Forest*) the innocent white child or the benighted Fitzcarraldo battling to introduce a bit of culture to the region; on the other hand, the indolent peasant, beaten by tropical nastiness into a miserable routine of unsuccessful hunting, gathering and swidden agriculture.

The third example is different, for it involves a notion of risk that is not, strictly speaking, Amazonian, although it draws its force through Amazonian association, and this is the idea that failure to attend to the conservation of Amazonian ecosystems will have global consequences. Thus we have the paradox that a place too risky to be of much more than passing and exotic interest becomes valorised because its threatened disappearance is now going to affect Europeans and North Americans (not to mention everyone else). There is a further paradox, however, which is that the risk represented in Amazonia's disappearance is not the same sort of risk identified by

Beck et al. as the hallmark of reflexive modernisation, for it is a system risk, not the risk of a fragmenting system.

It would be rash to confirm the accuracy of any of the modern/late-modern system risks located in Amazonianist discussions, but it is worth listing them. They include:

- Global warming (deforestation, removal of carbon sink, rising temperature, smoke, feedback re El Niño, etc.)
- Decline of bio-diversity (permanent removal of plant genera, species, sub-species, varieties; depletion of commercially valued species; depletion of gene-warehouse, etc.)
- Pollution (mercury, smoke, tailings)
- Disappearance of primate communities and species
- Eradication of fish stocks
- Desertification
- And so on.

Since *c.* 1970, Amazonia's risk profile has risen, not because Amazonia has transformed internally, but because change has been forced upon it, and the kind of risk which prevails is not characterised by uncertainty, but by certainty: the overt exploitation of scarce resources. The construction of the Transamazon Highway (1970) made terrestrial access possible for the first time, displacing an agrarian crisis from one part of Brazil and locating it (or adding to it) in another (Amazonia). The opening of Brazil to foreign capital (1964) forced national capital to seek investment opportunities within national boundaries (Amazonia). The concentration on export agriculture encouraged the expansion of food-staple frontiers (Amazonia). Inducements to national capital in the form of cattle-ranching subsidies encouraged deforestation (Amazonia). Twelve per cent of the region is now deforested, and virtually all of that has taken place in the past thirty years.

The point here is that environmental risk (in Amazonia, and projected onto the global stage) is not a natural phenomenon, but one with a well-documented cast of interests, and this leads one to question the very category of risk: this is not risk, it is business as usual.

Not surprisingly, following quickly in the steps of environmental risk were agents of risk management, and in the remainder of this chapter I want to focus on such managers.

RISK MANAGERS

Contrary to frequently alarmist views promulgated in the press concerning the disturbingly high level of environmental risk posed in and by Amazonian development, those who have carried out the research upon which risk estimates are based are more equivocal in their judgements, and in large measure this equivocation reflects the fact there are few baselines according to which phenomenal forms of environmental depredation can be measured. This doesn't make them any less alarmist or more sanguine. In fact, it probably makes them more pessimistic in the light of the fact that their specialist takes on the situation are so easily misrepresented. Given that inventories of plants, for example, are incomplete even as vast areas of forest are being cleared, claims about declining bio-diversity – and consequences which are likely to follow – are almost certainly true in gross terms, but gross terms may not be of greatest consequence. An example: brazil nut trees – a not inconsiderable Amazonian resource – require pollination by a class of bee which itself requires the presence of orchids which themselves require a particular kind of forest cover. The green or pseudo-green or cynical or uninformed cattle-rancher who scrupulously preserves brazil nut trees in his pastures while felling other big species is barking up the wrong tree of sustainability. Another example: progressive legislation concerning the minimum size for the taking of key fish species are easily circumvented: salted fillets replace fresh fish on the market.

A further example, and one widely covered in the press concerns mercury pollution which in Amazonia is very high: for every tonne of gold taken from Amazonia, a tonne of mercury is released into the environment: tonnes are released annually and have been since around 1980. There has as yet been no disaster on the scale of Minimata despite the extent of the pollution, but the reasons for this are not well understood. It appears that mercury is sequestered to a degree which prevents its wider distribution through food chains. More significant, perhaps, is the fact that although worryingly high levels of mercury have been found in Amazonian populations, given Amazonian life expectancy, the effects of mercury pollution *per se* are unlikely to be a significant factor in mortality. So, there is indeed risk, but its consequences have to be considered in light of a more general scheme about which the information is not available (or of interest, perhaps).

Body shop, risk and bad hair

The strongest part of the reflexive modernisation claim is that the idiom of risk provides a major contemporary metaphor. The weakest part is the assumption that descriptive adequacy also addresses underlying causes, what was referred to earlier as the joint dissolution of both agency and structure. I would argue that, despite the idiomatic claims of reflexive modernisation, it is business as usual and the emphasis on risk serves to obscure more than it reveals.

We have in the collaboration between Body Shop International (BSI) and the Kayapo a neat ideological conjunction: a corporation whose status within the church of capitalism derives from its (largely self-attributed) renegade posture and a native people able to stake long-repelled legitimate claims partially, but significantly, on the basis of tendencies toward internationalisation and globalisation (that is, they are self-consciously modern).

Following the successful repudiation in 1989 of attempts by the Brazilian government, in collaboration with the World Bank (allied with a group of private British banks), to construct a hydroelectric complex on various Xingu region rivers, a segment of the peoples known as Kayapo entered into a commercial ageement with BSI. The Kayapo would deliver brazil nut oil which BSI would market as an element of a hair-conditioning product. BSI provided the technology required for extraction of the oil, guaranteed a price significantly higher than the market dictated, and trading companies were established.

The consequences of this arrangement have been scrutinised and commented upon by various interested parties (for a recent overview, see Rabben, 1997): BSI itself, representatives of the Kayapo, appointed intermediaries (for example, the man who ran the trading company), anthropologists associated with the Kayapo (Terry Turner, Darrell Posey), journalists interested in indigenous rights, ethical commerce and rainforest politics, and the authors of a social audit commissioned by BSI, but not available for public consumption.

The commercial posture of BSI is overtly 'Third Way', associated with the diffuse tendencies of so-called ethical capitalism. In the specific case of BSI/Kayapo brazil nut oil hair-conditioner, the claim is made that risk of environmental and cultural depredation can be reduced by incorporating Kayapo commodity production into the structures of a beneficent commercial entity: through returning to the Kayapo fair payment for their brazil nut oil, the Kayapo are economically empowered and can conserve their traditional culture, BSI can improve its commercial position, and the environment can be preserved (in the sense that a renewable non-timber forest product can out-compete alternative forms of extraction, such as clear-felling).

BSI has been forthright in defending the rationale for its relationship with the Kayapo (and other remote suppliers of cosmetic exotica). Under the banners of 'trade not aid', 'fair trade' and now 'community trade', the company has argued that cultural assimilation and environmental destruction are forestalled by gripping the risk bull by the horns: think globally, act locally, as the bumper sticker has it.

Some, however, have questioned whether risk mitigation is so convincing an outcome, or even an issue. Stephen Corry of Survival International, for example, in a fierce piece in the *Ecologist* (1993) draws attention to the fact that in the absence of legal security of land claims, the assertion that economic prosperity translates directly into cultural integrity is feeble. And indeed, when one looks at the relative risks borne by the Kayapo and BSI in their alliance, the former are rather exposed while the latter are not. The track record of peoples dependent on integration in the world economy on the basis of a single commodity (much less one, dare I say, as inconsequential as hair-conditioner) is not heart-warming. More importantly – from the point of view of the risk discussion, and in light of the fact that brazil nut hair-conditioner is not in itself profitable for BSI – there is a compelling reason to ask: what really is the nature of this risk?

The prospects of mitigating environmental destruction in Amazonia (and by current extension, the globe) have been heavily subsidised by the notion of sustainable development. A key feature of this – in Amazonia, and elsewhere – is the promotion of NTFPs (non-timber forest products) such as brazil nuts. BSI has presented itself as ideologically sound through declining to advertise (a stricture which it seems to have broken of late), yet what it has advertised has been its position, if not its products. Through the promotion of 'trade not aid' rather than 'product' (hair-conditioner), BSI has been able to promote its merchandise not only on the basis of content (assuming that brazil nut oil hair-conditioner has some unique and desirable qualities), but also on the basis of appearing to be socially meaningful in an amplified sense. Thus while Timotei or Vidal Sassoon shampoos and conditioners are ideologically bereft or incomplete offerings, for they fail to address more than the immediate requirements of cosmetic products, something which addresses hair care and social responsibility simultaneously is clearly a superior product.

CONCLUSION

For some years, eco-politics in Amazonia has been a useful hook upon which to hang various projects, but strikingly absent in most discussions has been serious attention to two facts:

1. There is an integral social landscape in Amazonia (in addition to 'green hell').
2. Most of the negative environmental effects have their origins not in Amazonia, but in the uses to which the region has been put by external interests.

In July 1997, satellite surveys revealed 51,517 fires (as against an already depressing average over the period of 1991–96 of 39,889). The number of fires is not in itself unambiguously significant (El Niño, for example, is a predictable suspect). What is significant is that these fires – taken here as a particularly dramatic indicator of a more comprehensive assault on Amazonia – have taken place against a backdrop of unprecedented official acts of intervention to prevent them. The Brazilian government – supported by the usual array of concerned multi-lateral agencies – has installed a federal apparatus in the form of park services, biological reserves, land reform agencies, environmental overseers, SIVAM (a network of satellite monitors), etc. to ensure that such fires do not occur.

This is not a risk environment, it is a highly managed one, and the risk metaphor is a diversion which licenses precisely those interests which have already benefited from despoilation to continue to take advantage. Because Amazonia as a natural space continues to be fetishised, the critical impact of eco-politics has been undercut, and the attempt to segregate eco-politics by placing issues of ecological justice to the side or parking them in that abused realm of plain old politics, results in the unedifying spectacle of a convergence of heightened eco-discourse and heightened environmental and social degradation.

The proposal that there is a political 'Third Way' – a position made explicit in much of the risk society literature – has drawn support from many quarters, not least from within the ranks of the environmentalist movement, yet in the context of Amazonia the discrepancy between ideological appeal and on-the-ground reality is fairly jarring. If one regarded the Rio Summit of 1992 with scepticism, one was dismissed as an unhelpful cynic, yet, as is evident now, little regulatory force was attached to the Rio protocols. Similarly, the widely trumpeted creation of biological reserves, extractive reserves and demarcated Indian territories has been followed quickly by legal concessions to extract timber from biological reserves, and by government moves to revoke the protection of demarcation and a number of other retrogressive gestures.

Risk, then, is not so much an inappropriate notion as an incomplete one. Its elevation represents the outcome – or ideological manifestation – of movements, agents and structures in society which, despite their disavowal of *laissez-faire*-ism, are direct or indirect beneficiaries of high-risk content in their accounts of the major tendencies of social theory.

That risk should be elevated to the status of a defining feature of the age suggests two things: one, as noted earlier, is the prospect that as the West finds it more difficult to displace its crises onto others, it begins to adopt the posture of the beleaguered, out of control in a manner previously assigned only to inhabitants of the periphery (cannibals, miscreants, natives running amok, etc.). The second is that the globalisation of risk refers not to a unity, but a contradiction which now has extensive ecological fit. An example of this was provided by the Rubber Tappers' Union leader Chico Mendes when, prior to his assassination in 1998, he joined forces with the US-based Environmental Defense Fund for purposes of fund-raising. Mendes was a trade union activist, had been educated by a member of the Brazilian Communist Party, and had an analysis of Amazonian and Brazilian society which was unashamedly old-fashioned political, but for US purposes he was presented as a green, eco-political nature-lover. This was an explicitly 'Third Way' approach adopted by his colleagues who argued that Mendes' appeal as a green was considerable but as an Amazonian red, somewhat diminished.

The fetishisation of risk in the literature on reflexive modernisation appears in conjunction with the restructuring of the former Soviet Union, the ascendency of neo-liberalism and management science, and a notion of ecological globalism. In relation to the first, the appearance of risk as a focal concern may not be unrelated to the fact that key traditional demons are no longer available. In relation to the second, the elevation of risk provides legitimation to experts who can claim to coordinate public and private sector strategies (cf. the OECD's Multilateral Agreement on Investment). In relation to the third, the vast discrepancies between core and periphery access to material benefit are effaced by appeals to the collective benefits said to derive from attention to the interrelatedness of eco-carrying capacity.

REFERENCES

Anderson, P. (1986) 'Modernity and revolution', *New Left Review*, vol. 144, pp. 96–113.
Beck, U. (1992) *Risk Society: Towards a New Modernity* (London: Sage Publications).
Beck, U., Giddens, A. and Lash, S. (1994) *Reflexive Modernisation: Politics and Aesthetics* (Cambridge: Polity Press).
Berman, M. (1982) *All That Is Solid Melts into Air* (New York: Simon and Schuster).
Blaut, J.M. (1993) *The Colonizer's Model of the World* (New York: Guilford Press).
Boynton, R. (1997) 'New labour's new intellectual', *The New Yorker*, 6 October pp. 66–74.
Corry, S. (1993) 'The rainforest harvest: who reaps the benefit?', *The Ecologist*, vol. 23, no. 4. pp. 148–53.
Davis, M. (1996) 'Cosmic dancers on history's stage? the permanent revolution in the earth sciences', *New Left Review*, vol. 217, pp. 48–84.
Enzensberger, H. M. (1974) 'A critique of political ecology', *New Left Review*, vol. 84, pp. 3–31.
Hirst, P. and Thompson, G. (1996) *Globalisation in Question* (Cambridge: Polity Press).

Meggers, B. and Evans, C. (1957) *Archaeological Investigations at the Mouth of the Amazon*, Bureau of American Ethnology Bulletin 167 (Washington, DC: Smithsonian Institute).

Mongiovi, G. (1997) Review of Doug Henwood's book *Wall Street: How It Works and for Whom* (London: Verso) in *The Nation*, 8 September, pp. 29–31.

Rabben, L. (1997) *Unnatural Selection* (London: Pluto Press).

Reich, R. (1991) *The Work of Nations* (New York: Knopf).

Steward, J. and Faron, L. (1959) *Native Peoples of South America* (New York: McGraw-Hill).

Weiss, L. (1997) 'Globalisation and the myth of the powerful state', *New Left Review*, vol. 225, pp. 3–27.

Zizek, S. (1997) 'Multiculturalism, or, the cultural logic of multinational corporations', *New Left Review*, vol. 225, pp. 28–51.

CONTRIBUTORS

Janet Bujra is a Senior Lecturer in Sociology in the Department of Peace Studies at the University of Bradford. Her interest in the social aspects of AIDS builds on earlier research on prostitution, labour migration, domestic service and political action in East Africa. She has published widely on gender, class, ethnicity and development.

Pat Caplan is Director of the Institute of Commonwealth Studies, School of Advanced Study, University of London. She previously taught at Goldsmiths College. She has carried out fieldwork in Tanzania, Nepal and South India, and recently directed a large project on food and health in Britain. She has published numerous books and articles.

Simon Cohn is a Lecturer in the Department of Anthropology at Goldsmiths College. He has carried out research in a clinic for diabetics in South-east London, and has published on medical anthropology, and on food and identity.

Sophie Day is a Senior Lecturer in the Department of Anthropology at Goldsmiths College. She has carried out fieldwork in Ladakh in northern India, and on sex-workers in London and has published widely in the field of medical anthropology.

Paul Killworth has recently completed his doctorate at the University of Cambridge. He carried out fieldwork with an infantry battalion in Northern Ireland.

Stephen Nugent is Reader in Anthropology at Goldsmiths College. He has carried out extensive research on Amazonia, on which he has published two books and numerous articles. He is also interested in the media and popular culture, and has recently edited a book (with Cris Shore) on anthropology and cultural studies.

Alison Shaw is a Lecturer in Social Anthropology at Brunel University. She has carried out fieldwork in Pakistan and among British Pakistanis, on which she has published a book and several articles. She is currently researching Pakistani understandings of inheritance.

Jonathan Skinner is a Lecturer in Anthropology and Sociology at the University of Abertay, Dundee. He has carried out fieldwork on the Caribbean island of Montserrat. He is interested in colonialism, nationalism, British Overseas Territories, and postmodern theory.

Penny Vera-Sanso has taught anthropology at the University of London's Extra-Mural Department, at Goldsmiths College and at the University of Kent in Canterbury, where she is currently an Honorary Research Fellow. She conducted fieldwork in low-income settlements of Madras, India between 1989 and 1996, on which she is finalising a book.

INDEX

Index compiled by Auriol Griffith-Jones